SENSES *of*

STYLE

SENSES *of* STYLE

poetry before interpretation

JEFF DOLVEN

THE UNIVERSITY OF CHICAGO PRESS · CHICAGO AND LONDON

The University of Chicago Press, Chicago 60637
The University of Chicago Press, Ltd., London
© 2017 by The University of Chicago
Published 2017
Printed in the United States of America

26 25 24 23 22 21 20 19 18 17   1 2 3 4 5

ISBN-13: 978-0-226-51708-7 (cloth)
ISBN-13: 978-0-226-51711-7 (paper)
ISBN-13: 978-0-226-51725-4 (e-book)
DOI: 10.7208/chicago/9780226517254.001.0001

The University of Chicago Press gratefully acknowledges the generous support of the University Committee on Research in the Humanities and Social Sciences at Princeton University toward the publication of this book.

Library of Congress Cataloging-in-Publication Data
Names: Dolven, Jeffrey Andrew, author.
Title: Senses of style : poetry before interpretation / Jeff Dolven.
Description: Chicago ; London : The University of Chicago Press, 2017. | Includes bibliographical references and index.
Identifiers: LLCN 2017023893 | ISBN 9780226517087 (cloth : alk. paper) | ISBN 9780226517117 (pbk. : alk. paper) | ISBN 9780226517254 (e-book)
Subjects: LCSH: Style, Literary. | English poetry—History and criticism. | Wyatt, Thomas, Sir, 1503?–1542. | Wyatt, Thomas, Sir, 1503?–1542—Literary style. | Wyatt, Thomas, Sir, 1503?–1542—Influence. | O'Hara, Frank, 1926–1966. | O'Hara, Frank, 1926–1966—Literary style.
Classsification: LCC PN203 .D65 2017 | DDC 808—dc23
LC record available at https://lccn.loc.gov/2017023893

♾ This paper meets the requirements of ANSI/NISO Z39.48-1992 (Permanence of Paper).

Frontispiece: Joe Brainard and Frank O'Hara, "Untitled (Cherries)" (1964). Ink and collage on paper, 13 1/2 × 10 3/4 in. Thomas Wyatt's "If waker care" is the poem in the upper right, in Frank O'Hara's handwriting. Used by permission of the Estate of Joe Brainard and the Collection of Kenneth Koch.
Photograph: Courtesy Tibor de Nagy Gallery.

CONTENTS

PREFACE

Style abhors a preface, if only because style is already here. A few words of introduction may be useful all the same. *Senses of Style* is made up of almost four hundred remarks, ranging in length from a sentence to a page. Its ambition is to offer an account of literary style that comprehends the contradictions typically dividing treatments of the subject; to ground that account in the works and lives of two poets, Thomas Wyatt and Frank O'Hara; and (a literary-historical pretext, but a real question as well) to explain the fascination of the second poet with the first.

The book begins and ends with continuing, how style keeps things going and keeps them from falling apart. In between, it explores four ironies of style (part and whole, art and nature, individual and group, description and judgment) and four antitheses of style (substance, aesthesis, interpretation, and narrative). These shifts of emphasis are recorded in the footer on each page. The composition, however, is digressive and interruptive; ideas emerge, subside, and reemerge; the contradictory nature of the subject is allowed expression as the book's own self-contradiction. It attempts to acquaint the reader, as it goes, with the story of each poet's life as well as with the sound of his poetry, for style has a way of reaching out from art into life and back into art again.

The subtitle promises to treat "poetry before interpretation." What that claim means will emerge over the following pages, but it can be said at the outset to derive from a fundamental desire to distinguish reading for the style from other kinds of reading. Such a distinction is impossible to maintain as an absolute, and the blurring of style's boundaries with those of meaning, or beauty, or narrative is inevitable. This book is not least an exploration of the motives for such conflations and confusions. Nonetheless the claim *there are only interpretations* is as flattening as the claim *style is everything*, and to take either one as dogma is to sacrifice the distinct prospects afforded by the terms' mutual independence. In that sense, the book might be said to be a critique of style, in the Kantian sense: an account of the word's proper limits. But also an account of when and where the word is useful, and for what purposes, and what is at stake when its limits are tested, breached, redrawn. So, a pragmatist critique, if such a thing is possible, and one that chooses, when it must, philology over philosophy. Style means how we use it, if it means at all.

The remarks are numbered, and keyed to endnotes that provide citations, suggest other sources, and sometimes dilate on the remark's topic. Early modern texts have been quoted from modernized editions. Where those are unavailable, the spelling has been modernized ad hoc, preserving original punctuation. In a book about style, that inevitably means a loss in time-feel, but one I hope is outweighed by the gain in comprehension for the reader unfamiliar with the vagaries of period orthography. The pervasive influence of intermediaries such as amanuenses, scribes, and compositors on Wyatt's texts means little is lost of his language, or little that is not lost already. Titles, as well as early modern sources embedded in modern quotations, are given in their original spelling.

CONTINUING

§1 Some Preliminary Contradictions

Style holds things together, things and people, schools and movements and periods. It makes us see wholes where we might be bewildered by parts. — But it makes us see parts, too. Say you are asked to identify or describe a style, to account for an act of recognition. (*That sounds like Gertrude Stein,* or *that looks like a Holbein.*) You might pick out a detail like a figure of speech or a quality of line, and you might well find a name for it, isocolon or crosshatching. Style, with all of this specialized language, is manifestly an art, a technical accomplishment with terms and rules that can be taught and learned. — Then again, can't style feel like something you are simply born with? Something that is in your gait or your hands, something you couldn't lose if you tried? A long habit, or even your nature, whether you like it or not. Style's idiosyncrasy is the individual signature that modernity, and not only modernity, wants from every great artist. — And yet, is it not style that dissolves the artist into her time, his country or city, her circle of friends? Everyone and everything has a style, a style that is nothing more or less than location in social and historical space. None of us can escape that space, nor could we ever finally want to. — All the same, even if everything has a style, isn't it true, or isn't it often said, that some people have style and others not? Far from being universal, style can make severe discriminations.

§2 What to Do

Faced with these contradictions, it will be tempting to abandon the word altogether. Alternatively, and particularly if you are a philosopher, or a taxonomically minded critic, you might seek to impose some discipline. In the words of one art historian, "The first step is to restore limits and shape to the shapeless objects of verbal abuse; to rediscover the purposes to which the word in question was appropriate; and to demonstrate its present unacceptable uses." There is another option, too: a shrug, a wry smile, or a barely perceptible nod of acknowledgment, as though to say, *I already knew all that.*

§3 Trying to Keep Going

"Oh," wrote Frank O'Hara to his friend Don Allen, in September 1961.

> I've been going on with a thing I started to be a little birthday poem for BB and then it went along a little and then I remembered that was how Mike's Ode got done so I kept on and I am still going day by day (middle of 8th page this morning). I don't know anything about what it is or will be but am enjoying trying to keep going and seem to have something. Some days I feel very happy about it, because I seem to have been able to keep it "open" and so there are lots of possibilities, air and such. For example, it's been called "M.L.F.Y.," "Wherebye Shall Seace" (from Wyatt), "Biotherm," and back and forth, probably ending up as "M.L.F.Y." The Wyatt passage is very beautiful:

> "This dedelie stroke, wherebye shall seace
> The harborid sighis within my herte."

Here is O'Hara at his desk in the middle of things, ten years into his life in New York, at the end of a summer of gradual farewell to his lover Vincent Warren and burgeoning friendship with Bill

Berkson. What makes him happy is the going on and keeping on and still going, "enjoying trying to keep going," and his letter is a continuation of the poem it describes, carried along by the same glad parataxis. (Parataxis: the rhetorical term for the flat syntax of *and* after *and*.) The reader is invited into his writing life, how he almost always prefers making a new poem to revising the last one ("I don't believe in reworking"), his impatience with intermissions ("what's so great about *sleep*?"), his readiness to mingle art and life freely, in the interest of keeping them both moving along ("life and art, friends and lovers"). As he had written two years before in a poem called "Adieu to Norman, Bon Jour to Joan and Jean-Paul," "The only thing to do is simply continue." The title itself allows barely a comma between goodbye and the next hello.

§4 Continuing (1)

It is easier to have a style than not: ease and fluency are among the primary motives for style, and also avoiding the jeopardy of decisions you have not already made.

§5 Wherebye Shall Seace

Which makes Thomas Wyatt's lines something of a surprise; they sound so abruptly different. They were likely written sometime in the 1530s, though the dating of Wyatt's poems is an uncertain affair, as is, often enough, his authorship. If Wyatt did write the lines, he might have done so at court, or on embassy in Barcelona or in Nice, or in prison. They are old-fashioned in diction, darkly suspended in syntax, and plainly melancholy. They are about a longing for finality, for a merciful, terminal blow. O'Hara knows how different they are and he warns Allen: "MLFY, I hasten to add, is not like that at all, so don't get your hopes up."

§6 We Will Begin Again (1)

In the event, O'Hara called his poem "Biotherm." (Biotherm is a "marvelous sunburn preparation" favored by Berkson's glamorous, socialite mother.) The Wyatt lines nonetheless found their place about two pages into the twelve the poem takes up in Allen's edition of the posthumous *Collected Poems*. By that time, its appetite for borrowed language is well established. It is jagged across the page, it interrupts itself, leaps and dodges, and quotes freely from books and conversation. It is in perpetual, unreciprocated conversation with a *you* who usually seems to be Berkson. After one of many interruptions O'Hara gathers himself to ask, "but we will begin again won't we," and then answers himself:

> well I will anyway or as 12,
> "continuez, même stupide garçon"
> "This dedelie stroke, wherebye shall seace
> The harborid sighis within my herte"

Continue, stupid boy: the request is not any less urgent for being so offhanded. Wyatt's lines are an answer. But what kind of answer? Does the older poet oblige, offering another way of carrying on? Or does he intervene as the bad conscience of the poem's concatenative appetites, a rebuke to gallic nonchalance and a reminder of some more final finality? Either way, "Biotherm" does not cease here. Far from it. There is another "and" to start the next line, and ten pages left to go. What to make of the interruption, indeed whether it is an interruption, will depend on the sense of O'Hara's style: whether it is broken by Wyatt's lines or continuous across them, whether, when O'Hara writes with Wyatt, or even, as here, quotes him, he is writing like himself.

§7 Continuing (2): Synchronically

If style is continuing, one mode of that continuing is across social space: synchronic style, the kind that affords a sense of being oriented in the present. In the poem "My Heart"—looking back six years, to 1955, when O'Hara, who worked the front desk when he first got to New York, had just returned to the Museum of Modern Art as an assistant curator—he explains that he wears work shirts to the opera. ("I / don't wear brown and grey suits all the time, / do I? No.") At the opera, there are other men in work shirts, in among the tuxedos and the suits and the women in gowns and dresses and skirts and, here and there, in the middle of a well-dressed decade, smart pants. He and his friends are like one another, and they recognize each other by virtue of sharing a style. They are also different from other patrons. Aesthetically, socially, erotically, their distinctive continuity orients them in the world. Such social space can align with real space, with the cheap seats or, more broadly, with a neighborhood or a nation. It can also be the imaginary landscape of affinity that makes people who share a mixed space with others feel as though they are somehow particularly there together, situated or moving particularly in relation to one another, among other communities different and indifferent.

§8 Everything Has a Style

Everything has a style. Take a shard of pottery, and place it in the history of Athens; take a safety pin, and stick it in your ear.

§9 Continuing (3): Diachronically

Style also continues across time. Its diachronic continuity applies to institutions, neighborhoods, and nations, which retain their identity by the persistence of stylistic self-resemblance, continuing to be more or less like they used to be. It applies likewise to individuals, who remain recognizable to others and to themselves in how they act and what they make. "My ship is flung upon the gutter's wrist / and cries for help of storm," O'Hara wrote when he arrived in New York City in 1951, in a sonnet sequence that he eventually called "A City Winter." They are proper sonnets, in rhymed pentameter, the sort of inherited form he would mostly abandon as time went on. The startling imagistic juxtapositions, however, reflect his early exposure to poets like Mayakovsky and the French surrealists, who interested him throughout his writing life. They are among the ways O'Hara always sounds like himself. Wyatt counts among such lifelong continuities too. "A City Winter" is the first of many poems that owe a debt to the sonnet that begins "My galley charged with forgetfulness," with its conceit of the self as a ship on a storm-tossed sea. The connection stretches across O'Hara's career, and across a much longer span of time, too, back to

Wyatt and to Petrarch before him. The archaic-sounding "cries for help of storm" is part of O'Hara's advertisement of an open traffic with the past.

§10 Parties (1)

Style continues inside occasions, too: conversations, parties, giving them their particular feeling, at the time and afterward even more. There is a silent count at a good party, maybe the music helps or maybe it's just the talk, everybody keeping it going, noticeable sometimes only when it's broken.

§11 Style as History (1)

Not that synchronic and diachronic style are ever truly separable. The past is present in the present—where else would we find it? It has social meanings, defining affinities and differences among communities now. To choose to sound like the past is to place yourself among the people who know it or care about it, whether they are antiquarians, nationalists, nostalgics, reenactors, or poets. O'Hara was never one to reject the history of his art. Quite the contrary: "all of the past you read is usually quite great," he told the readers of Allen's 1960 anthology, *The New American Poetry*. "Quite great": that sounds particularly like O'Hara, deflationary camp with a stubborn seriousness in it, and the puckish atavism of his good manners, always at his disposal, whether or not he chose to use them.

§12 Continuing (4)

Sir Thomas Wyatt's word for continuing is "remain." He often uses it to talk about love, in the idiom of unrequited longing he learned from translating Petrarch. (He was one of the first poets to bring Petrarch into English.) "I was content thy servant to remain," he complains, vowing to leave a woman who repaid him with cruelty; "I your thrall must evermore remain," he complains, vowing to stay by another. He uses the word for his injuries, too: "But yet, alas, the scar shall still remain," he wrote after a period of imprisonment.

That was in 1536, after his release from the Tower of London; or perhaps it was 1541, after his release, again, from the Tower of London. To remain, at all events, is not exactly to continue. The word has for Wyatt a sense of stubborn integrity, but also weariness, and fear of being left behind. Its constancy is often a protest against what he calls "newfangleness," against fashion and change of fashion. There is in his "remain" a Stoic determination that was part of his education, as a reader of Seneca and Boethius and an early English student of the humanists' Latin canon. But there is also a helpless allegiance to virtues that have gone out of date, and perhaps a certain grim pleasure, or pride, in endurance. ("Restless to remain, / Against my will, full pleased with my pain," his admirer, self-proclaimed inheritor, and elegist Henry Howard, Earl of Surrey, would later write.) What the word offers above all is a constancy of posture, dependable if not comfortable, a way of being, and certainly a way of writing.

§13 Style Is a Way

If style is a way, perhaps that is because there are many ways to the same destination, as there are said to be many styles for the same subject. Style can be a way without a destination, too, and then there are even more ways, and they can continue indefinitely, in any direction. *Way* is one of the basic style-words in English, along with *how* and *like*. Some antitheses might be said to be *thing*, *what*, and *different*, respectively, or perhaps, instead of *different*, *love*.

§14 Remaining Despairing

Among Wyatt's translations from Petrarch is the sonnet O'Hara so admired, "My galley charged with forgetfulness." It ends:

> The stars be hid that led me to this pain.
> Drowned is reason that should me comfort
> And I remain despairing of the port.

The source is "*Passa la nave*," a poem that concludes with the onset of despair: "I begin to despair of the port [*tal ch'i' 'ncomincio a desperar del porto*]." Wyatt, by contrast, ends in the middle, and his remaining despairing is a kind of continuing. He is not exactly enjoying trying to keep going, as O'Hara would have it, but not exactly not, either.

§15 A Minor Puzzle of Literary History

Frank O'Hara was constant to Sir Thomas Wyatt throughout his writing life. He likely first read Wyatt's poems at Harvard, where he studied on the GI Bill after a tour in the Pacific. (He served, appropriately enough, as a sonar operator.) Among his teachers was Hyder Rollins, who had prepared a modern edition of the 1557 miscellany where many of Wyatt's poems were first printed. Rollins knew the texts and also the wilderness of manuscript and print from which they had to be rescued. Wyatt first appears in O'Hara's writing three years after Rollins's course, in the poem "After Wyatt." (O'Hara had just arrived in New York; it was the fall of 1951.) Soon he was at work on "A City Winter," with its debt to "My galley." That poem is the one his friend and protégé Ted Berrigan spoke of years later when he observed that O'Hara's "models are impeccable and he returned to them time and time again, Wyatt being one of them . . . a particular poem of Wyatt's, one particular poem, will lead Frank to writing a number of different poems until he eventually comes up with a poem like 'To the Harbormaster.'" It is a minor puzzle of literary history, this affinity between the gay curator-poet from the New York City of Eisenhower, Kennedy, and Johnson, and the courtier-poet of the court of Henry VIII, supposed lover of the king's consort, later wife, Anne Boleyn. It is not a matter of a one-poem stand, nor a few scattered allusions, but something more like a way of writing, even a way of living; a way, for O'Hara, of continuing. And of course a way of continuing for Wyatt, too, whose poems have another life in O'Hara's.

§16 Reaching You (1)

The end of "To the Harbormaster" plays a variation on the final suspension of "My galley":

I trust the sanity of my vessel; and
if it sinks, it may well be in answer
to the reasoning of the eternal voices,
the waves which have kept me from reaching you.

This not-quite-reaching-you is O'Hara's version of remaining despairing of the port. The eternal voices of the waves postpone the
final union, and the poem ends in refusing an ending. It refuses its
"you" as well, who was Larry Rivers in 1954 but also, half remembered, Petrarch's Laura. It does, however, choose Wyatt. It chooses
him not as an object, but as a model. If not love, then likeness.

PART AND WHOLE

§17 Style and Likeness (1)

I like you; I am like you. The coincidence in English, of liking and likeness, is the heart of the matter; though it is open to question whether style should be said to have a heart, or a matter, for that matter.

§18 The Other Enemy (1)

Frank O'Hara, writing in his college journal in 1948:

> I must take pains not to *intend* anything but the work itself, to let the work take shape as it comes. . . . I must think only of and for the emergent work and not allow messages or ideas as such to displace the validity of the work with their sham importance and subtle derangement of emphasis.

Here is a basic attitude to which O'Hara would be loyal all his life: a suspicion of whatever a poem might be about, messages and ideas, what one might call (for its traditional distinction from style) *content*. After making this proclamation to himself, he begins a new line in the notebook: "The other enemy: style."

§19 Style and Likeness (2)

Likeness is a place to begin, not least because it has already begun: to experience something as *like* is to have experienced something like it before. (So, style is already continuing.) That experience does not necessarily entail recollection of a reference point. A hunch, an intuition, a little déjà vu will do. Nor is it always easy to say where the likeness is, even when two like things are side by side. If it is sometimes obvious enough (*they are both red!*), likeness can also be elusive, a feeling that things just go together, matching, like parts of the same outfit or pieces of furniture from the same room, like but not obviously resembling each other. The problem is puzzling to reflection. You could find yourself saying, *no two things are truly like*, convinced that proper scrutiny discloses only differences; or you might say that *all things are like all other things*, which is equally true, since any two things are both things, only the first of the commonalties that could be proposed. In such speculations it is possible to chase away the original feeling for their likeness, that sense of a shared style, altogether. Style can be like that.

§20 The Time of Style (1): Already

Style is already.

§21 He Can Tame Lions

Thomas Wyatt, not yet Sir, was probably born in 1504, the son of Sir Henry Wyatt, who was an unusually durable counselor both to King Henry VII and Henry VIII. (Loyal to Henry Tudor, the future Henry VII, Henry Wyatt was imprisoned in his youth by Richard III and tortured; the instrument of torture, a cruel device called the barnacles, became an element of the Wyatt arms and an emblem of the family's faithfulness.) Not much is known about Thomas's childhood, spent at Allington Castle in Kent, forty miles from London. There is a story in the family papers that he kept a greyhound and a lion whelp, and that one day the lion, having grown into "courage and heat," attacked the boy who had raised him. The greyhound held the lion at bay, while Wyatt, "in a most present and undaunted courage, drew forth his rapier and ran it into the rebel's heart." Henry VIII, the young Henry, poet, musician, scholar, still the graceful image of the humanist prince, supposedly took notice: "Oh, he can tame lions!" The brave boy he praised may or may not have been the "Wyot" who was admitted to the Middle Temple to study law in 1517. Firmer evidence finds him at Christ's College, Cambridge, at the end of the decade. Soon after, he was at court, dispatched on the king's business in 1523 to transport a considerable sum of gold to Scotland for the English garrisons there. These are most of the details that survive from those earliest years, some stations, events, discrete parts of a continuous life.

§22 Parts of Style (1)

If someone says, *what do you mean, like*, you might answer by pointing to common parts, or elements. The year 1959, the year that Billie Holiday died, and the year O'Hara fell in love with Vincent Warren, was also the year that Macmillan first published Strunk and White's *The Elements of Style*. The book trades on the intuition that style can be described and improved if you first take it apart. Its bantam seventy-one pages are a mix of grammatical doctrine and donnish scolding, promising control over composition as a set of discrete virtues and vices, in terms both formal and moral. ("Use the word *not* as a means of denial or in antithesis, never as a means of evasion.") The book sold two million copies in that first year, and millions more since, being now in its fourth edition. It is possible to pick out the elements of any style ad hoc: they can be adventitious, idiosyncratic, the things that happen to get noticed first. Other elements will be defined in advance by a technical matrix, a descriptive system with an internal organization that bestows names and defines relationships. In the case of the *Elements*, the systems of grammar and rhetoric are ready to hand. Strunk and White bear witness to the reach even into the popular imagination of the idea that style is a profitable subject for analysis.

§23 Frank in Parts (1)

O'Hara was always cagey about the technical aspects of his art. "Would that you were here for midnight beers and liberated discussions of art, sex, friends," he wrote to Kenneth and Janice Koch after a move to Greenwich Village, then added, "and above all techne, which alone is said to free the poet from his limitations." His skepticism does not mean that his poems cannot be taken apart. Marjorie Perloff does an efficient job of it in her study *Poet among Painters*, describing his characteristic idiom as "a system of nonsequiturs, making use of false connectives and demonstratives, pronouns with shifting referents, dangling conditional clauses, incomplete declarative sentences, confusing temporal and spatial relationships, and so on." The terms here are those of late-century descriptive grammar, mixed with some reckoning of the consequences for the reader, "false" and especially "confusing."

§24 And So On (1)

Perloff's list trails off: or does it simply continue? She assumes, after a few examples, that the reader will know how to carry on. Wittgenstein writes: "I believe that I faintly perceive a pattern in the segment of the series, a characteristic feature, which needs only an 'and so on' in order to reach to infinity."

§25 The Product of My Own Time

The only way to be quiet
is to be quick, so I scare
you clumsily, or surprise
you with a stab

. . .

      To
deepen you by my quickness
and delight as if you
were logical and proven,
but still be quiet as if
I were used to you; as if

you would never leave me
and were the inexorable
product of my own time.

§26 Frank in Parts (2)

Perloff's elements are apparent at the beginning of O'Hara's writing life. In 1951, he was at the University of Michigan for a year of graduate school between his studies at Harvard and his moving to New York. In January, he wrote a poem that he called "Poetry." "The only way to be quiet / is to be quick," it begins, and it takes a few lines to speculate about how time feels to the praying mantis, the cricket, and the zebra. Then it turns to you: a *you* who might be Larry Osgood, O'Hara's fellow student and lover at Harvard, or perhaps the jazzman turned painter Larry Rivers, whom O'Hara had met, epiphanically, on a visit to New York the month before. ("Into this scene Larry came rather like a demented telephone.") Biography is one honorable answer to the question, *what is this poem about?* Another is to say something thematic, for example, that it tries to reconcile the suddenness of love with the habit of companionship; permanence, with being present, immediate, and up-to-date. If those remarks are attempts at what the poem means, however, there is still the question what is it like, and whether it is like what Perloff says O'Hara's poems are like. Certainly the temporal relationships are confusing. In its ambivalent longing for immediacy and custom, thrill and happiness, a variety of tenses and moods coordinates the relationship to the *you*. The last sentence is no sentence but a string of dangling conditional clauses, *as if, as if, as if.* Those *as if*'s count as false connectives, if that means that they promise a cumulative argument but don't add up. By Perloff's lights—and she is one of his best critics—typical O'Hara, from the start.

§27 I Find No Peace

I find no peace and all my war is done.
I fear and hope, I burn and freeze like ice.
I fly above the wind yet can I not arise.

And naught I have and all the world I seize on.
That looseth nor locketh, holdeth me in prison
And holdeth me not, yet can I scape no wise;
Nor letteth me live nor die at my device
And yet of death it giveth me occasion.
Without eyen I see and without tongue I plain.
I desire to perish and yet I ask health.
I love another and thus I hate myself.
I feed me in sorrow and laugh in all my pain.
Likewise displeaseth me both death and life,
And my delight is causer of this strife.

§28 Knowing What You Are Doing (1)

"The mystery of Wyatt," wrote an anonymous reviewer for the *TLS* in 1929, "is simply whether he knew what he was doing or whether he did not." It is hard to say whether any given Wyatt poem is early or late. O'Hara dated most of his pages, but Wyatt's poems are harvested from manuscripts and miscellanies and commonplace books that passed through many hands, and dates are not recorded there. "I find no peace" comes near the beginning of the so-called Egerton manuscript, named for the man who bequeathed it to the British Library. Wyatt seems to have kept it for himself as a fair copy of his own work. It translates, roughly—with Wyatt, always roughly—Petrarch's "*Pace non trovo.*" The unremitting appetite for excruciated paradox made the poem a touchstone for later imitators. George Puttenham, the Elizabethan author of *The Arte of English Poesie*, cites the first two lines of Wyatt's version to prove that a pentameter line can be made up of monosyllables; he shared the disposition of his contemporaries to find in Wyatt a wellspring of the skill in versification celebrated at century's end. (Wyatt and Surrey had "greatly polished our rude and homely manner of vulgar poesy from that it had been before, and for that cause may justly be said to be the first reformers of our English meter and style.") Criticism since, however, has tended to emphasize the verse's irregularity. The third line, for example, seems to have six stresses; many lines have extra syllables, if you are looking for a count of ten. When the poem was first printed fifteen years after Wyatt's death, in Richard Tottel's miscellany *Songs and Sonnets*—the book Hyder Rollins would edit four hundred years later for Harvard University Press—that third line was tacitly corrected, becoming the fluent "I flý alóft, yet cán I nót aríse." The resulting poem sounds, as Tottel surely wanted it to sound, and as Puttenham found it, much like the younger, better-born Surrey, who precedes Wyatt in the anthology and who is often credited as the pentameter's first modern practitioner.

§29 Style as Deviation (1)

False, shifting, dangling, incomplete, confusing, and so on. Perloff is a sympathetic critic, but her account of the distinctiveness of O'Hara's voice sounds like a catalog of vices. Descriptions of style often do, as though style could only be defined as a lapse, a deviation, from good usage. That's how W. H. Auden, another New Yorker of the 1950s, heard Wyatt: "one must say that Wyatt failed to do what he was trying to do." But this, Auden thought, made him good for us, and maybe that was the good O'Hara found in him. "What for Wyatt was a failure," Auden concluded, "is for us a blessing."

§30 Style as Failure (1)

Can there be a style of failure? The question probes another contradiction. On the one hand, the answer must be yes. For better or worse, you can have a habit of incontinent oath-swearing, or of drinking too much and speaking too sharply. *There he goes again.* Anything can be style, whether or not it is desired or desirable. On the other hand, if it were to be said of such lapses, *that's his style*, there would likely be some irony in the tone. For style usually carries some implication of self-command, or if not command, then at least the relative ease of an accustomed way of doing things. To have a style can simply mean that you have settled into habits that make you familiar to yourself and to others. If that is what style is, a good-enough way of continuing, then a style of failure makes less sense. Failure would have to lie instead in the rupture of the style, the moments and actions that don't fit, that make you feel anxious and exposed.

§31 On Rachmaninoff's Birthday

Quick! a last poem before I go
off my rocker. Oh Rachmaninoff!

. . .

       Oh my palace of oranges,
junk shop, staples, umber, basalt;
I'm a child again when I was really
miserable, a grope pizzicato. My pocket
of rhinestone, yoyo, carpenter's pencil,
amethyst, hypo, campaign button,
is the room full of smoke? Shit
on the soup, let it burn. So it's back.
You'll never be mentally sober.

§32: Style as Failure (2)

And another question, striking deeper. Is not any style a failure of a kind? At the moment of its emergence, perhaps a style can only distinguish itself by failing, failing at least to be what was expected of it. This is the risk taken by the genius iconoclast, also the risk of being the first one to wear a work shirt to the opera, or one of the first few. If it weren't failure to someone, could it be style to anyone? Any new style must somehow convince us that it is not a botched attempt at something more familiar; that its difference is a matter of skill, not incompetence; that we might just want to try it ourselves, or that someone might.

§33 Some Pronouns

There is no *you* in Wyatt's "I find no peace," nor in most of his love sonnets. There is always an *I*, sometimes a *she*. She was not his wife. Wyatt was married young, in 1520, to a woman named Elizabeth Brooke, around the time that he was probably studying at Cambridge. They had a son, also Thomas, but there is good evidence that husband and wife were estranged by the middle of the decade. Soon after that Wyatt's travels as a diplomat began, first to France in 1526, the next year to Italy, where he may have started reading Petrarch. The Italian poet's theologically excruciated unrequitedness was a resource he would adapt to a courtier's distinctive range of opportunity and frustration. One rumor from the time has clung to him, one in special: that he was, sometime in the years before the king took his fatal interest, the lover of Anne Boleyn.

§34 Whoso List (1)

> Whoso list to hunt, I know where is an hind,
> But as for me, helas, I may no more.
> The vain travail hath wearied me so sore,
> I am of them that farthest cometh behind.
> Yet may I by no means my wearied mind
> Draw from the deer, but as she fleeth afore
> Fainting I follow. I leave off therefore
> Sithens in a net I seek to hold the wind.
> Who list her hunt, I put him out of doubt,
> As well as I may spend his time in vain.
> And graven with diamonds in letters plain
> There is written her fair neck round about:
> "*Noli me tangere* for Caesar's I am,
> And wild for to hold though I seem tame."

§35 I Put Him out of Doubt

"Whoso list" is one of the first poems copied into Egerton. "*Noli me tangere* for Caesar's I am," says the collar around the hind's neck in the famous final couplet, "And wild for to hold though I seem tame." Is it about Anne? It is certainly like Wyatt. It begins with a characteristic, nearly scornful bravado, like several other poems scattered among the manuscripts, "Deem as ye list," "Grudge on who list," "Stand whoso list." (Also one of the King's own ballads: "Grudge who likes, but none deny.") The poem leans upon commonplaces, as Wyatt often does: to try to hold the wind in a net was proverbial. It probes and retreats, tests and relents, or perhaps just changes its mind, or mood. Its lability gives the impression of an utterance in real time, some mix of urgent persuasion and internal debate. If the poem has an interlocutor, imagine the challenge, for that poor man, of gauging whether he is a confidant or a rival. Wyatt is on the balls of his feet, assured, even commanding, and then, abruptly, on his heels, and already, precociously weary, helas, as though he has suddenly aged. Or is that weariness just a ruse? "I put him out of doubt."

§36 Have You Forgotten

"Have you forgotten what we were like then"? The question opens O'Hara's poem "Animals": in those days, "we could manage cocktails out of ice and water":

> I wouldn't want to be faster
> or greener than now if you were with me O you
> were the best of all my days

O'Hara's *you* is a flexible instrument: it is usually intimate; sometimes named, sometimes not; ambiguously available to the reader, to guess at or inhabit. It is held open in a particular way, even held ajar. Who knows who might decide to come in? Already in 1950 he was working out a voice that made room for intimacy and new possibility at once, that would begin to admit, with his arrival in New York, so many new friends. There was Larry Rivers, with whom he had a sudden romance and a long, collaboration-filled friendship; Joe LeSueur, his roommate in a succession of apartments from 1955 to 1965; the painters Jane Freilicher, Grace Hartigan, and Fairfield Porter; the poet James Schuyler, another roommate in the early years. Why then does the *you* in "Animals" seem already to be lost? You *were* the best of all my days. Nostalgia is a great sharpener of stylistic perception, returning to the past as a lost way of life, a whole of which one is no longer a part. It activates the sense of style as history. O'Hara was twenty-four. It would prove to be quite like him to feel nostalgia already for the present.

§37 Parts of Style (2): Rhetoric

What are the parts of style? Taken by size, the largest are the parts of rhetoric, largest in the sense that the technical vocabulary of rhetoric can describe effects of speech from the scale of a single word up to a whole oration. Grammar governs sentences. Rhetoric would govern everything.

§38 Advance-Guard Writing

For the happy few of the avant-garde, according to Paul Goodman, alienation was a basic condition of life:

> (1) society is "alienated" from itself, from its own creative develop-
> ment, and its persons are estranged from one another; but most of the
> members of society do not feel their estrangement; (2) the artists, how-
> ever, feel it, regard themselves as estranged; and (3) society responds
> to them not with snobbery and incomprehension, as to foreigners,
> speaking a foreign tongue, but with outrage, embarrassment, and ridi-
> cule, as to an inner threat.

In consequence, "Advance-guard works tend to be impatient, frag-mentary." The remedy, Goodman wrote, is "the physical reestablishment of community," a community that is "clearly an act of love, embarrassing in its directness." O'Hara got his hands on the essay right away. "The only pleasant thing that's happened to me since you left gal is that I read Paul Goodman's current manifesto in *Kenyon Review*," he wrote Jane Freilicher in the summer of 1951. "If you haven't devoured its delicious message, rush to your nearest newsstand! It is really lucid about what's bothering us both besides sex, and it is so heartening to know that someone understands these things."

§39 Parts of Style (3): Rhetoric

Rhetoric came to Wyatt and his age as an ancient art with a modern prestige. It was one of the three *artes* that made up the classical trivium, along with grammar and logic, but the movement that has come to be known as humanism pushed it to the center of intellectual life. The humanist project, across editions of ancient authors, textbooks, schoolrooms, and much of the European continent, was the adaptation of classical eloquence to the challenges of present-day affairs. The humanists' rhetoric was imagined as a practical art, involved with deliberation and counsel; they looked back on the medieval dialectic as an exercise in unworldly philosophical vanity. For all that, rhetoric was not much less technical in the teaching:

> memorize the rules of poetry and all its patterns; have at your fingertips the chief points of rhetoric, namely propositions, the grounds of proof, figures of speech [*figurae*], amplifications, and the rules governing transitions. For these are conducive not only to criticism but also to imitation.

These are the injunctions of the Dutch scholar Desiderius Erasmus, at the beginning of his *De Ratione Studii*, which he wrote during five years spent at Cambridge from 1509 to 1514. Wyatt arrived at the end of the decade, in Erasmus's long wake. Something basic about humanist teaching is apparent in even this brief charge: that formal rhetoric sees texts in parts, parts for analysis, for good reading, and also parts for imitation, for making a new text in the manner, in the style, of the old. Schoolmasters and rhetoricians called this discipline *imitatio*. Wyatt would have encountered such pragmatic study of Seneca and Cicero and Horace as the coming thing at Cambridge, particularly at Christ's. He was reputed to be a quick study: some time later, as he began to make his way at court, Thomas Cheney wrote to Cardinal Wolsey that he had "as much wit to mark and remember everything he seeth as any young man hath in England."

§40 Parties (2)

If you went to one of Oscar Williams's parties on Wall Street, with the *Partisan Review* crowd, you would find yourself talking about "sensitive literary matters—style, poetic innuendos, psychoanalysis, alcoholism—all this, as liquor flowed and words and ideas became more and more confusing and elliptical." So John Gruen reported. He went himself, it seems, more than once, but he professed to take a dim view. "In phrases of convoluted impenetrability, these 'younger writers' of the fifties would dissect matters of style and give heavy vent to opinions." Williams was a poet and anthologist, responsible for such well-upholstered volumes as *Golden Darkness* and *Master Poems of the English Language*. Gruen was a critic, composer, photographer, and friend of O'Hara's. It should be said, the *Review* published O'Hara as early as 1952, but Gruen makes it stand for the academic verse culture of the decade, which has sometimes appeared to critics, at least in the middle distance, as the Age of Lowell. (Robert Lowell, who told Bobby Kennedy, "I have always been fascinated by poets like Wyatt and Raleigh, who were also Statesmen"—not the main reason for O'Hara's interest.) Style is an ever-less-technical concept over the course of the twentieth century, its more formal departments increasingly *arrière-garde*. O'Hara never trusted such analysis anyway. "The encouragement of a taste for technical facility . . . makes it easier for the poet to write while it makes it easier for the public to like what he writes."

§41 Parts of Style (4): Rhetoric

The parts of rhetoric most traditionally associated with style are what Erasmus calls the *figurae*, the figures of speech, both tropes (figures of meaning, like metaphor) and schemes (figures of arrangement, like anaphora). They could be learned in any number of Latin textbooks, but by the middle of the sixteenth century they were being brought to the vernacular in manuals like Richard Sherry's *A Treatise of Schemes and Tropes* (1550) and Thomas Wilson's *The Arte of Rhetorique* (1553). They had long been in use in English poems:

> Without eyen I see and without tongue I plain.
> I desire to perish and yet I ask health.
> I love another and thus I hate my self.
> I feed me in sorrow and laugh in all my pain.
> Likewise displeaseth me both death and life,
> And my delight is causer of this strife.

These lines make up the sestet that completes Wyatt's sonnet "I find no peace." Their painful formalism, a rack on which to stretch the sentiment, is achieved by crossing antithesis, the juxtaposition of opposites, with isocolon, a scheme that balances parallel phrases in what Sherry calls "even or equal" members. The end-stopped lines reinforce the symmetries: the opposites "perish" and "health" are paired structurally, and rhythmically, with the opposites "other" and "self." The connoisseur might notice how the antitheses redouble, as the relatively neutral pair "desire" and "ask" becomes the compoundingly antagonistic "love another" and "hate myself."

§42 Style and Explanation (1)

Wyatt's patterning is already in Petrarch. The Italian's poems are self-conscious exercises in bringing the structures of classical eloquence to the vernacular: "*et ò in odio me stesso et amo altrui.*" Wyatt has taken his liberties, however, if *liberty* is the word. The helpless *et* in Petrarch, "I hate myself *and* I love another," becomes in translation a grim law: "I love another and thus I hate myself."

§43 What Secret Pleasures

Their intimacy sweetly bore upon them a pain
which soared when they were together,
yet spent itself on the scenery when they were apart.
No one could have guessed what secret pleasures,
that ardent profile whose public expression is hate.

§44 Style and Pain

Pain may finally conquer language, but style will go first.

§45 Style as Gesture (1)

"Scheme," says Richard Sherry, "is a Greek word, and signifyeth properly the manner of gesture that dancers use to make . . . but by translation is taken for the form, fashion, and shape of any thing expressed in writing or painting." The association of a figure of speech with a gesture is an ancient commonplace: a gesture is extra, ornamental, mere; less serious and consequential than an action. Wilson's *Arte of Rhetorique* defines gesture as "a certain comely moderation of the countenance, and all other parts of man's body, aptly agreeing to those things which are spoken." Gesture is to action, one might say, as *figura* is to *sententia*, as ornament is to idea. It is a discrete element of social life, and it is possible to isolate and identify a particular wave of the hand, or nod, a way of holding your cigarette. (O'Hara was famous for the last: a much-reproduced photograph of him on the telephone, cigarette dangling, is a generational emblem of casual appetite.) But if a gesture is discrete, something you can point to, it also has a strong association with habit and with character. *Gesture* derives from the Latin *gerere*, to bear or carry, to carry on, to continue, a carrier of style, continuing.

§46 Embassy

At the beginning of 1527, the courtier John Russell, who had served, like Wyatt's father, under Henry VII and VIII, was dispatched on an embassy to Rome. England's survival throughout the sixteenth century depended on its management of relations with the great Continental powers, France and the Holy Roman Empire (the latter united with the Spanish Empire by Charles V, heir to both). All his life Henry VIII feared a grand alliance against him. The papacy was a check on Imperial ambition in Italy, and Russell's job was to shore up that resistance by promising English help and raising support among the other Italian city-states. On his way out of London, the story goes, he met Wyatt, "and after salutations was demanded of him whether he went, and had answer, to Italy sent by the king. And I said Sir Thomas, if you please, will ask leave, get money and go with you." Here is the bluff, prompt, improvisatory Wyatt remembered in so many sources. In Rome, the two men convinced the pope to hold out for help from Venice; riding east, however, Russell broke his leg in a fall and had to turn back. Wyatt went on. Now England's principal emissary, he persuaded the Venetians, but only after great delay, and a similar mission to Ferrara came to nothing. In the meantime, the pope had agreed to an armistice with the empire. Wyatt continued his roving, "desirous to see the country"; dangerous country, for he was captured by Imperial troops in March, and ransomed only at great expense. He made his way back to Rome and departed the city with Russell days before its sack, armistice notwithstanding, on the sixth of May. The embassy was a failure. Perhaps it was in these months that he first read Petrarch.

§47 Parts of Style (5): Grammar

Next among the parts of style: the parts of grammar, smaller because they are all found within the boundaries of the sentence. Grammar serves the critic Chris Stamatakis in a shrewd assessment of Wyatt's tendency to "favour an indefinite mood (typically the subjunctive) over the indicative." It is also the language of Perloff's précis, with its list of shifting pronomial referents, dangling conditional clauses, and incomplete declarative sentences. The move from the gestural parts of rhetoric to the parts of grammar is a shift in the senses and the motives of style, from a criterion of persuasion to a criterion of correctness. The test of good rhetoric is its work in the world, its power to persuade, and among the schemes and tropes there are almost as many names for disorder and interruption (*catachresis, hyperbaton*) as for pattern and equipoise (*conjunctio, progressio*). Grammar, by contrast, is concerned with the norms of speech and the competence of speakers, without regard to situation or ends. The two will often disagree: good rhetoric can be bad grammar, if it breaks grammar's rules; good grammar can be bad rhetoric, if it fails, in its propriety, to persuade.

§48 Wyatt's File

"There was never file," wrote Wyatt,

> half so well filed
> To file a file for every smith's intent
> As I was made a filing instrument
> To frame other, while I was beguiled.

After Wyatt's death, John Leland, the self-proclaimed king's anti-quary, made a collection of Latin funeral songs, the *Naeniae*: "*Anglica lingua fuit rudis & sine nomine rhythmus: / Nunc limam agnoscit docte Viate tuam*"; "The English tongue was rude, its verses vile; / Now, skillful Wyatt, it has known your file." It is unlikely that Leland had such confoundingly ungrammatical lines as the above uppermost in mind when he wrote his encomium.

§49 Style and Action (1)

The grammar of action is subject and verb. ("An action is not a matter of taste," wrote Harold Rosenberg, in his 1952 manifesto on action painting: "You don't let taste decide the firing of a pistol or the building of a maze.") The grammar of style is adjectives, adverbs, prepositions; it cannot be counted upon to shore up the first person as a verb does. Consider the peculiar grammar of the sentence *I imitate you*. Which pronoun is the real subject, the real agent, and which is the object?

§50 Parts of Style (6): Grammar

Rhetoric is every way arguable, by turns ostentatious and covert. It is not easy to number schemes and tropes either by hand or, yet, by machine. Grammar, by contrast, aspires to be an objective and comprehensive system of classification that can account for anything in a well-formed sentence. Accordingly, its features can be more readily tallied, and the tallies compared. The parts of grammar allow for the measurement of style, its quantification, without so much interference from what the stylist has to say or what might come of it.

§51 Style as Deviation (2)

Grammatical correctness as a standard of style can carry with it the ideal of a convergent style, a single good style, hedged round with infelicities and barbarisms. This is the style of the prescriptive manuals. (So Strunk and White: "The colloquial *have got* for *got* should not be used in writing.") Less judgmentally, but still judgmentally, the grammatical paradigm may imply a neutral norm from which the departures of style can be measured. Style is deviation: one of the concept's most familiar definitions. Roland Barthes allows as much when he says that "style is a distance, a difference"; but he asks, "in reference to what?"

§52 Style as Deviation (3)

> Johnny and Alvin are going home, are sleeping now
> are fanning the air with breaths from the same bed.

The rhetoric is striking, in the marked triple apposition; the grammar too, or at least the punctuation, in the dropped comma and the missing *and*; and the picture of two men in bed together. That casual courage in the representation of homosexuality is also part of O'Hara's style, as is the fact that he is somewhere else, up late, writing. All are, as the linguists would say, marked: distinctive, notable.

§53 Parts of Style (7): Earlobes

The earlobe owes its privileged place in the history of style to the writing of Giovanni Morelli, whose *Die Werke Italienischer Meister* (1880) is illustrated with drawings of ears after the likes of Bellini and Mantegna. "My adversaries like to consider me a person who is unable to discern the spiritual meaning in a work of art and for this reason gives special importance to external matters," he wrote, with a characteristic relish for controversy: "the shape of a hand, of an ear, and even, *horribile dictu*, to such an unpleasant subject as fingernails." He was, in fact, trained in anatomy, but these bloodless dissections were at the service of a passion for the history of art. He eventually became notorious for the claim that apprentices, copyists, and forgers are most successful in imitating the most meaningful details of a painting, the ones that attract the attention of the commentators and the interpreters, expressive eyes or fine gestures of the hand. To catch them out, look to the earlobe—to the parts that matter least, which they will execute from their own idiosyncratic habit rather than with self-subduing care for their model. Morelli's sketches of these unregarded parts are strategic redirections of attention to what ordinarily most escapes attention, and to what is therefore, for purposes of attribution, most telling. One can distinguish a true Mantegna from a fake not by ear, but scientifically, by the ear.

§54 Style and Distance (1)

Style disappears as you get truly close, disappears under conditions of intimacy or of close combat. You might long for this, to get past style by closing in.

§55: Parts of Style (8): Earlobes

Sigmund Freud thought he recognized a fellow traveler in Morelli: "It seems to me," he writes in "The Moses of Michelangelo," "that his method of inquiry is closely related to the technique of psychoanalysis. It, too, is accustomed to divine secret and concealed things from despised or unnoticed features, from the rubbish-heap, as it were, of our observations." The historian Carlo Ginzburg reads Morelli and Freud together, and adds Arthur Conan Doyle, in order to tell a story about the development of semiotics as a tool of the humanistic disciplines, the discovery of the special signifying power of the neglected detail. "In each case, infinitesimal traces permit the comprehension of a deeper, otherwise unattainable reality." But Morelli's earlobe could just as easily be said to belong to another story, one that leads in the opposite direction: not toward psychoanalysis as a search for symptom, but toward the statistician's trust in the neutral feature, beneath any conscious determination. Sometimes an earlobe is just an earlobe. If the forger's idiosyncrasies betray him, it is not of interest to Morelli's stylistic forensics what special preference or secret fetish has provoked the swerve from his model. That telltale pouch of flesh is cut off from the rest of the body painlessly, dispassionately. It functions best, for the purposes of attribution, because it has no charisma of its own, none of the willful manipulations—of self, of others—in the attentive and mirroring eye.

§56 The First Limit of Style: Incoherence

Everything has a style. Even the most functional object, if it is discovered by an archaeologist, or worn on the street, gives of a way of life; think of that safety pin in the ear. Nevertheless, there are limits to when it will be useful, or feel right, to use *style*, limits to when *style* is the proper aspect or the appropriate word. One such limit is incoherence. It may be possible to imitate a manner of distress, distraction, or madness—of not following from yourself, the frightening failure of that taken-for-granted *and so on*—but it is difficult, difficult to assume the fractured manner of a self in disarray, and to the extent that the disarray seems real, it will feel wrong to speak of its style. If style affords ease, the relative ease of knowing how to go on, how could anyone want a style that undoes itself? And that wanting is so important to style—your wanting, or somebody's. Likeness and liking are so hard to separate. Could you speak of a style of madness? You could, but wouldn't it be kinder to speak of a kind?

§57 Wyatt in Parts

There are not many things in a typical Wyatt poem, not many props or objects, nor in the run of poems written after Petrarch. The things there are, often parts of the body, tend to come apart:

Avising the bright beams of these fair eyes,
Where he is that mine oft moisteth and washeth,
The wearied mind straight from the heart departeth
For to rest in his worldly paradise

These lines begin Wyatt's translation of Petrarch's sonnet "*Mirando 'l sol.*" The decomposition of the self is a hallmark of the Italian's idiom. It is radicalized by his English imitator. The lines mean something like: *when I consider the beams of her fair eyes, where I can see the reflection of the love god who often makes me cry, then my wearied mind departs my heart to go and rest in the paradise of her gaze* (or perhaps *her heart*, or *her mind*). The machinery is unwieldy, with the lover split up into eyes, heart, and mind, which are variously sense organs, places to go, and ambassadors between them. The result, in the view of another of Wyatt's editors, F. M. Padelford, is "incoherency and elusiveness." The critic Elizabeth Heale generalizes: "it is impossible to know how deliberate Wyatt's alterations to the original are, or to what extent they are a result of accidental touches or mistranslations." The parts are all in Petrarch's inventory. Their radical disarray is Wyatt's, his style or his spell against style.

§58 Parts of Style (9)

To see something in parts involves a certain resistance to its charisma. (All styles have charisma, at least for someone—*charisma* defined, for the moment, simply as the solicitation to imitate.) Resistance, but not necessarily hostile or even skeptical resistance. Naming parts can be an act of praise as well as critique. Still, the namer declines to be carried along. It is as though to observe the divisions within an object of attention necessarily establishes a division between the object and the observing subject. Any dividing line you draw, anywhere, you also draw around yourself.

§59 Parts of Style (10): Statistics

Smaller than an earlobe, even, is a letter. Let us suppose that works might be attributed by counting the relative frequency of letter use. Subtle alphabetical biases—a penchant for n, a distaste for t— might yield a signature, twenty-six-part ratio, consistent across any individual's writing and distinct from the writing of others. The method, proposed by Anthony Kenny thirty years ago, has not found favor among stylometricians, nor did Kenny pursue it, but it can stand for an interest like Morelli's in strategies of attribution that elude conscious manipulation. Unlike Morelli's ears, the evidence is statistical. It escapes desire first by relying on an inconspicuous atom, the humble letter, and second, because the number of instances necessary exceeds anyone's unassisted capacity to form a total impression. If the letter-count strategy has not proved out, computational stylometrics as a discipline has become more and more capable of parsing such telling but effectively invisible features. One promising correlation with authorship turns out to be the relative frequency of so-called function words—articles, pronouns, particles, and other words that have (as one historian of the enterprise puts it) "relatively little meaning on their own." Computer algorithms for the recognition of natural language increasingly allow for tagging devices of syntax, too, so that habits of sentence-building become more reliably discernible. The rhetorical schemes will yield themselves up to census as the machines learn to read them.

§60 Of You in Me

When your left arm twitches
it's like sunlight on sugar
to me and my tongue seeks
the sea of your skin, its oily
calm of green light on the floor
of the ocean
             as in parting,
there's a flutter between us
while I haul down a flag and
you look absently out of
my heart so you won't see
what light one fears in the
sea that I don't want you
to know is of you in me

§61 Style and Form (1)

The promise of statistical analysis is the promise of a measure that could never be faked, because it could never be conscious: who has such control over her writing, balancing the letters with one another by design? Not only could style so defined never be forged, but it could never, or never consciously, be imitated. At the limit of this line of investigation lie patterns of stylistic correlation that have no bearing on our interests at all, as makers or as readers. Machine learning, set to the task of finding patterns across large corpuses of text, will likely be able to define structures and families by criteria we have never thought of, and would never think of. They may likewise discover, following those criteria, affinities that run athwart the questions of identity, genealogy, and origin, temporal or spatial, that are so often the questions of style. Michael Witmore has speculated in this direction, about the potential of such analysis to transcend itself in the direction of the text's independent, post- or simply un-human ontology. Texts may show linguistic patterns beyond rhetoric: useless, meaningless, irrecuperable for interpretation; merely true.

§62 Parts of Style (11): Statistics

The text that relates to itself and to other texts by criteria and in patterns that transcend human powers of recognition—perhaps that text has crossed from style into beauty, the severe beauty claimed, for example, by the unhearable intricacies of the most austerely mathematical serial music, or the inaudible harmonies of the circling spheres. But it would not be beauty for us. Notice how much easier it is to credit a beauty that is not for us, not for any humans, than to credit such a style. (Is beauty ever for us?— but style is always.)

§63 Little Pieces of It

O'Hara wrote his long poem "Second Avenue" in 1953, when he left MoMA to join the magazine *ARTnews*. He spent the next two years there editing and reviewing, more and more involved in the lives and works of the artists around him. In the middle of it, he went to lunch with Kenneth Koch: his Harvard friend, "excitement-prone Kenneth Koch," who was getting his PhD from Columbia, and who had already helped introduce him to the French poets, Rimbaud, Apollinaire, the surrealists. The poem duly contains what O'Hara later called "a true description of not being able to continue this poem and meeting Kenneth Koch for a sandwich while waiting for the poem to start again."

> Candidly. The past, the sensations of the past. Now!
> in cuneiform, of umbrella satrap square-carts with hotdogs

and onions of red syrup blended, of sand bejewelling the prepuce
in tank suits, of Majestic Camera Stores and Schuster's,
of Kenneth in an abandoned storeway on a Sunday cutting ever more
insinuating lobotomies of a yet-to-be-more-yielding world
of ears

Koch, O'Hara goes on to explain, was himself "continuing to write
his long poem as he waited." (That poem was another exercise in
continuing, "When the Sun Tries to Go On.") O'Hara was not often
induced to comment on a poem he had finished; his remarks were
extracted from him by the *Time/Life* editor Rosalind Constable
four years later, and not published until after his death. He gamely
glosses a few passages, but he has misgivings. "I don't know if this
method is of any interest in taking little pieces of it. You see how
it makes it seem very jumbled, while actually everything in it either happened to me or I felt happening (saw, imagined) on Second
Avenue." It betrays the poem, or at least "seems quite . . . batty,"
to itemize its elements. This in spite of the fact that it is conspic-
uously a poem of odds and ends, lots of bits strung together by a
mix of vernacular *and*s and a higher-level, anaphoric rhetoric "of
umbrella satrap square-carts . . . of sand bejeweling . . . of Majestic
Camera Stores."

§64 Style Hides (1)

Analysis is a failure of style, or better, a text that succumbs to analysis has failed; perhaps, a reader who subjects it to analysis has
failed, too. The text (or artifact, or outfit) has failed to be seamless
(assuming, of course, that the seams are not part of its style). The
reader has failed to accept the offer of free passage, of fluency, of
continuing, and has chosen instead to stop and reflect, to interrupt
the charisma of the object to study its elements. In some grander
sense, both have failed the potential of style itself to be the whole,
of style to be everything, choosing instead another kind of knowledge, or even just knowledge itself. Nature hides, says Heraclitus.
Style hides, too. They both hide particularly, or only, from finding.

§65 No Other Way

So chanceth it oft that every passion
The mind hideth by colour contrary
With feigned visage, now sad, now merry;
Whereby if I laughed any time or season,
It is for because I have n'other way
To cloak my care but under sport and play.

§66 The Hermeneutic Circle

Need there be a choice between part or whole? Could there be? Surely there is a way of negotiating between them, between analysis and—whatever it would be, fluency, knowingness, the alreadyness of recognition. One way to begin is by

> first observing details about the superficial appearance of the particular work . . . then, grouping these details and seeking to integrate them into a creative principle which may have been present in the soul of the artist; and finally, making the return trip to all the other groups of observations in order to find whether the "inward form" one has tentatively constructed gives an account of the whole.

Leo Spitzer offered these instructions in 1948, while Frank O'Hara was at Harvard; Spitzer had spent his war at Johns Hopkins, having fled Nazi Germany in 1933 via a three-year stint at the Istanbul State University. His *Stilstudien* had been published two decades before, when he was still at the University of Marburg. *Linguistics and Literary History*, written for an American audience, offers a summa of his method. It has a characteristic motion: the mind goes from a detail, to a preliminary relation with other details; then to a new detail, to test that understanding; back again to an evolving integration of the work, a gathering whole; and so on. Motivating that circuit is the premise that there is a whole to be gathered. "The 'axiom' of the philologian," as Spitzer puts it, is that "details are not an inchoate chance aggregation of dispersed material through which no light shines." They are rather parts, even images of a totality. Together this circular motion and its fractal account of culture describe what Spitzer calls the hermeneutic circle.

§67 Wholes of Style

As there are kinds of parts, so there are kinds of wholes: a culture, a period, a nation, a place; a sentence, a work, an oeuvre; a race, a climate; a workshop, a coterie; an individual.

§68 Jujubes (1)

What do the following parts have to do with one another?

Oh! kangaroos, sequins, chocolate sodas!
You really are beautiful! Pearls,
harmonicas, jujubes, aspirins!

Are they parts at all? Parts of what—of a moment, of a mind? Or is each a whole? Are they somehow like one another? Or are they just next to each other? Just next to each other: why *just*?

§69 Ornament and Cosmos (1)

Any part of style identified as such will be vulnerable to the charge that it is trivial, excrescent, mere ornament, just as style can always be dismissed as mere style. In his appalling, mesmerizing denunciation "Ornament and Crime," the proto-high-modernist architect Adolf Loos calls ornament a waste of labor and a sign of backwardness. His functionalist austerity might be said to hate style altogether: "Every age had its style, is our age alone to be refused a style? . . . Weep not! See, therein lies the greatness of our age, that it is incapable of producing a new ornament. We have outgrown ornament." But the word *ornament* can be traced back to the Greek *kosmos*, and its Latinate derivatives *ornatus* and *decoratio*. Kosmos has the double sense of a general order, and a particular sign of that order; the totality of the universe, and a signet ring. That ancient idea of the synecdochic ornament becomes what Gérard Genette calls a "methodological postulate" for the study of style in the nineteenth century. "What is true of individual elements is equally true of larger units."

§70 The Time of Style (2): Already

Spitzer again: "Why do I insist that it is impossible to offer the reader a step-by-step rationale to be applied to a work of art?" Why is there no method for finding the detail that is the beginning of the recognition of a style, of the recognition that there is a style? "For one reason, that the first step, on which all may hinge, can never be planned: it must already have taken place."

§71 Ornament and Cosmos (2)

Genette's postulate has a complex genealogy: part art-historical (the idea of a period style), part philosophical (the hermeneutic circles of Schleiermacher and inheritors like Heidegger and Gadamer). It is an enabling idea for Erich Auerbach, the German Jewish philologist who shared Spitzer's intellectual formation, and who also shared an escape route through Istanbul to the United States. "In any random fragment plucked from the course of a life at any time," Auerbach wrote from his desk on Beyazıt Square in the early 1940s, "the totality of its fate is contained and can be portrayed." His magisterial history of Western literary representation, *Mimesis*, depends on the idea that any detail is an epitome. With this assumption came the reassurance that there was a whole to reconstruct out of a shattered Europe, a whole contained in any of its fragments. Auerbach's method of using a text to capture a discrete stage in the history of representation asserts the "vital unity of individual epochs, so that each epoch appears as a whole whose character is reflected in each of its manifestations." History, then, is a whole, or at least a series of wholes. Not only does style provide the terms of its wholeness, but if civilization itself were to be ruined, even the smallest part would suffice for its resurrection.

§72 Jujubes (2)

Consider the jujube, how it is like. A rose jujube is like a rose jujube is like a rose jujube, and very like a spearmint. They are all like lifesavers, and also like marbles, or shards of colored glass. (That is, they all look alike.) A jujube is also a little like a sequin, or a pearl, or an aspirin; and like a chocolate soda, because you might get them both at the same soda fountain. (They sit side by side in the world.) The jujube is like 1950, a little symptom of a newly optimistic era's taste for sweets and bright colors, and its forgetfulness, for the time being, of South Asia, where the jujube tree grows. (So, the likeness of a tic to a personality, or of a clue to a crime.) The jujube is like New York, a little hard candy lens through which to see the city, and more than that, a rose-flavored capsule of amber that contains everything of that time and place. (The likeness of the microcosm to its cosmos.)

§73 The First Irony of Style

Style wants to be taken whole; or at least, taken without halt or interruption, taken for granted, continuingly.—But any effort to talk about style, or to point it out, or to contain its charisma, will press toward the seeing and the naming of parts. Sometimes the talk will count as continuing the style it describes. Sometimes not. The contradiction of part and whole does not have the status of a proper paradox or antinomy, for neither term, part nor whole, can do without the other. Perhaps the better word is *irony*, for the management, sometimes conscious, sometimes not, of a tacit dilemma. Style is obviously made up of parts. How else would we talk about it? How else would we study to imitate it, or teach others?—And yet, to itemize a style is to disable its spontaneous charisma, and even to turn it into something else. (Method, perhaps.) It is possible to declare for one attitude or another, but also to keep them in a kind of practical suspension, available at need. So, part and whole: the first irony of style.

§74 Wait a Minute

But might it be said that the very distinction between part and whole is itself on the side of the part, on the side of partitioning?

STYLE V.
SUBSTANCE

---

§75 Quiet of Mind (1)

By 1527, Henry's first queen, the Spanish Katherine of Aragon, had already come to know the vulnerability of her place in the king's court and in his bed. She had not given him the male heir he sought, and she was forty-one years old. Diplomatic efforts to dissolve the marriage were already under way in Rome. Always a sober figure amid the French ostentations of English aristocracy—she had been brought up in the austerity of the Castilian court—she took to wearing mourning black, attended by a loyal group of ladies in waiting. (A young woman named Elizabeth Darrell, whom Wyatt would come to know, was among them.) Eventually the king would repossess her jewels to give to Anne. Katherine took comfort in a circle of humanist advisors, and in the classical tradition's store of Stoic counsel: a good life is a life indifferent to the vicissitudes of fortune, a life in which you do not hold too tightly anything you might lose. Some time that year she asked Wyatt to make a translation for her of Petrarch's *De Remediis Utriusque Fortunae*.

§76 Style and Substance (1)

There is another way to cut style: not into its parts, but free from its substance. That cut enacts a pragmatic, dualist theory of language, rudimentary but durable, according to which what is said and the way it is said can be separated from one another. Translation is saying the same thing in different languages. Style works the same way within a given language; it is supplementary, ornamental, and therefore the same thing can be said, the same action performed, the same image made, in varying styles. Just as the word *style* is defined by its ironies, so it is defined by its antitheses, and of those, style and substance, the *how* and the *what*, is the most basic.

§77 Quiet of Mind (2)

Wyatt was a likely choice for a translation job, a young man making his way, known to be good with languages. Queen Katherine had been generous to his friends John Poyntz and John Leland; he himself had been to Petrarch's Italy. The gift was ready for New Year's Day 1528, but as its preface explains, it was not exactly what the queen had asked for. Instead of Petrarch, Wyatt translated Plutarch's essay *De Tranquillitate Animi*, which he titled *Of the Quyete of Minde*. He had made a start on the Petrarch, he explained, but the labor became tedious "by superfluous often rehearsing of one thing," a redundancy that the eloquence of the original Latin could disguise, but that his poor native English laid bare. Plutarch's essay offered the same "fruits . . . handsomely gathered together, without tediousness of length," while still "containing the whole effect of that your highness desired of Petrarch." The gift makes two substitutions: Plutarch for Petrarch, and his English for the original Latin. (Wyatt worked from Guillaume Budé's Latin translation of Plutarch's Greek.) He assures Katherine that the whole effect of his source is nonetheless preserved.

§78 Style and Substance (2)

The opposition between *how* and *what* has many variants: style and essence, the outer surface and its inner nature; style and matter, the way something is made and the stuff it is made from; style and content, the container and the contained; style and subject, what something is like and what it is about; style and doctrine, as the humanists might say, or style and proposition, with the moderns. In each case the distinction raises the question of the independence or interdependence of the two terms. Is style dictated by its substance, matter, content, subject? Or can any substance take any style? The question could be said to be a question about freedom, style free and style bound.

§79 Happiness (1)

Joan Mitchell, the Joan of "Adieu to Norman, Bon Jour to Joan and Jean-Paul," was the host of a party in honor of the marriage of Jane Freilicher and Joe Hazan, in February 1957; O'Hara read (and, Brad Gooch maintains, wrote) a poem in their honor on the spot. He did not easily surrender his friends to marriage,

> but ideas are obscure and nothing should be obscure tonight
> you will live half the year in a house by the sea and half the year in
>   a house in our arms
> we peer into the future and see you happy and hope it is a sign that we
>   will be happy too, something to cling to, happiness
> the least and best of human attainments

O'Hara told the composer Ned Rorem, a couple of years later, "like Kenneth Koch once said, when I am unhappy I am terribly anxious to get happy and when I am happy I am terribly anxious that I don't lose it."

§80 Quiet of Mind (3)

"We accuse wicked fortune and our destiny when rather we should damn our selves of folly," Wyatt wrote, "as it were, to be angry with fortune that thou canst not shoot an arrow with a plow or hunt an hare with an ox, and that some cruel god should be against them that with vain endeavor hunt an hart with a drag net, and not that they attempt to do those impossibilities by their own madness and foolishness."

§81 Happiness (2)

To be happy is be fortunate, or so the etymology implies: the *hap* is the root of *happen* or *happenstance*. Modernity has smoothed the word out into a kind of cheerful quiet, continuous rather than arbitrary and episodic, and in so doing has made us responsible for its maintenance. Frank O'Hara was no Stoic, but he may have longed to be — may have longed for something like that quiet of mind.

> I am sober and industrious
> and would be plain and plainer
> for a little while.

He could hardly have found a better model of failure in that enterprise than Thomas Wyatt.

§82 Quiet of Mind (4)

It is folly to blame fortune for our suffering; we might as well try to hunt a rabbit with an ox. Such proverbs are typical of the Stoic counsel of *The Quyete of Minde*. Also of its style, which was obdurately Anglo-Saxon, an emphatically English Plutarch for the Spanish queen. Wyatt was keeping a difficult balance, as a favorite of Katherine's circle who could feel the north wind blowing. The questionable control of syntax is typical too, and the censure it has attracted. "Its sentence structure [is] loose and, frequently, incoherent," writes one modern critic; "each sentence [is] primitive in structure yet involutedly struggling with an unwieldy rush of minor clauses," writes another. Several speculate that it was written in haste, a judgment that dogs the poems, too. That impression is no accident of Wyatt's style, but a true signature, not the offhanded *sprezzatura* of a generation after but the hurry of a strong mind taxed. So much of his work sounds like that. Still, if the little book was made "not precisely (I confess) without error as one should have done that had been of perfect learning," he reminds Katherine that he seeks "rather the profit of the sentence than the nature of the words."

§83 The Second Limit of Style: Plainness

Everything has a style. Nonetheless, at one limit of the antithesis of style and substance is the dream of stylelessness, of a language that is pure substance. Rhetoric calls this aspiration a plain style, though it often reflects a desire to escape from rhetoric altogether. So Wyatt again: "Rather the profit of the sentence than the nature of the words." "Sentence" here means *sententia*, opinion or thought, and of that, he takes only the profit, a double abstraction, or perhaps concretion. What does this *sententia* come down to when it is stripped of the clothing of style? Perhaps just information, a modern category, or perhaps just logic, the bare syntax of argument. Perhaps an ideal that could be called classical, the form that subtends all styles, the purity from which all style is a difference, and the criterion by which to measure style's pandering deviance.

§84 The Aspect of Style (1)

Given any whole, there would seem to be parts that count for its style, and parts that don't. So, the lapels of the jacket are style, the weight of the fabric that warms the wearer, not. The tail fins yes, the chassis no; the cornice, but not the brick. It is easy enough, however, to undo the distinction in practice. Brick has a style, when you compare it to clapboard, stone, or glass. It is a way of building, with its own charisma. No practicality of construction or of dress is secure from being a statement of identity and affiliation. It may be true that some things are more readily seen as style than others, but still, a categorical distinction, one that sorts the things of the world into those that can carry style and those that cannot, is a doomed project. Better to think of style as a way of seeing, a register of experience—an aspect under which anything at all can appear to us, or not. If that is true, substance, too, is an aspect, and anything we can call substance we can call, in another mood, style.

§85 But Only Wind

> Throughout the world, if it were sought,
> Fair words enough a man shall find.
> They be good cheap; they cost right naught;
> Their substance is but only wind.
> But well to say and so to mean—
> That sweet accord is seldom seen.

§86 Making an Oration

A traditional rhetorical education depends upon the power to conceive of ideas in a styleless state. The good student knows composition to have five stages. The first is *inventio*, invention, "the finding out of apt matter": the stuff of argument, the ideas and reasons, "things true, or things likely, the which may reasonably set forth a matter." The definition here is Thomas Wilson's, from his *Arte of Rhetorique*, but any number of other early modern manuals would serve. Cicero's *Orator* and the pseudo-Ciceronian *Rhetorica ad Herennium* are the common wellsprings. Next after invention comes *dispositio*, disposition, "an apt bestowing, and orderly placing of things, declaring where every argument shall be set." (Wilson again.) In this phase the elements of the argument take their proper order, the order of their logical and evidentiary consequence. Only then, once the things are discovered and set in place, does style lend its dress. *Elocutio*, sometimes *eloquentia*, is "an applying of apt words and sentences to the matter." Here are the schemes and tropes, the elements of style deployed as a tactic of persuasion. They are added to the matter, not of it. Next comes *memoria*, memorization, and finally *pronunciatio*, the performance, "framing of the voice, countenance, and gesture, after a comely manner." The more sophisticated theorists remind their readers that the division of matter from eloquence is an artificial one. "It might be thought that . . . they interact so closely that any distinction between them belongs to theory rather than practice," says Erasmus. "Even so, I intend to separate them as a teaching procedure." Teaching procedures, of course, can matter more to habits of thinking than the theories that support them.

§87 I Speak as One

I speak as one whose filth
is like his own, of pride
and speed and your terrible
example nearer than the sirens' speech,
a spirit eager for the punishment
which is your only recognition.

§88 The Time of Style (3): After

According to the theory of rhetoric, style is not *already*, not the
network of affinity waiting for the instance, already in place when
we begin to speak. It is *after*: after the idea, after the substance and
its arrangement; after *inventio* and *dispositio*; something added on
to something that existed before it. Common sense and common
usage lend support to this way of thinking, when we treat style, for
example, as clothing put onto a naked body that was already there.

§89 Mine Own John Poyntz

My Poyntz, I cannot frame my tune to feign,
   To cloak the truth for praise, without desert,
   Of them that list all vice for to retain.
I cannot honour them that sets their part
   With Venus and Bacchus all their life long,
   Nor hold my peace of them although I smart.
I cannot crouch nor kneel to do such wrong
   To worship them like God on earth alone
   That are like wolves these silly lambs among.
I cannot with my words complain and moan
   And suffer naught, nor smart without complaint,
   Nor turn the word that from my mouth is gone.

§90 The Third Limit of Style: Helplessness

Everything has a style. One way to imagine escaping from it
would be to give up, to speak the plain truth because you cannot

do otherwise. Wyatt's poem takes the form of a verse letter to his friend John Poyntz, a fellow courtier who shared his commitment to a Stoical humanism. (*Felix qui poterit* was Poyntz's motto, happy who will be able.) The letter is a satire, one of three Wyatt wrote, two of them to Poyntz, and it deplores the vices of the court, the drunkenness and lechery and deceit. Wyatt cannot get the trick of that life, and the poem's terza rima tercets are an inventory of his incapacities. He cannot pretend to sufferings he does not feel, nor keep silent in true pain; he cannot recall, nor will he repent, a word once spoken. He cannot give false counsel for advantage. The poem could be read upside-down as a how-to manual for getting along in court, in its specific, detailed, and nearly exhaustive catalog of vices. But exhaustion saves its speaker: "My wit is naught. I cannot learn the way." Weariness allows him to abjure control over what he says, able neither to tune his song for the occasion nor restrain it for his own protection. The poem could only be called styleless if style is always mendacious, the art of bending and concealing the plain truth, and if Wyatt's candor therefore immunized him. But it can certainly be called plain, and Wyatt is at pains to write an English that could be the voice, or the sound, of true counsel: his Anglo-Saxon vocabulary, his paratactic structures. (The rhyme does sometimes torture the syntax, but mostly into awkwardness rather than sophistication.) It is as though that plain sound could truly be defined by negation, the stripping away, or falling away, *I cannot, I cannot*, of strategy and ornament to find the truth beneath it.

§91 Style and Truth (1)

Can style be true or false? Can it be truth or fiction? It may seem plausible to say that a true style is one that is proper to its subject, a false style one that violates that propriety, and that an inappropriate, an indecorous style might be a fiction, even a lie. (A lie like Anne Boleyn wearing Queen Katherine's jewels.) So, the style is a proposition, and the substance is what the proposition is about. Such a structure of correspondence is one of the readiest ways to moralize style. Either the style fits, or else it lies.

§92 To the Film Industry in Crisis (1)

the Tarzans, each and every one of you (I cannot bring myself to prefer Johnny Weissmuller to Lex Barker, I cannot!)

§93 Synonymy (1)

Can two sentences, made up of different words, mean the same thing? Much of what is said about style would seem to depend upon the idea that they can, to depend upon the possibility of synonymy, saying the same thing in different ways. How would it be possible to recognize two different styles, two ways, two *hows*, unless they were styles of the same thing, the same *what*?

§94 De Copia

"Always, as long as I live, I shall remember you," writes Erasmus in his *De Copia*. "Never, as long as I live, shall I fail to remember you." He provides another two hundred variations before the last good-bye. "As long as I shall be allowed to have the pleasure of my soul, to speak after Sallust's fashion, I will not cease to take pleasure in recollecting you." The idea of a style that can vary independently of the subject, substance, meaning, and so on is of pragmatic value to the orator and the teacher. It epitomizes the technical conception of style, and style's freedom of choice, a free style. Nor is Erasmus's choice of a theme an accident. When is style's implicit promise of continuing, of a way of going on, more important than in the management of an *adieu*? "Adieu to Norman, Bon Jour to Joan and Jean-Paul."

§95 Synonymy (2)

"The more we reflect on it," Graham Hough protests, "the more doubtful it becomes how far we can talk about *different ways of saying*; is not each different way of saying in fact the saying of a different thing?" There have been attempts to put the concept of synonymy on a more solid conceptual footing. E. D. Hirsch argues that the difference between "spilled milk" and "spilt milk" may be salient in some situations but not in others. (Yes, in the drawing room; no, in the nursery.) When not, the two are synonyms. Others have attempted to define aspects or levels of language that are deep enough to remain constant in spite of superficial, stylistic difference. Richard Ohmann suggests that generative grammar may offer a ground of meaning against which stylistic difference may be judged. The deep structure stays the same, while the style varies. He acknowledges the "ontological queerness of disembodied content—propositions, for instance—divorced from any verbal expression." But at the same time he worries that failure to find such a basis "leads to the altogether counterintuitive conclusion that there can be no such thing as style, or that style is simply a part of content."

§96 Meditations in an Emergency (1)

> Each time my heart is broken it makes me feel more adventurous (and how the same names keep recurring on that interminable list!), but one of these days there'll be nothing left with which to venture forth.

§97 Synonymy (3)

Style requires synonymy, but there are no true synonyms. Nelson Goodman proposes another way out of the problem, by relaxing the categories: "distinctness of style from content requires not that exactly the same thing may be said in different ways but only that what is said may vary nonconcomitantly with ways of saying." Or, in Antoine Compagnon's approving paraphrase, "to save style, one is not obliged to believe in exact and absolute synonymy, but only to admit that there are highly diverse ways of saying very similar things, and conversely, very similar ways of saying highly diverse things." This relaxation is the pragmatism of the thesaurus, which treats a synonym as a word that is pretty close, sometimes interchangeable, but still usefully different.

§98 Synonymy (4)

What is the difference between style and substance? One answer, always at the ready, is that one is masculine and one is feminine. That is, style is feminine, ornamental, yielding, while substance is masculine, anchoring, authoritative. Unless, of course, style is the masculine signature inscribed by the stylus upon impressionable, feminine matter. Gender has its preferences with style, but they are not always predictable. Style, for its part, is accommodating, being barely a synonym with itself.

§99 The Anxiety of Appropriation (1)

Can I take away your style? No: style is not a commodity. The more people do it, or have it, whatever the right word is, the more there is to go around, and the more it is a style.

§100 Synonymy (5)

The attempt to relax the categories of style and content without abrogating them shifts the ground of thinking from philosophy to rhetoric, the criteria from logic to persuasion. If such open categories still count as philosophy, it is philosophy of a certain style, closer to art history or literary criticism, a dancing partner with language rather than a dancing master. Just as the philosopher may seek to reveal the structures of thought that underlie style's charismatic filiations, so style can round on philosophy, to make a map of the philosopher's places and affinities, a map that purports better to explain how philosophy works than its own, internal reckoning can. The question is again one of aspect, seeing each as the other. It is not out of bounds, if we are talking style about philosophy, to observe that Goodman kept company with artists, and ran a gallery in Copley Square while completing his doctorate in philosophy at Harvard; or that Compagnon's *Literature, Theory, and Common Sense* was titled, in the original French, *Le Démon de la Théorie*.

§101 The Long Love

The long love that in my thought doth harbour
And in mine heart doth keep his residence
Into my face presseth with bold pretence
And therein campeth, spreading his banner.

§102 Style and Skill (1)

Differences of skill, like differences of style, are most readily assessed if the occasion is held constant: given two performances of the same task, two cadenzas or two bow shots, one can be said to be more skillful than the other. The difference between skill and style lies in the *more*. Skill is easy to quantify by degree, assuming as it does an ideal efficiency. Style resists such measurement, not always, nor perfectly (someone can be said to have *more style* than someone else), but it nonetheless tends away from a single criterion. If skill can be represented as a gradient, style wants a map.

§103 Love That Doth Reign

Love that doth reign and live within my thought,
And built his seat within my captive breast,
Clad in the arms wherein with me he fought
Oft in my face he doth his banner rest.

§104 Style and Skill (2)

Wyatt and Surrey both translated Petrarch's "*Amor, che nel penser mio vive e regna*": "Love who lives and reigns in my thought," in Robert Durling's modern translation. (Their nineteenth-century editor Nott, swayed more by Surrey's self-advertisements than by the historical record, imagined the poems written in "friendly competition . . . as a sort of exercise of style.") Surrey's "Love that doth reign" is closer to the Italian. It is also smoother, a steady run of iambs, its principled liberties taken only with the flexible first foot, "Lóve that doth reígn," "Óft in my fáce." It is altogether more skillful than Wyatt's "The long love." Which is to say, it is more interested in verse as a skill; it solicits evaluation according to norms. Of Wyatt it might be said that the pentameter is not a norm, but one of many available effects, given his general commitment to a decasyllabic line. He writes five iambs when he wants to, and they give him moments of particular poise or conviction, but they never become a stable criterion by which to judge the rhythmic variety of the rest. For Surrey, they did. He was an earl, scion of the Howards, one of the most powerful families in England. Some of the country's noblest blood ran boiling hot in his veins. For him, the five-iamb line is like that seat built within the breast, or like the too-great house he would build for himself, near the end of his short life, at Kenninghall.

§105 Where Is Your Love

I am standing here with my harp in the frigid light.
I hear you by my side, but where are you? where is your love?
I sense, O my friend, that in the distant air
a great height is descending to make war upon me.
I have been alone for a long time.

§106 Style and Skill (3)

Humanist and courtier John Cheke's elegy for Surrey celebrated his tongue as "a subtle tool to file the rough-hewn to the best, / Of style a stream to flow." Fellow poet George Turberville asked, "What should I speak in praise of Surrey's skill / Unless I had a thousand tongues at will?" Surrey came first in Tottel's *Songs and Sonnets*, as he would have wished it: the full title was *Songs and Sonnets Written by the Right Honorable Lord Henry Howard Earl of Surrey, and Other*. Surrey was the measure, and for more than two centuries after, Wyatt's verse was filed to fit.

§107 Style as Hearsay (1)

"We'll open with a question," said Joan Mitchell, another painter friend, the host of the wedding party where O'Hara read out his call for happiness. "Is style hearsay?" The scene was the Club, at

39 East Eighth Street, since 1949 the intellectual headquarters of the abstract expressionist painters. The occasion was a panel about "Hearsay," and the participants were Mitchell; her fellow painters Mike Goldberg, Norman Bluhm, and Elaine de Kooning; and O'Hara. Near the end of the transcript comes the following exchange:

> MIKE: About Dada—style becomes inevitably the structure on which one hangs nothing, not even oneself.
>
> NORMAN: Joan says style's not a structure. It's a skin. It's not inside. It's outside.
>
> ELAINE: Fairfield says it *comes* from inside. When asked: Where does it go, Fairfield says—I don't care; anywhere it likes.
>
> MIKE: Style is some thing one builds brick by brick on which one *hangs* the skin.
>
> NORMAN: There's only one reason I don't like that word, skin. It reminds me of architecture.

The Club could be a serious place, hosting discussions of "Nature and the New Painting" (an essay of O'Hara's) or "The Image in Poetry." The problem of style and substance is a serious problem: the very definition of a serious problem, if seriousness is a matter of making sure that words and things are securely attached to one another. Mike turns the problem inside-out, or upside-down, putting the style underneath, as a structure; for good measure, he strips away the cloak or clothes that might have hung off it. Norman, citing Joan, turns everything right-side-out and -up again: style is the exterior, the skin, as usual. Elaine ratifies that restoration by explaining, via the painter Fairfield Porter, that outward style is an expression of what is inside. Then Mike takes them back to the idea that style *is* the inside; now it is as substantial as bricks. The question is left hanging, what to make of the skin. Norman only remarks that it reminds him of architecture. (He had dropped out of architecture school before the war, and it was apparently a bad memory.)

§108 Style and Freedom (1)

Call style that can be varied independently of content *free style*. Free style is the pedagogical premise of the rhetorician. Call style that is constrained to express its content *bound style*. Bound style is the dream of the Stoic, or perhaps it is the hope that the Stoic is left with, waking from the dream of having no style at all.

§109 Style as Hearsay (2)

Elaine de Kooning prepared the script for the hearsay panel, culling the lines from three garrulous evenings of private conversation leading up to the event. It is a send-up of the high-toned art and poetry gossip that swirled around the Club: "Joan says Norman said," "George says Mayakovsky says," "Milton says somebody told him somebody in the New Testament said," "Ernestine Lassaw told Franz Kline and Tom Young that Bob Rauschenberg told her that Joseph Cornell saw," and so on. It shows a community acutely concerned with style, with craft ("Elaine says sharpening pencils is practically a lost art") and its limits ("the cult of ineptness"), and with competition ("the race to master and surpass the 'look' of others"). All of it is playfully distributed through the network of second- and third- and fourth-handedness that is both the recurring joke and the structure of the occasion. In these chains of report, styles are mixed into something like a collective, a house idiom, capacious enough to hold them all together and to absorb *Paradise Lost* and the Bible too. At the same time, as playfully as the banter may juggle style and substance, it respects the difference. Part of the fun is listening for the voices of the participants across all the mediations of their transmission. O'Hara is on hand, but also often cited: Norman says "Frank says: Style at its lowest ebb is method. Style at its highest ebb is personality."

§110 Wyatt by Subtraction

Hyder Rollins: "Few of his poems show traces of humanistic influence; of those that do, two epigrams translated from Ausonius and Pandulpho, two moral songs from Seneca and Boethius, two satires suggested (though perhaps indebted through the Italian) by Horace, and a tiresome 'Song of Iopas' indebted to Virgil make up the known total." A. C. Spearing: "There is no Chaucerian name-dropping, no Lydgatean moralizing, no Skeltonian bandying of quotations and technical terms, no scholasticism, no encyclopedism, no informativeness, little classical mythology, no sustained allegory, almost no personification, no elevated diction, no amplification . . . no Muses . . . no appeals to Apollo, no apostrophic prologues, above all no sense that the poem is ratified by its place in the literary tradition that its words evoke." Thomas Greene: "an idiom that is radically anti-Latinate and calls attention to its own parochial rusticity. . . . He suppressed classical mythology; he avoided descriptions of nature and of women; and he led the English lyric a few steps further toward its eventual parting from music. He seems deliberately to have muted whatever imagistic brilliance he found in the *Canzoniere*. . . . The drabness of Wyatt's language is of course essential to his moral style."

§111 Style Is Everything (1)

Oscar Wilde—"the divine Oscar," as young O'Hara called him—did not much respect the difference between style and substance. "In all unimportant matters, style, not sincerity, is the essential. In all important matters, style, not sincerity, is the essential." His double aphorism sounds like the playful juggling of brick, skin, and self on the hearsay panel, but it is not, really. The terms do not trade places; rather, sincerity, or call it seriousness, is twice discarded. The art of Wilde's aphorism is to take the idea of the essential, the essence, with all its ancient philosophical seriousness, and turn its inside out, without turning its outside in—there is nothing left but outside. Stripped of its wit, you might say style is everything. That position is one way out of the problem of style and substance. Wilde takes an insouciantly unmetaphysical view of the world, and makes the wager that you can get by on style alone. Who needs *what* if you have enough *how*?

§112 The Metaphysics of Style

Style has no metaphysics; though metaphysics may have a style, so long as there is more than one of them.

§113 Free Style

Larry Rivers was sick. This was sometime in the 1950s. Not desperately sick, just laid up in bed, and housebound. John Ashbery knew it, and he didn't visit—he had breakfast with Jane Freilicher instead—but he felt bad afterward, and wrote his friend an apologetic letter.

> Rumor hath it that you are sore annoyed with me for not going and having breakfast with you that day when you were indisposed. But, my dear fellow, surely you remember that before I made the fatal phone call to Jane you had unequivocally stated that you would be unable to have it with me! It was only then that I received the inspiration to call her. Of course, I should have stayed with you and smoothed the pillow of your illness, but it seems to me that I offered to and you uttered a demurrer. And I was so hungry! Please, please, in these days of factions let there be no feelings of rancor 'twixt you and me.

The letter begins up high: the diction is fancy and old-fashioned, Shakespearian at first, then maybe Edwardian ("my dear fellow"); there is a showy metaphor ("pillow of your illness") and an unexpected legalism ("demurrer"), which also sounds French. Then the tone drops: "And I was so hungry!" Then, just as abruptly, back to the altitude of *Romeo and Juliet*, with the talk of rancor and factions. The point of the performance is free play. Ashbery can travel up and down the spectrum of diction and syntax, from faux-formal to plain Jane; in a space of such freedom, slights can easily be forgotten. He is no more locked into a particular style than Rivers is locked into his resentment. What virtuosi, of words and of friendship! And as Rivers explains, it worked, a small job easily done. The letter survives (he quotes it in his autobiography) as an exhibit in the everyday, solvent dexterities of a circle of wit, free style freely given.

§114 The Aspect of Style (2)

To say style is an aspect is to invoke a philosophical tradition of seeing-as: the word *Aspekt* is used by Wittgenstein, and often attached to the famous duck-rabbit drawing (figure 1) he adapted for his *Philosophical Investigations*. His claim is that you can see the image as a duck, looking left, unfazed by the dent in the back of his head, or as an ingenuous, stargazing rabbit. Just not both at the same time. But try looking at it for its style—looking under the aspect of style. It may help to have another instance to hand, the first appearance of the image (figure 2), in a German comic magazine in 1892. How easy, and how not wrong, it is to say that one is looking at the same thing in different styles. That difference and that

FIGURE 1. Duck-Rabbit from Ludwig Wittgenstein's *Philosophical Investigations* (1953).

FIGURE 2. "Rabbit and Duck" from *Fliegende Blätter* (1892).

sameness are what it means to see now under style's aspect. (The two images are not themselves different aspects; it is their juxtaposition that proposes the aspect of style for both, that prompts the recognition of their stylistic difference.) According to the critic Richard Lanham, the difference is between looking *through* (reading for the referent, duck or rabbit) and looking *at* (for the style, for the different ways of making a duck-rabbit). Looking *at* the images, at the way each was drawn and made, distracts us from asking what they mean. But there is something more to the style-aspect than just looking *at*. It is also looking *out*, looking outward, to the object's coordination with other instances, be they diagram or illustration or cartoon, twentieth-century or nineteenth; the movement not through the object of attention, but radiating out from it to the likeness and differences elsewhere, actual and possible. The aspect of style is its continuing, seeing-as as seeing-like.

§115 Bound Style

Ashbery's letter has an interesting coda.

> This letter, in a style I have not indulged in since the age of sixteen, may be a product of the dexedrine I have been taking to lose weight and of several gallons of black coffee, and some typhoid and smallpox shots I had this morning.

It is a style (or styles) he has not indulged in since adolescence. Why fall back on them just now? Because of the dexedrine, he explains, to lose weight; the coffee, to stay alert; the typhoid and smallpox shots. Rivers himself, of course, has been sick. This little game of style dances across some serious business, and the performance is coordinated, playfully, with forces that may not be so easily controlled, age, illness, drugs and the need of them. Of which the style might be an involuntary symptom.

§116 This Painful Fit

> And for the end of this my song,
> Unto your hands I do submit

My deadly grief and pains so strong
Which in my heart be firmly shut.
And when ye list, redress my wrong
Since well ye know this painful fit
Hath last too long.

§117 Style as Symptom (1)

To call style a symptom is to treat it as a trace or a clue, but instead of connoisseurship, the project is diagnosis. Style manifests some underlying disease; perhaps the self itself is a disease, suffered by an innocent organism that might otherwise flourish. Style so borne is not ease, but a set of discomforts, constraints, and compulsions. Disease also carries with it the idea of contagion, from person to person, as though style might be catching, which it is.

§118 The First Antithesis of Style

The problem of style and substance is really two problems. First, whether style can be separated from substance at all, and what it means to do so. Second, if the separation is allowed, the attendant problem of free style and bound style. And then, third, or perhaps first, the problem of the problem. How could style be a problem at all? Isn't it rather a solution, as Oscar Wilde would want us to see? If in fact style is a way, it is perverse to turn that way into an obstacle or a knot. — Nonetheless, the phrase *the problem of style* has recurred as topos and even title over many decades of scholarship and criticism. (J. V. Cunningham's *The Problem of Style*, in 1966, or John Middleton Murry's *The Problem of Style*, in 1922, or Georg Simmel's essay, *"Das Problem des Stiles,"* in 1908, and so on.) For some spirits, free style, style that can vary independently of its object, is an abject submission to circumstance, mere weather. The only true freedom is the integrity of a style anchored constantly in a substrate of character, bound style. — But the opposite argument is even easier to make: how could style be free, if it cannot change? What can be said, from here, is only that the problem of style is a problem of freedom.

ART AND NATURE

§119 Style Is Everything (2)

Wilde once again: "In all unimportant matters, style, not sincerity, is the essential. In all important matters, style, not sincerity, is the essential." *Art* might be substituted for *style* and *nature* for *sincerity*; in the same suite of aphorisms, Wilde allows that "a really well-made buttonhole is the only link between Art and Nature." He had little interest, however, in the nature side of the divide. "The first duty in life is to be as artificial as possible. What the second duty is no one has as yet discovered." Wilde's blithe monism declares for one side of the second irony of style, art and nature. Art is enough. The technical senses of *art*—the Latin *ars* is the usual translation of the Greek *techne*—were not necessarily what he meant by artificiality. He had a certain distaste for ostentatious technique. Then again, art's ambition to find a method for elegance is an unending source of technical elaboration, and Wilde would not have been entirely dismayed to be admired for a tailor's way with a chiasmus. Such elaboration begins in the intuition that style has parts. It is structured by the idea that style has levels.

§120 Levels of Style (1)

The levels of style, you learn in school: high style and low style, and usually a middle style between them. The canonical statement belongs to Cicero, the very soul of style, most eloquent of the Roman golden age rhetoricians so admired by the sixteenth century. (It was a matter of active debate: should one use any Latin words that Cicero had not? Any constructions? Eloquence reached with him "such a peak of perfection," Erasmus wrote, with a sigh for his own age, "that there was no possibility of further development.") The *Orator* explains: first there is the *genus grande*, high style, which shows "splendid power of thought and majesty of diction"; it is forceful, versatile, and serious, and rouses strong emotions. Some orators achieve its effects by poised and rounded sentences, a syntax of premeditation. Others use a rougher vocabulary, and blunter, less regular sentence structures, the heat of an urgent occasion. Both heighten intensity. At the bottom of the same ladder, the *genus humile*, low or plain style, "explaining everything and making every point clear rather than impressive, using a refined, concise style stripped of ornament." The low style will make use of familiar maxims; it may have about it the sound of someone paying more attention to thought than to words, but this, Cicero says, will be a *"neglegentia . . . diligens,"* a careful negligence. The low style is no less a matter of art than its opposite. Between them, on the middle rungs, a style *"medius et quasi temperatus,"* moderate and tempered, the middle style, which uses "neither the intellectual appeal of the latter class nor the fiery force of the former." These three styles would come to be identified with three canonical motives: the high style, moving its audience (*movere*); the middle, pleasing (*conciliare* or *placere*); the low, teaching (*docere*).

§121 The Middle

"Perhaps it is to avoid some great sadness," O'Hara begins,

> as in a Restoration tragedy the hero cries "Sleep!
> O for a long sound sleep and so forget it!"
> that one flies, soaring above the shoreless city,

veering upward from the pavement as a pigeon
does when a car honks or a door slams

He wrote these lines on a dare: James Schuyler and Joe LeSueur
were teasing him over breakfast about his "unquenchable inspiration"; Schuyler recalled how "the cigarette smoke began jetting
from Frank's nostrils and he went into the next room and wrote
SLEEPING ON THE WING in a great clatter of keys." His poems
chase exaltations (the vaulting sprung rhythm of "Ó for a lóng
sóund sléep") and affirm ordinariness (the spondaic come-down of
"cár hónks or a dóor sláms"). What they avoid most is the middle:
the middle moods, the small pleasures and sorrows of the everyday,
the middle style of which it might be said that his friend John
Ashbery became the perpetual, infinitely modulating master. For
O'Hara, there was a great sadness in the middle, sadder than ec-
stasy and sadder than despair.

§122 Altitude

You don't need school to tell high style from low, any more than to
tell the soprano from the bass. What makes the high style high?
Some share of the difference is authority, the commanding or hor-
tatory aspect of the high style, spoken from a podium, a pulpit, a
horse, a judgment seat. The spine is straight and the lungs are full.
The posture of the high style is one of confident altitude. The sentences are longer; they take more time, ask more patience of the
audience. Energy is being spent, for a purpose. The low style, by
contrast, will tend toward the deferential bow or the nod of shared
confidence. The volume is lower, spoken not to followers or adversaries but to superiors, companions, confidants. It is brief and
to the point. Energy is being conserved, again for a purpose. The
pitch of speech itself will figure: a high pitch carries far, asks attention, while a low pitch subsides into the murmurous background.
The low style is safely grounded, while the high is aloft, and in its
height dangerous to others and also vulnerable. All are positions of
the body, in itself and in relation to other bodies.

§123 Levels of Style (2)

Another version of the ladder is articulated by Thomas Wilson, writing in 1550:

> There are iii manner of styles or inditings, the great or mighty kind, when we use great words, or vehement figures: The small kind, when we moderate our heat by meaner words, and use not the most stirring sentences: The low kind, when we use no metaphors, nor translated words, nor yet use any amplifications, but go plainly to work, and speak altogether in common words.

Cicero cares most of all for syntax, the grand periods of which he was master. Wilson's hierarchy is built of words and figures, small verbal units rather than grand gestures. (Notwithstanding the handsome tricolon of the description above.) He has a pragmatic, one might say English commitment to the common language in which interlocutors go plainly to work together; he finds a virtue in the language's constraints on word order, better for plain talk than Latin's prodigious flexibility. All is at the service of decorum, propriety, fitness, finding the right style to get what you want, under the circumstances. "Comeliness therefore must ever be used, and all things observed that are most mete for every cause, if we look by attempts to have our desire."

§124 I Tell Thee It Is Mine

Say you are playing bowls on the level sward of one of the green courts at Hampton Palace, one of the king's great pastimes. The year is 1527, or thereabouts; Katherine will be queen yet for six more years. The object is to cast your ball closest to the jack, and to displace the balls of your competitors. Your ball is closest, but the king claims the advantage: he says, plainly, "Wyatt, I tell thee it is mine."

§125 Style as Structure (1)

Style is a structure. Its three levels are a repertory for practical situations, with the sense of time-as-opportunity, so beloved of the orators, that is captured in the Greek term *kairos*. There is an endless repertoire of strategies for making the necessary adjustments, with each scheme and trope effecting a delicate calibration of altitude and attitude. Less organized across the tradition are the factors that define the situation of speech. There is no canonical number or division, but a fair count would be five:

occasion

speaker **level** audience

topic motive

This ad hoc diagram offers the prospect of mastery. A noble speaker will tend to use a high style, though perhaps not when addressing a servant; a humble subject may petition authority in a high style, out of a sense of occasion, or she may prefer to be modestly, deferentially plain. The same recommendations obtain for a ceremonial occasion, a weighty topic, a serious purpose. The five factors can be rotated and rearranged to reflect their relative importance. There is always some animal sense of looming or cowering in the hierarchy, but its formalism can help reconcile participants to the particular dignity of their positions, and the positions can shift (in the agon of argument), or can be shared (when kings talk to kings, or friends to friends). The point of the system is to be legible, predictable, and to provide all participants with a way to continue.

§126 Style as an Image of Order

If there is a proper style for any occasion, for any moment—a style that will work, if you can find it; ideally, work for anyone—then the concept of style will serve as the image of an integral culture. Social life is not a series of crises or unpredictable contests. Rhetoric is the adequate art of its every occasion. Any contradictions can be harmonized by eloquence. In this sense the technical ideal, style as an art, gives a picture of a society whose variety and contradictions, and whose members, can be arranged at any given moment along a single, vertical axis, from high to low. Also, therefore, a society that does not need to change, at least not in its structure.

§127 Yippee!

It is an inner necessity of many O'Hara poems to break decorum, especially their own decorum.

> disbelieving your own feelings is the worst
> and you suspect that you are jealous of this death
>   YIPPEE! I'm glad I'm alive
>   "I'm glad you're alive
> too, baby, because I want to fuck you"

There is an aphoristic seriousness to the first line. The second is a gnomic, graceful alexandrine. (O'Hara's French was good.) Its very grace provokes the ensuing outburst, and then the answer—is it a proposition, or somebody else's line coming to mind? The decorum broken is not just aesthetic. It is also social decorum, what follows from what with whom, what you can say when; what you can say, and still be loved for it. There is a bid for freedom in this discontinuity. Freedom from style? Just as importantly, a bid for intimacy: I can say anything to you! Can't I?

§128 I Hope It Will Be Mine

It is said that Wyatt stole a jeweled lace from Anne Boleyn, in an opportunistic moment of courtly gamesmanship. (Perhaps it was a bid for her attentions; perhaps it was a reminder of a former intimacy. The story comes from the same not entirely reliable cache of family papers that yields the meeting with Russell on the Thames, and the encounter with the lion.) By the time of their game of bowls Henry had taken his own fateful interest in Anne, and had won a ring to wear on his finger. With this finger he gestured to his ball: "Wyatt, I tell thee it is mine." Wyatt produced the telltale lace from his doublet to measure his own claim. "And if it may like your majesty to give me leave to measure it," he said to the king, "I hope it will be mine." Wyatt's perfectly polite antagonism, with its *may* and *hope*, is finely judged, a modest elevation ambiguous between tribute and challenge. "Conversation with the king," Stephen Greenblatt has written, "must have been like small talk with

Stalin." If his grandson George Wyatt is to be believed, that day Thomas got away with it.

§129 Style and Truth (2)

All style is false. The problem is not the mis-fit between style and substance; that is, truth is not to be sought in the agreement of the one with the other. Substance, content, the *about*—this alone is truth, and any style at all, layered or plastered or painted on top, must falsify it. Or, more generously, style is an accommodating fiction that allows the truth to make its way in the world. But still, some kind of fiction, some kind of deception.

§130 Levels of Style (3)

Style is an art. But there are not enough levels—how could three suffice? Quintilian, a century and a half after Cicero, wonders if such divisions will always be too crude for the subject. (There are four winds, "but really there are many in between, which have their own names and are in some cases peculiar to certain areas or rivers": winds from different compass points, and with different local habitations, names, maybe accents.) Demetrius adds a fourth genus, the forceful. Hermogenes of Tarsus, in his *On Types of Style*, is the most taxonomically expansive of the ancients. What he offers is less a hierarchy than an orchestra of styles, for combination in different proportions by particular orators. There are seven types, grandeur, clarity, beauty, rapidity, character, sincerity, and force; each has its own roster of subtypes, grandeur, for example, being divisible into solemnity, asperity, vehemence, and brilliance. There is a question of the point at which this repertory becomes coextensive with the available adjectives in literary Greek, but Hermogenes insists that his types remain a structure, not merely a descriptive repertory. "Since it is not possible to understand or appreciate a mixture, in reference to style or anything else, until we recognize the various elements out of which the mixture was created," he argues; "we must ignore the style of individual writers." The structure comes first.

§131 PS

O'Hara, in a letter to Grace Hartigan in the summer of 1957: "PS
We must have a long talk in a dune; boy, have I been depressed
lately, it almost makes me think I have a sensibility!"

§132 Imitation (1)

"Indeed," Hermogenes says, "imitation and emulation of the ancients that depend upon mere experience and some irrational
knack cannot, I think, produce what is correct, even if a person
has a lot of natural ability." *Imitatio* is an art: the technical refine-
ment of the use of the ancients, breaking down their styles, building them up again piece by piece. It is a defense against imitation,
against the inchoate operations of charisma on the voice, against
inclination and tendency and tropism.

§133 Levels of Style (4)

Or are there too many levels? Aristotle needed only two, two kinds
of speech, rhetoric and clarity. Which is to say that he makes the
distinction between style and no style, art and artlessness, between
persuasive language and its philosophical content. Rhetoric itself
is a necessary, if unfortunate, concession to public life: "For it is
not enough to know *what* we ought to say; we must also say it *as* we
ought." Any effective speech will be a mean between the style and
substance, a mean of the sort that also characterizes his account
of virtue as the middle path between two extremes. The reckoning
of that mean is ultimately a practical matter, responsive to *kairos*
precisely because it is not a discrete category, but a ratio. G. L. Hendrickson argues that the mean enters rhetoric as a proper third
term with the articulation of the *genera dicendi* in the *Rhetorica
ad Herennium*, long taken to have been written by Cicero. "The inevitable rise," as he puts it, "of a tertium quid," a compromise, a
third way.

§134 After a Diverse Fashion

The octet of one of Wyatt's sonnets:

> Each man me telleth I change most my device,
> And on my faith me think it good reason
> To change purpose like after the season.
> For in every case to keep still one guise
> Is meet for them that would be taken wise;
> And I am not of such manner condition
> But treated after a diverse fashion,
> And thereupon my diverseness doth rise.

No model has been discovered for this poem; it seems to be Wyatt's own, start to finish. *How do you expect me*, it asks, *to be constant, when I am treated so variably?* It is a plain-style complaint from a frustrated Stoic, but it reserves some strategic ingenuity for itself, a subtle show of the speaker's unused resources. The irony of "on my faith" is brazen; "keep still one guise" (just one disguise?) only slightly less so. "Manner condition," in its ostentatious redundancy, may be eking out the line, or it may be an advisedly gratuitous flourish, as though to accuse the reader of a taste for such empty aureation. The level fluctuates almost with the length of the words. The sonnet is a courtly artifact, agile, inward, polite, obscurely threatening.

§135 Style as Structure (2)

Style is an art. Is it therefore a structure? The ancient and the modern terms, *art* and *structure*, share a dependence upon analysis, conceiving a situation in terms of its parts and their relation. An art puts this analysis to practical work, making something, as a musician makes melodies or a rhetorician sentences. Structure, in the sense afforded by twentieth-century structuralism, offers something more like a model, descriptive and predictive. It implies the completeness of a set of relations among elements, be they elements of a poem, a painting, a family, or a culture, and it requires no specific end, nor a god to watch over it, nor a form to aspire to. A structure operates without recourse to transcendental explanation. Everything is laid out on the flat of the tabletop or the blackboard.

§136 Style and Freedom (2)

"The purpose of these instructions," writes Erasmus, of his rules and examples, "is . . . to give you the choice, once you understand the principles, of emulating the Laconic style," the low style, "or of imitating the exuberance of Asianism," the high, "or of expressing yourself in the intermediate style of Rhodes," the middle. Erasmus's ideal student has a choice because he understands the principles. The variables of the situation are all available simultaneously: speaker, audience, topic, occasion, motive. If some are set, some are free, and none binds the others a priori. The situation is undetermined by the past and open to the future. In its presence to the now, it might be said to stand outside of time: history is not understood, in the scene of speaking, as a force flowing through the present, nor as a momentum of events that mocks agency, nor as a deep structure, but as a set of present considerations. Nothing is hidden in time. The orator is therefore free to operate within and by means of that structure, to the best of her ability. If that is not enough to realize her ends, at least the futility is not decided in advance.

§137 Free Choice (1)

Our motive's not
despicable, in play
we separate desire from the mirage
of sentiment and
ideal choice.

§138 Style and Freedom (3)

Style is a structure. The freedom of structure, or its promise of freedom, is not the freedom of the poet as inventor, as architect of a second nature or as an unacknowledged legislator. It is the freedom of the well-taught rhetorician, the limit of the technical conception of style, of style as *ars* and art. That freedom is also the reason why style-as-structure is such a durable idea: it brings the problem of style fully into consciousness, allowing for nothing that can make a difference that is not here and now, available to choose or not.

§139 Always One

> But you that blame this diverseness most,
> Change you no more, but still after one rate
> Treat ye me well and keep ye in the same state;
> And while with me doth dwell this wearied ghost,
> My word nor I shall not be variable
> But always one, your own both firm and stable.

§140 Style and Freedom (4)

Another voice from the 1950s, Roland Barthes:

> Whatever its sophistication, style has always something crude about it: it is a form with no clear destination, the product of a thrust, not an intention, and, as it were, a vertical and lonely dimension of thought. Its frame of reference is biological or biographical, not historical: it is the writer's "thing," his glory and his prison, it is his solitude. Indifferent to society and transparent to it, a closed personal process, it is in no way the product of a choice or of a reflection on Literature. . . . It is the decorative voice of hidden, secret flesh; it works as does Necessity.

Style is a structure, he says a moment later; but a carnal structure, *"une structure charnelle."* It takes its place in a three-part scheme, one of many Barthes would confect and discard over the course of his career, always a couple of steps ahead of would-be epigones. There is *language*, the horizon of historical possibility, what can be written at a given moment given the conventions in place. There is *writing*, which is the territory of choice, the possibilities of genre and mode open particularly to modern writers, the choice of classicism, say, or Marxism. *Style* is not the overarching system within which these constraints are arbitrated. Instead it is the third of three contending forces. What the word captures, for Barthes, is the determination of biology and of personal, intimate experience, both of them too deep for history to reach, or for literature as a merely social form. Style is solitary and intransigent and vested above all in bodies that cannot change. Style is what we are given to desire before we get to choose.

§141 They Flee from Me

They flee from me that sometime did me seek
With naked foot stalking in my chamber.
I have seen them gentle, tame, and meek
That now are wild and do not remember
That sometime they put themself in danger
To take bread at my hand; and now they range
Busily seeking with a continual change.

Thanked be fortune it hath been otherwise
Twenty times better, but once in special,
In thin array after a pleasant guise,
When her loose gown from her shoulders did fall
And she me caught in her arms long and small,
Therewithal sweetly did me kiss
And softly said, "Dear heart, how like you this?"

It was no dream: I lay broad waking.
But all is turned thorough my gentleness
Into a strange fashion of forsaking.
And I have leave to go of her goodness
And she also to use newfangleness.
But since that I so kindly am served
I would fain know what she hath deserved.

§142 Once in Special (1)

One of the poems for which Wyatt has come to be best known recalls a moment when the women at court were at his beck and call: they flee him now, but once they sought him out; more than twenty times over, he was their patron, their master, and their willing quarry. Still, there was one in special whom he finds he cannot forget, and the middle of the poem is the reverie of a singular occasion. It was no dream. But what happened, what happened? Somehow, by his own courtesy—he marvels at it now—she graciously let him leave, when he wanted to stay; her new manners got the better of his skill. "Fashion" and "newfangleness" are style words, and style is how Wyatt experiences the loss. He has slipped behind the times, he no longer knows the moves, and he is left to ask what she deserves. Perhaps that means, *what punishment suits her crime*, if crime it was. Or perhaps he is asking after something, for want of a better word, deeper than that: a kind of deserving that might hold steady, might remain, amidst so much change; that is not subject to fashion; that is not style at all. Love?

§143 Free Choice (2)

"O'Hara's work is characterized by its insistent and explicit thematizing of the process of choosing," writes the critic Michael Clune. It is not the object that ultimately matters, but the act. For Oren Izenberg, this constant expression of preference elevates "valuing as such in order to demonstrate that *that* is an activity . . . not bound by particular histories or restricted to particular communities." O'Hara's ambition is to escape style, to be "a poet who 'chose' everything, and as a result made no stylistic choices at all." Clune again: "O'Hara opens a way from individuality to collectivity, from the personal to the abstract, through the representation of personal choices that do not refer to particular persons. . . . This is free, or abstract, choice." And as Maggie Nelson points out, Joan Mitchell was fond of saying that "abstract is not a style."

§144 A Ferocious Desire

Anne Boleyn spoke very good French; at the age of thirteen she had been sent to the court of Margaret of Austria, in the Low Countries, to learn the graces of the Burgundian court, and sometime later she joined the household of Queen Claude, the young wife of the

King of France. Her much-admired skill in dancing and music was welcome when she returned to England, and as Henry's infatuation grew, he lavished her with gifts of jewelry and clothing, gowns in tawny velvet with black lambs' fur, in white satin, in sliver-lined purple cloth of gold, and so on. "She was the model and the mirror of those who were at court," wrote Nicholas Sander, fifty years later, "for she was always well dressed, and every day made some change in the fashion of her garments." Fashion: the English court had long imitated the elegance of Burgundy. No one in England was more fluent than Anne, and in 1533, she was at the apex of her favor. One morning in February she accosted a courtier outside her chamber, possibly Wyatt, who had possibly been her suitor, once, and possibly her lover. "For the last three days she had had such an incredibly ferocious desire to eat apples," she told him, "as she had never felt before, and . . . the king had said to her that it was a sign that she was with child."

§145 Emotion Itself

Ashbery to Rivers, sometime in the 1950s: "'They flee from me who one time did me seek': isn't that emotion itself, not the memory of it."

§146 Style as Expression (1)

Barthes's sense of style might be reformulated, if one were to let go, for a moment, of the lonely verticality of desire, of its secrecy and universal, private perversity—but what is left? of Barthes, at least?—all the same, it might be reformulated as the idea that style is expressive. That is, style is an outward manifestation of something inward, something that is not itself style but that determines style and pushes it out into the world. Here is the dualism of style and substance, not free, but bound: style is determined by the self behind or beneath it, by the nature of the author. If so, style is communicative, and interpretable, insofar as there is a something, a self, behind or beneath or inside it that attention to its surface might reveal. Which is to say that style begs for explanation and explaining is the right thing to do with it.

§147 Style as Expression (2): Personality

Expressive of what? One answer is *personality*, a word that comes to join its elder colleagues *self* and *character* in the nineteenth century. Style is the way you show who you are. That definition might suit O'Hara in some moods, or at least Norman says that "Frank says: Style at its lowest ebb is method. Style at its highest ebb is personality." But to say that style *is* personality is not the same as to say that style *expresses* personality. The former is close to Wilde: style is everything. The latter is a claim that has a different appeal, the anchoring of style in something other than style. It participates in the commonsense dualism of style and substance, and suits some philosophical accounts, those that are structured by a problem of reference.

§148 My Heart (1)

I'm not going to cry all the time
nor shall I laugh all the time,
I don't prefer one "strain" to another.
I'd have the immediacy of a bad movie,
not just a sleeper, but also the big,
overproduced first-run kind. I want to be
at least as alive as the vulgar. And if
some aficionado of my mess says "That's
not like Frank!," all to the good!

§149 Style as Expression (3): Personality

Style is "a way of *doing* certain things," and "an author's way of doing these things is an expression of her personality." So the philosopher Jenefer Robinson in her well-anthologized article "Style and Personality in the Literary Work." She cites Richard Wollheim's maxim: "We are interested only in the paintings of painters." That is, we are only interested in works that express the self of the maker, and a painter is "someone with a formed style." (A phrase to detain a moment, for its savor of paradox: "formed style.") What forms that style, Wollheim calls psychology. "Style—individual style of course—*has psychological reality.*" The practical yield of this "generative" account of style, this account of where style comes from, is that it offers the viewer of the painting the power to explain what she sees, and to explain it by going in deep rather than out wide. Style is not just for classifying, not just for grouping things together and telling them apart, for knowing your way around. You can look at the painting of a painter, or the poem of a poet, and ask of any of its features, *why?* Indeed, *why* is the most rewarding question to ask. The explanation will be psychological. To be properly interested in style is to be interested in the outside as an expression of the psychological interior, the interior which is its explanation.

§150 Style and Explanation (2)

Ah, but style never explains. If you have to ask. . . .

§151 Style and Mood

If you have a style, you must have a self, a self, moreover, that does not easily change. Where else could a recognizable style come from? Robinson writes: "Thus stylistic qualities are likely to be qualities of mind, moral qualities and deep-seated character traits, rather than mood or emotional qualities such as 'angry,' 'joyful,' and 'afraid.'" There is some reassurance here: style is not just a mood, the volatile, emotional equivalent of shifting fashion; indeed, style might be relied upon to control those passing states, the fluctuations of energy and of optimism that can derail the most ordinary day. "The paintings of painters": not just the paintings of people, but of people whose activity gives them a practical identity, a place in the world. *Who are you? I am a painter.* (Cf. O'Hara's "Why I Am Not a Painter.")

§152 Discipline and Personality

O'Hara found a formulation he liked in Apollinaire: "*Discipline et personnalité, voilà les limites du style comme je l'entends.*" "Isn't that cute?" he wrote to Kenneth and Janice Koch in January 1957.

But "I can't decide what it means. If only the *personnalité* came first I would understand." He used the same line writing to James Schuyler: "I just read this marvelous sentence from an Apollinaire letter: '*Discipline et personnalité, voilà les limites du style comme je l'entends . . .*' Isn't it the end?" The quote made the rounds. Schuyler put it in an *ARTnews* review of the painter Milton Resnick that March: "his credo might be Apollinaire's: discipline and my own personality."

§153 Style as Expression (4): The Body

Expressive of what? Another answer is the body. "A hand that taught what might be said in rhyme," said Surrey of Wyatt's gift. (But did Wyatt want to teach anybody anything?) The hand is one place a writer's style is specially situated, being, after all, the socket for the stylus. Another is the breath: "it seemed to me that the metrical, that the measure let us say, if you want to talk about it in Olson's poems or Ezra Pound's, comes from the breath of the person," O'Hara told an interviewer, "just as a stroke of paint comes from the wrist and hand and arm and shoulder and all that of the painter." The body is solid, fixed, the stable site of nature and fate over against the mind's art and choice. What E. H. Gombrich calls "physiognomic style" is the authority of nature at its maximum, a body before art, which art can translate but not efface or replace.

§154 Etymology

Style is from *stylus*: not the stylus at rest, on a single point; but the stylus in motion, continuing, in the particular way dictated by the hand that guides it. The Greek *character* is the engraver's chisel.

§155 Quiet of Mind (5)

"So all things is not for every man," wrote Wyatt. "But he that will obey the poesy of Apollo [know thyself] must first know him self, and so take advice of his own nature and as she leadeth to take an order of life, rather than passing from one to another to force and constrain his nature. An horse for the cart, an ox is meet for the plow, after a ship that saileth a dolphin is mete to swim, and to hunt the boar a fierce dog."

§156 Style as Expression (5): The Body

What is the body? Perhaps, whatever resists the perfection of technique. The body is what guarantees the idiosyncrasy of the artifact. The rest is versatile, malleable mind; technique, after all, can be learned by anyone. The body—the real body, not just the idea of it—is only what cannot successfully be reduced to method, and if the same can be said of style, then style is the body and the body is style and art must be something else again.

§157 Free Choice (3)

O'Hara goes out to eat:

> we go eat some fish and some ale it's
> cool but crowded we don't like Lionel Trilling
> we decide, we like Don Allen we don't like
> Henry James so much we like Herman Melville

The preference for Allen over Trilling and Melville over James is a kind of declaration of independence. Free choice! But then, aren't those the choices Frank O'Hara and LeRoi Jones, the other half of the poem's *we*, would be expected to make? It is hard to avoid one style except by another. As Izenberg allows, "O'Hara has proved to be one of our most imitable of poets," for all his unease with style, "providing a set of moves, gestures, and features that are, perhaps too easily, reproduced and transported."

§158 The Nature of Things

Wyatt's *nature* is *natura rerum*, the nature of things, their essential character. What modernity knows as the natural world, with its rocks and stones and trees, counts as natural for Wyatt because it is true to itself. By 1536, *Of the Quyete of Minde* was almost a decade behind him. Katherine's marriage to Henry had been undone three years before, and in January, in exile at the royal castle of Kimbolton, she died. But there was no male heir from the new queen Anne, only a daughter, Elizabeth, and some miscarriages. In May, Wyatt's mentor and protector Thomas Cromwell, the king's chamberlain, moved to imprison her, accusing her of adultery and casting her in the Tower. Six men went with her, including her brother Viscount Rochford, Francis Weston, William Brereton, Henry Norris, Mark Smeaton, and Thomas Wyatt.

§159 The Anxiety of Appropriation (2)

Can you take away my style? It is curious that the styles most in demand often belong—is that the word, *belong*?—to people who do not have much else that others want, to borrow or to buy.

§160 Thou Hast Said True

When Anne was informed who had joined her in the Tower, she asked Lady Kingston, wife to her jailor, whether there was anyone to make their beds for them. "Nay, I warrant you," Kingston replied. Anne quipped back, "they might make ballets well now," punning ruefully on "pallets" and "ballads," "but there is none but Rochford that can do it." Kingston corrected her: what about Master Wyatt? "By my faith," replied Anne, "thou has said true."

§161 Style as Expression (6): The Body

"A common tendency in the physiognomic approach to group style," wrote Meyer Schapiro in 1953, "has been to interpret all the elements of representation as expressions." Every visible trait, that is, has a root in the nature of the group. Schapiro put in his time at the Cedar Tavern and the Club; along with Harold Rosenberg and Clement Greenberg, he was one of the most important critic-advocates of the abstract expressionists. He handed on that phrase "physiognomic style" to Gombrich, who was still more caustic. "More often than not," Gombrich wrote of the anthropologists of style, "they are simply arguing in a circle and inferring from the static or rigid style of a tribe that its mentality must also be static or rigid." A different idea of the body is in play here, not the individual with his or her muscles and tendons, nerves, old injuries, and intransigent perversities, but the fixed bodies of race and nation. "The less collateral evidence there is, the more easily will this kind of diagnosis be accepted," Gombrich continued, "particularly if it is part of a system of polarities in which, for instance, dynamic cultures are opposed to static ones or intuitive mentalities to rational ones." These three critics of the 1950s, Schapiro, Greenberg, and Rosenberg, were Jewish, as was Gombrich; the memory of the war was fresh; they mistrusted the way expressivism could so easily become essentialism. Schapiro took arms a few years later against A. L. Kroeber's popular *Style and Civilizations*, which was published in 1957. Of the book's treatment of India, he wrote, "Kroeber offers as a formula of total style the tendency to abstract systematization found in Indian chess, arithmetic, and logic." But what about other areas of Indian life? "Do Gupta sculpture, Ajanta painting, Hindu poetry . . . show this abstract systematization? Is this their style? Kroeber does not say; and one may doubt it very much."

§162 Yourself the Cause

> Then if an heart of amorous faith and will
> May content you without doing grief,
> Please it you so to this to do relief.
> If otherwise ye seek for to fulfill
> Your disdain, ye err and shall not as ye ween,
> And ye yourself the cause thereof hath been.

§163 Openness

The fourth issue of LeRoi Jones's little magazine *Zazen* contained poems by Charles Olson, Gary Snyder, John Wieners, and O'Hara, among others. "I was 'open' to all schools within the circle of white poets of all faiths and flags," he recalled in his *Autobiography*, published in 1984, long after he had changed his name to Amiri

Baraka. It was a "kind of openness" that he got from O'Hara, he told an interviewer at around the same time. But the *Autobiography* continues: "what had happened to the blacks? What had happened to me? How is it that only the one colored guy?"

§164 Style as Symptom (2)

Why, why, why?—it is another of Petrarchism's hallmarks to cry out for an explanation, to seek a cause for all this suffering. Such a call might be an attempt to stand outside the genre, to master it by finding a vantage elsewhere. It is also perfectly conventional, another Petrarchan symptom, and a way of continuing in the tradition. All style requires, to absorb such attempts to break it, is that they happen more than once.

§165 Style and Explanation (3)

Explanations can be immanent, or transcendent; they can occupy the same world as what they explain (as storytelling tends to do), or they can point or stand elsewhere (like astrology, or physics). Another way of putting it: an explanation can share a style with what it explains, or not. It can sound like, or sound different. The desire to explain is often a desire for difference, in the fear that to sound *like* is to be entangled, compromised, complicit. You might ask for an explanation simply in order to stop the action, as explaining a joke will still the laughter. The rhythm is interrupted. Explanation may pause thoughtfully, step back, even take the time out of the situation altogether in order to offer an abstracted picture, or it may replace time in its flow with explanatory time, a sequence of events or a chain of causes summoned from the past. In its refusal of local rhythm, transcendent explanation is the enemy of style.

§166 My Heart (2)

yet I do not explain what exactly makes me so happy today
any more than I can explain the unseasonal warmth
of my unhabitual heart pumping vulgarly the blood

§167 Style and Explanation (4)

Does explanation itself have a rhythm? Is there a way speech sounds when it answers to a *why*? Or is it only necessary that explanation interrupt the rhythms it explains? If it does have a rhythm or rhythms of its own, perhaps the most characteristic would be the stepwise regularity of logical argument, which is mechanical; or a puncturing, epiphanic intervention, which is divine. Perhaps they could be counted styles of explanation. Neither of them, however, is an easy way to live.

§168 Grudging

It is not clear that Wyatt was ever accused of adultery with Anne. "I grant I do not profess chastity," he would write five years later, "but yet I use not abomination." (The "Queen's abomination" became the name for Anne's supposed crimes.) By May 10, 1536, his father Henry had received a letter from Cromwell promising his son's safety, and in due course Thomas was set free. The others were executed on May 17, and Anne's death followed two days later. No explanation for Wyatt's imprisonment or for his release survives. In prison again, the next time, he was obliged to address the suspicion that he held a grudge against his king. "If they take grudging for being sorry or grieving, I will not stick with them. I grant it." But he insisted his imprisonment had left no rancor, only regret. "If they use that word grudging including a desire to revenge, I say they lie."

§169 Style and Truth (3)

A true style is a style that keeps decorum not with its subject, but with itself: what we seek in style is its self-consistency, its predictability, the implicit promise that the future will be like the present and the past. There is an ethics of style here, if we follow the etymological cue to take ethics as habit. The truth of style would then consist simply in its being like itself, being true to itself, continuing; and falsehood (like failure) could only be a fracture or a multiplication of styles.

§170 The Lie of Style

Or is consistency the great lie of style, chronic and constitutive, the lie style always tells against the contradictions of desire?

§171 In Memory of My Feelings (1)

Grace

to be born and live as variously as possible. The conception
of the masque barely suggests the sordid identifications.
I am a Hittite in love with a horse. I don't know what blood's
in me I feel like an African prince I am a girl walking downstairs
in a red pleated dress with heels I am a champion taking a fall
I am a jockey with a sprained ass-hole I am the light mist

in which a face appears

and it is another face of blonde I am a baboon eating a banana
I am a dictator looking at his wife I am a doctor eating a child
and the child's mother smiling I am a Chinaman climbing a mountain
I am a child smelling his father's underwear I am an Indian
sleeping on a scalp

§172 And So On (2)

There can be something obscurely discouraging about getting to know a style, someone else's or your own: *oh, so it is going to be like this*.

§173 Style as Expression (7): The Body

"In Memory of My Feelings" was written in the middle of 1956, when the surrealisms of "Second Avenue," what Ashbery called his "French Zen" period, were mostly behind O'Hara; he was more and more writing in the city vernacular for which he is best known. With elements of both, "In Memory of My Feelings" is something of a pivot poem. Its polymorphic, polyphonic identifications range across categories of sex, race, nation, and history; among the fantasies and fever dreams, one finds such passing caricatures as the

Indian sleeping on his scalp. Ethnic shorthand is never stable in O'Hara's poems, but it is not alien. When he wrote about black men, there was a strain of primitivism that fascinated him poetically and erotically. "I call / to the spirits of other lands to make fecund my existence," he cried out in his ode "Ode: Salute to the French Negro Poets"; "I consider myself to be black," he wrote some years later. Racism and homophobia both made for "lives in the darkness," and O'Hara sought solidarity there. But a side effect of versatility, and sometimes of appetite, is caricature, holding the other constant in order to be sure of escaping from yourself.

§174 Sighs Are My Food

Rain, wind, or weather I judge by mine ears.
Malice assaulted that righteousness should save.
Sure I am, Brian, this wound shall heal again
But yet, alas, the scar shall still remain.

§175 Style and Scar (1)

There is no saying where Wyatt was when he heard that foul weather, whether inside the prison walls or not, or when he wrote them, in the Tower in 1536 or after, or during or after the later stay in 1541. They are addressed to his friend Francis Bryan, notorious libertine and co-religionist, called the king's "vicar of hell" for his readiness to undertake his master's dirty work. Prison was close to both men as a metaphor and as a practical fate. The image of the scar would come back to the Earl of Surrey in a poem written at another time of trouble: "Yet Solomon said, the wronged shall recure; / But Wyatt said true, the scar doth aye endure."

§176 Style as Expression (8): Personality

"There was also a whole drink mythology connected with Frank," Bill Berkson recalled. "He used to say that he drank to kill boredom. He used to say, 'I drink to the extinction of my personality.' It was like Max Jacob saying that personality was the persistence of error. That it was a persistent error. So Frank sat there with his gigantic persistent error, because his personality was of the largest scale. And he drank to destroy the error." Drink can be a habit, a part of a personality, and can leave scars.

§177 Style and Scar (2)

A scar is a good problem for the study of style. It is part of my body, but not the way my hand is, nor my signature. Is the scar integral to my nature? Or an abiding insult to or distraction from that nature? Is it a symptom? If so, of what? Is it something I might even choose to wear? Like a tattoo, or a piercing, or the mark of an old duel? How can I make it mine?

§178 Graven with Diamonds in Letters Plain

W. H. Auden chose Ashbery's *Some Trees* for the Yale Series of Younger Poets prize in 1955; he turned down O'Hara's manuscript, and warned him to "watch what is always the great danger with any 'surrealistic' style, namely of confusing authentic non-logical relations which arouse wonder with accidental ones which arouse mere surprise and in the end fatigue." O'Hara wrote to Kenneth Koch: "I don't care what Wystan says, I'd rather be dead than not have France around me like a rhinestone dog-collar."

§179 The Second Irony of Style

"*Discipline et personnalité, voilà les limites du style comme je l'entends.*" Personality may promise style as a mode of freedom, a freedom that is spontaneous, improvised, unhabitual. ("Style at its lowest ebb is method. Style at its highest ebb is personality.")—If for *personality* one substitutes *nature*, however, the freedom seems somewhat less. ("Every man . . . must first know him self and so take advice of his own nature.") Style-as-nature is lodged in the physical body and shaped by the body's capacities and constraints, in handwriting or brushstrokes; it is a symptom; you cannot get rid of it, it gives you away; it expresses the self shaped by experience, the self of inclination, habit, compulsion, beneath mood and pose; its tenses are past and future, what can't be changed and what will follow by necessity.—Then again, discipline might offer its own freedom from such a nature, particularly if one calls that discipline *art*. Style-as-art is teachable and learnable; it has a method, rules of *imitatio* that govern the impulse to imitation; it is a situation, a complex interaction of variables to which the orator must be present and alert; it is a structure, for those variables can be systematized and manipulated; it is a tool of persuasion; its tense is the present, with all of the present's open possibility.—"If only the *personnalité* came first I would understand." The real appeal of the formulation may be the space that lies between the two limits, between art and nature, a space in which style might be free to move.

STYLE V.
AESTHETICS

---

§180 Style Hides (2)

Style hides: it hides from definitions and from specifications. It also hides us, or covers or clothes us, protects us from the exposure of our self-differences, from shame.

§181 At the Old Place

Down the dark stairs drifts the steaming cha-
cha-cha. Through the urine and smoke we charge
to the floor. Wrapped in Ashes' arms I glide.
(It's heaven!) Button lindys with me. (It's
heaven!) Joe's two-steps, too, are incredible,
and then a fast rhumba with Alvin, like skipping
on toothpicks. And the interminable intermissions,

we have them. Jack, Earl and Someone drift
guiltily in. "I knew they were gay
the minute I laid eyes on them!" screams John.
How ashamed they are of us! we hope.

§182 Style and Shame

The real shame is not in being discovered to be gay, but in being discovered to have been pretending otherwise; this is the wit and the polemic of "At the Old Place." Shame is the feeling of being exposed as different, especially different from how you want to be. A contradiction is brought into public view, and the experience is of being fixed or frozen in the gaze of others. (Dreams of nakedness, trapped in plain sight: is it shameful simply to be immobilized? Perhaps you can only abide such stillness if you think you are beautiful; and held still under scrutiny, how long can anyone maintain that conviction?) What the dance floor at the Old Place offers is the freedom of a community of camp, and the fluid dancing and the rotation of partners and even the intermissions are part of it. A "mixture of frivolousness, bathos, high-pitched boredom, and self-satire," Helen Vendler says; Joe LeSueur quotes her approvingly when he writes about the night, though he demurs about his two-steps. To escape shame, at all events, it is not enough to be clothed. We've all been made to feel ashamed of what we're wearing. The clothing has to go together, and go with you, and happiest of all if it goes with where you are and whom you're with.

§183 Style and Form (2)

Style and form: not only do they get along, but they would seem to need each other. Meyer Schapiro describes the characteristic form, or is it style, of their collaboration: "By style," he explains, "is meant the constant form . . . in the art of an individual or a group." What makes a style possible is the constancy of its form, where form is some perceptible shape that looks or sounds the same from case to case. That form might be the totality of the work, like the form of a sonnet or a sonata. But a style might also be achieved by a combination of parts, "a system of forms," now plural, "with a quality and a meaningful expression through which the personality of the artist and the broad outlook of a group are visible." The forms might be turns of phrase, musical cadences, brushstrokes, forms as elements of style. What comes of it all is a "formed style," Wollheim's phrase, and his sense too that style mediates between the formal detail and the larger constructs of self and culture. The form is what you can point to in order to substantiate a claim of shared style; its elements, to cite Wollheim again, may be "formally or formalistically identified: line, hue, tonality, firmness of line, saturation of color," and so on.

§184 Fashion Drawings

Grace Hartigan was talking with O'Hara about a painting by Jane Freilicher; she told her journal later, "Jane's picture pointed up as Frank said 'the danger of painting from experience (or observation) instead of talent or *style*.'" For O'Hara, style might be the enemy, when the threat was sounding too much like yourself, but it could be an ally against the encroaching world. "I thought of this as we went thru the Metropolitan," Hartigan continued. "I think Manet has great 'style' and I even enjoy his pastel portraits of women which Larry says look like fashion drawings. They are too 'chic,' but I love the arrogance and the elegance." Style gives permission for traffic with fashion. Rivers may dismiss the Manet portraits, but Hartigan allows as she enjoys them—only to brush them away, "too chic," then woo them back with "arrogance" and "elegance." It was January of 1954, and in those days she still sometimes exhibited her own paintings under the pseudonym "George."

§185 Style and Form (3)

To say that style is a constant form allows style to share in form's dependability, dignity, and moral worth; further away from fashion, perhaps closer to law or to nature. The two, style and form, are integrated as aspects of aesthetic experience, and become difficult to tell apart. (Though a *formed style* sounds more . . . respectable, somehow, than a *styled form*.)

§186 Wyatt's Forms (1)

Sonnet and song; ballade, rondeau; canzone, strambotto; epigram: all are forms, in the familiar, present-day sense of *form* as a conventional literary shape, defined by the arrangement of its lines and rhymes. They come from France, Italy, ancient Rome, worlds of Wyatt's travel and reading; they were all part of the life of the court, its pastime and good company. As King Henry wrote of his games, songs, and sonnets:

> My heart is set!
> All goodly sport
> For my comfort.
> Who shall me let?

Who shall hinder me? "Grudge who likes," he adds. Wyatt's kinds are forms under the aspect of the rules of their construction. (The rules would not be written down for English, in any systematic way, until later in the century.) They are also forms in the sense that they are the shape-making principles that bring order to the matter of language. Are they styles? Certainly they *have* different styles, for instance the strambotto, a lighter Italian eight-line, three-stanza form, suited to sociable occasions; and the epigram, with its Roman models, and sober detachment; and a song like Henry's. But to say so refers them to the company they keep, rather than any abstracted account of their principles.

§187 Style as Example (1)

> you were there I was here you were here I was there where are you I
>   miss you
> (that was an example of the "sonnet" "form") (this is another)
> when you went I stayed and then I went and we were both lost and
>   then I died

§188 Style and Truth (4)

If style is extra, a supplement, perhaps it is always out of place: matter out of place, as Mary Douglas says of dirt. You might feel this way about style if you understand truth to be by definition plain, or clean, likewise if you understand beauty that way. Style is painted on, and insofar as it clutters or encrusts the truth, necessarily false. It has traffic with cosmetics and with the misogyny that is fascinated by cosmetics. Some of the bias against style is grounded in such disgusts.

§189 Life Is Beautiful (1)

In some moods, everything is beautiful. "How beautiful it is / to visit someone for instant coffee!" Instant coffee, indeed. Beauty seems to consist, at such moments, in the caffeinated immediacy of attention. And what is beauty but attention itself? Not fixed and rigid focus, but a concentrated distraction, perceiving the object in different ways and from different vantages, keeping moving as you go. A still eye quickly goes blind, but O'Hara's was always moving, refreshing. "And here I am," he sings in his "Autobiographia Literaria," right at the start of his career, "the / center of all beauty! / writing these poems! / Imagine!"

§190 Once in Special (2)

"And she me caught in her arms long and small": this line from "They flee from me" is one of the most strangely moving in Wyatt. He is not a descriptive poet; by present-day standards of pictorial vividness, none of his contemporaries was. Even so, the sensuous austerity of "long and small," long and slender, is arresting. To call the pair of adjectives formal is to say that it is unencumbered by particularity, very nearly ideal, the barely pliant marble of a Galatea just come to life. To call it beautiful would be to have a certain idea of beauty in mind. A certain idea of beauty in mind.

§191 Style and Form (4)

Form is vertical. Style is horizontal.

§192 Life Is Not Beautiful

In another mood, O'Hara wrote to Larry Rivers, "How I wish I had hundreds of your pictures to stare at for the next few years. Life simply is not beautiful and there's no sense pretending it is."

Beauty is not a part of life, to be found everywhere you look for it. It is an alternative to life, even a reproach. The same note sounds in the poem "Radio," from 1955, where he complains about the dreary music on the Saturday afternoon broadcast, "when tired / mortally tired I long for a little / reminder of immortal energy," for Grieg and Honegger. What saves him from despair is the painting on his wall:

> Well, I have my beautiful de Kooning
> to aspire to. I think it has an orange
> bed in it, more than the ear can hold.

The painting is not part of the decor. It is an aspiration; there is some sense that it is not already there when he comes home, indeed somehow not there even yet. He thinks it has an orange bed in it, but how can he be sure? The painting overwhelms the ear, a synesthetic confusion, and possibly a sublimity. It is an alternative to everything else, a rescue from the world.

§193 Style and Form (5)

Form is singular. Style is plural.

§194 Style and Form (6)

"When a thing is perfectly beautiful," writes Simone Weil, "as soon as we fix our attention on it, it represents unique and single beauty. Two Greek statues; the one we are looking at is beautiful." Some share of this effect is absorption: the experience of beauty, on just about any account, is one of acute and focused attention. Some share is beauty's alliance with love, and love's idealized choice, now or forever, of one object above all. Some share is beauty's relation to form. The word *form* bows to its Platonic inheritance when it is used this way, the idea that beautiful things are beautiful by virtue of participating in the transcendent form of beauty. One beauty is incarnate in all of them. That conceptual movement, ascendant, convergent, and idealizing, is the opposite of the map-traveling and map-making collations of stylistic recognition.

§195 The One Warm Beautiful Thing

when I want only to lean on my elbow and stare into space feeling
the one warm beautiful thing in the world breathing upon my right rib.

§196 Thou Shalt Be Judge

When he was released from the Tower in 1536, Wyatt retreated to his house in Kent. Not fastidious France, nor elegant Spain, nor carousing Flanders,

> Nor I am not where Christ is given in prey
>> For money, poison, and treason at Rome—
>> A common practice used night and day.
> But here I am in Kent and Christendom

It has seemed likely, to many critics, that he wrote his epistolary satires there in Kent, far from court, during a caesura in his diplomatic career and a volta in his writing life. There was little left to win by the courtly gamesmanship of songs and sonnets. It is John Poyntz to whom he writes, among the closest of his many friends. ("I never saw man that had so many friends," Cromwell had written him.) But the end of the poem abjures their familiarity:

> But here I am in Kent and Christendom
>> Among the Muses where I read and rhyme,
>> Where if thou list, my Poyntz, for to come,
> Thou shalt be judge how I do spend my time.

What Wyatt needs from this friendship is not sympathy, no intimate *you know what I mean*. Instead, "Thou shalt be judge." What the men share are criteria, the laws by which a way of life might be condemned or exonerated. Friendship ought to be set on a foundation of principle. The poem is rangy and intemperate in its satire, but it asks at the end for a verdict, as though to be rescued from its excesses. *There is more to our bond than the way we talk.*

§197 Life Is Beautiful (2)

That painting of the orange bed was lent to O'Hara by his friend Fairfield Porter, and Willem de Kooning, who made it, was a friend too. "After all it's life we're interested in, not art," said Larry Rivers to O'Hara at the cocktail party where they first met. A couple of weeks later, when he visited Rivers's studio for the first time, "with its big splashy canvasses and the beginnings of full-scale female nudes in plaster hanging from pipe-and-flange armatures, he said with no air of contradiction or remembrance, 'After all it's *art* we're interested in, not life.'" Rivers's main interest, O'Hara concluded, was obviously in the immediate situation.

§198 Wyatt's Forms (2)

Consider another line from the satire: "My Poyntz, I cannot from me tune to feign." *From me*: does that mean, I cannot find it in myself to play the game, or I cannot depart from myself to do it? Another line, from a sonnet: "Thou hast no faith of him that hath none." Does that *of* mean faith *in* him, or faith learned *from* him? Another: "Though I my self be bridled of my mind." Is the speaker's mind bridled by someone else, or is his mind the bridler? And one more: "She from myself now hath me in her grace." By my consent, or at my expense? These blurred prepositions are everywhere in Wyatt, obfuscations that as ever confound the distinction between strategy and accident. (And do they confound it strategically, or accidentally?) They are aspects of his style, at least if one is prepared to relax the bond between style and self-mastery. They are formally identified, by attention to the grammatical patterning of his sentences. Are they therefore formal? Are they forms?

§199 Style and Form (7)

Roland Barthes says: "Form is what is between the thing and its name, form is what delays the name." His form is evidently not the kind that prompts recognition of what the thing is, as *eidos* is for Aristotle. He follows another line, descended from Kant. In *The Critique of Judgment*, form is how a thing presents itself when regarded without interest. It is, in Kant's famous phrase, a "purposiveness without a purpose," as though one were to take an object—say, an urn—and subtract from it any perception attached to its pleasures or its practical affordances. Not for holding water, nor for ornamenting a mantelpiece, nor for tickling the fancy nor anything else. What is left, is form: an immanent abstraction, the purified line or shape or pattern that is also the object's essence. To that form, it is not possible to attach concepts, which are the determinate shapes of the understanding, the *what-it's-for* and *whom-it's-for* and *where-it's-from*. To do so would be to see the form in terms of its uses and pleasures. On the contrary: aesthetic experience is characterized by that condition of not knowing, by the "free play" between those concepts and the imagination. (The imagination is, for Kant, the faculty of representation.) The understanding tries to name the thing, but fails, again and again. From this account descends the modern idea that art can be known, as Jacques Rancière would have it, by its difficulty in being known, or as Barthes would say, by delaying the name. When we encounter someone or something beautiful, we do not know what to say, let alone what to do.

§200 Style and Form (8)

The word *form* is as contradictory as *style*; it is used for outward shape and inner essence, for the transcendence of eternal ideas and the taxonomy of worldly kinds. It is not, however, a word that characteristically evades or ironizes its contradictions, so much as it reconciles, even synthesizes them. *Form* has an elevation about it, an open aspiration to bridge the here and the beyond and to hold them together.

§201 Meditations in an Emergency (2)

I can't even enjoy a blade of grass unless I know there's a subway handy, or a record store or some other sign that people do not totally *regret* life.

§202 The Fourth Limit of Style: Nature

Everything has a style, except nature. Nature is the paradigmatic occasion of aesthetic experience in the tradition of Kant. The manifest and unfathomable organization of a great forest or a sea, even the form of a single tree, make the best examples of purposiveness without a purpose. They give the overwhelming sense of being *for* something, and yet we confront that feeling without any account of what they are for. That, again, is to know them formally. (The *for* in *form* is a perpetual, nice irony, from the Kantian perspective.) It is of course possible to have a natural style. That would mean something like a style that is native, unforced, unmethodical, a style that has the continuity and self-resemblance that nature, which is never ashamed, might offer to us in our abashedness. A natural style has the qualities of "natural painting," as O'Hara defined it in the essay discussed at the Club in 1955: "called such because the talent of the painter seems to encounter no obstacles, to appear before our eyes as characteristically as his handwriting." It is also possible to adopt a style in imitation of nature, like the vaulting trees of gothic architecture, or the embowering ornament of art deco. But to speak of nature itself as having a style—it is not quite right, to say that crowd of poplars shares a style, or that wave after wave rolls in with this season's signature lunge or slouch. Why not? Nature happens in a different time, to be sure. If stylistic change is sensitive to time at the scale of human events, evolution will not be hurried or willed. At the root of the difference is the fact that though we may imitate nature, and each other, nature does not imitate itself—not the way we do—nor does it imitate us. Its self-likeness is of a different kind.

§203 Once in Special (3)

But since that I so kindly am served
I would fain know what she hath deserved.

§204 Knowing What You Are Doing (2)

No one knows what to do with art. Ravishment may spoil beauty; interpretation risks exhausting it, or replacing it. Buying beauty simply installs the problem above the mantelpiece. There is still nothing obvious we can use it for, or do with or to it. (*For, with, to*: none of them is quite right; does aesthetic experience beg for a new preposition?) It is not enough just to look and look and look, is it? Beauty is not knowing what to do, whereas style is knowing; style already knows.

§205 The Other Enemy (2)

O'Hara praised the painters who turned away "from styles whose perceptions and knowledge are not their own occasion"; from styles, that is, that expressed a knowledge that could be distinguished from their paintings. (Recall his college journal entry: "I must think only of and for the emergent work and not allow messages or ideas as such to displace the validity of the work.") The panel that took up O'Hara's essay "Nature and the New Painting" at the Club was a distinguished group, Alfred Barr Jr., the director of MoMA, and the critics Clement Greenberg and Hilton Kramer. O'Hara continues: "Stylistic preoccupation often makes for sameness, the trap of the look, of performance. There is an initial perception which becomes a method: the perception of what painting is, or how it is done." He allowed: "that is a great pleasure but it is not the highest art can afford. We like to think that an opera singer or a pianist will sustain the level of execution through successive performances—that is not what we hope for the painter." (Recall his college journal entry: "The other enemy: style.")

§206 Knowing What You Are Doing (3)

Style may not be knowledge, but it is knowing, knowing in two inseparable senses. First, style, having it yourself and recognizing it in the world, is an orientation, knowing your way around; to know a style is to have concepts for what you see. Not reflective, analytic concepts, but the kind of background concepts closest to the word's etymology, *con-capere*, holding things together, or continuing. Second, style is knowing in the sense that it already knows. The languid, bored connoisseur is an obvious case. She has seen it all. But it is in the nature of stylistic recognition to be unsurprised, to take the situation for granted. That is not to say that a new style, or a style out of place, will not startle, but insofar as it is seen as a style (as opposed to a singular, aesthetic event), it tends already toward un-surprise, toward coordination with other cases and other possibilities. When style is understood this way, aesthetic form cannot be the principle of its networks of likeness. On the contrary, form, as the true object of aesthetic attention, is the key term in the disruption of a regime of mere style.

§207 It Makes Me Work

"It makes me work all the harder at art to know nature so far ahead," wrote O'Hara to Fairfield Porter, "especially in conception (dear God! what's happening to me?). I'm sure the preceding sentence is to be blamed on Henry James, whose *Golden Bowl* I just finished this morning to my staggering exhilaration and bewilderment."

§208 Beauty and Mood

Among the things to fear in beauty is its brevity. *Ars* may be *longa*, but its material situation is fleeting, the evanescence of performance or pigment or health. It is always possible to blame the object for falling from grace over time. Perhaps it is more frightening when the change is in the observer. That shift from object to subject, from the *it* to the *I*, is one of the basic themes of modern aesthetics. Kant called this shift the reflective character of the judgment of beauty; reflective, as opposed to objective, for everything happens within the subject. ("Here I am, the center of all beauty!") If Kant's is the right way to think about beauty, then beauty's limit may be set not by the object's frailty but by our own, our survival or even our reserves of energy, whether we're up to it today or not. Wyatt might call such frailty weariness: "But as for me, helas, I may no more." O'Hara might call it being "tired mortally tired." It would be possible, taxed by the demands of beauty, its singular intensity, its restlessness, its war with ordinary life, to long for the more generous temporality of style, perhaps even for temporality per se, which style requires, and which beauty sometimes seems to scorn.

§209 The Resting Place of Love

> But if my hope sometime rise up by some redress,
> It stumbleth straight for feeble faint, my fear hath such excess.
> Such is the sort of hope, the less for more desire,
> Whereby I fear and yet I trust to see that I require:
> The resting place of love where virtue lives and grows,
> Where I desire my weary life also may take repose.

§210 Style and Form (9)

Another way of putting it: if beauty is disinterested, and *form* is the name for how we encounter the beautiful object when interest is suspended; if beauty is the singling out of its object to no purpose; then the form makes an opposite of style: style which is above all interested, *inter-est*, being in the middle of things.

§211 Jujubes (3)

To see a jujube as beautiful, in its distinctive form, that bright-colored conical cross-section with the sweet dimple on top, is to see it as a singular instance of an ideal. The world in a polyp of corn syrup! To recognize its style is to know its place in the candy shop and in the pockets and pantries of its consumers. To say that its style is beautiful is to treat its likenesses as instances, to hold it at arm's length, for appreciation. To settle for, or settle into, style is to forget about such reproaches to the quotidian, and just buy some or leave a pack lying around or eat them, perhaps with a friend. Having a jujube with you, and washing it down, maybe, with a Coke. Once again, a question of aspect.

§212 The Second Antithesis of Style

Style is the opposite of beauty. To say so rejects the notion of a beautiful style, of a style that has a beautiful form. —But it is not necessarily to do so on ontological grounds, to say there is such a thing as beauty, distinct in the world, and such a thing as style, distinct again. Nor is it necessary to deny that the words are used companionably, for often they are. The force of the opposition is meant to show the two terms at maximum contrast. That contrast is not between properly beautiful objects on the one hand, and on the other, properly stylistic, or ornamental, or merely fashionable objects, objects of which it is right to say they have style, wrong to say they are beautiful, or vice versa.—On the contrary, any object, any part of any object, can be seen as form or as style. The difference is between two attitudes, or orders of experience, two aspects. When the terms are held apart they show more of and more about the world.

INDIVIDUAL AND GROUP

§213 Style and Freedom (5)

Beauty is the best way to experience freedom. For Kant it was so; the free play of our faculties, the suspension of our concepts and of our knowingness, offers an experience of what it is like to act in the world without prejudice, without special interest. Other familiar intuitions conspire with this idea: art's for-its-own-sakeness, its autonomy, or the way beauty suspends time, and with it dictatorial cause and effect. From that vantage, the interests of style could never be free.

§214 My Rococo Self

I am sober and industrious
and would be plain and plainer
for a little while
                    until my rococo
self is more assured of its
distinction.

§215 Individual Style (1)

It is always possible to go back to Cicero; the humanists usually did. "Isocrates had grace of style, Lysias precision, Hyperides penetration, Aeschines sonorousness, Demosthenes force," he observes in his *De Oratore*, which was written about ten years before his account of the levels of style in the *Orator*. Those Greeks were the orators in whom the Roman found his tradition. "Which of them is not eminent? and yet which resembles anyone but himself?" *Quis cuiusquam nisi sui similis?* Like the *genera*, these questions have had a long afterlife; they are a persistent counter-song to the three-part harmony of high, middle, and low. Persistent enough for Carlo Ginzburg to call them a "new cognitive model," one that played an important role in the development, he argues, of historical awareness itself. What if style were not a matter of regular and durable structures, but of idiosyncratic influences, each bound to its own time?

§216 Imitating Yourself (1)

To have a style is to be like yourself. An obvious idea, but strange as soon as it is said, since it seems both to close and to open a seam at once; in asserting self-likeness, it lets go of self-identity.

§217 Individual Style (2)

"Behold in painting Leonard Vncio, Mantegna, Raphael, Michelangelo, George of Castelfranco," says the Count Ludovico, fifteen hundred years after Cicero. A group of aristocrats is waiting out a season of plague in the hills above Urbino; the count is expertly guiding the company's discussion of the perfect courtier. "They are all most excellent doers, yet are they in working unlike, but in any of them a man would not judge that there wanted aught in his kind of trade: for every one is known to be of most perfection after his manner." Urbino and his companions are the dramatis personae of Baldassare Castiglione's elegant courtly survival manual, *The Book of the Courtier*. The translation here is Thomas Hoby's, from 1561, but the book was first published in Venice in 1528. Wyatt likely read it, and certainly would have done well to; his patron Thomas Cromwell was thought to have a copy, and the emperor Charles V reread it regularly. "Behold," says Ludovico, expecting his audience to be able to call those painters before their eyes, and expecting the differences to be obvious. "Every one is known to be of most perfection after his manner." *Quis cuiusquam nisi sui similis?*

§218 Group Style

The following lines are Thomas Wyatt's, on the best authority:

> Ah, Robin,
> Jolly Robin
> Tell me how thy leman doth
> And thou shalt know of mine.
>
> "My lady is unkind, perdie!"
> "Alack, why is she so?"
> "She loveth an other better than me,
> And yet she will say no."

What authority? The stanzas appear in the Egerton manuscript, Wyatt's manuscript. Egerton was drafted by several hands, and this poem was set down by one of his amanuenses, like "They flee from me" and many others. Wyatt's own distinctive script is nonetheless prominent in its pages, and some poems, in particular his psalms, seem even to have been partly composed there. Another hand again has written "Wyat" in the margin. Many other such songs appear in Egerton, and the open vein of complaint is familiar. Together, such evidence is close to the gold standard for editorial attribution. And yet many such songs appear elsewhere, too; they are scattered through the commonplace books and miscellanies of the period. A version of this one appears in Henry VIII's songbook, which may have been compiled as early as 1509, when Wyatt was five years old. Shakespeare's clown Feste sang another version when *Twelfth Night* was first performed in 1602. It may well have been a popular song; Wyatt may have got it from the composer William Cornish, who set it, or Cornish from Wyatt, or both of them from somewhere else.

§219 Manuscripts

Thomas Wyatt and Frank O'Hara both inhabited manuscript cultures: Wyatt perforce, O'Hara more idiosyncratically, willfully, with his mostly casual attitude to publication and his habit of sending poems into the world by pressing them in someone's hand or folding them into a letter. Hyder Rollins likely taught O'Hara something at Harvard about the long history of what had become an avant-garde tactic, the retreat into private circulation, Goodman's "physical reestablishment of community." Was that among the affinities that drew O'Hara to Wyatt? The Henrician court, in retrospect, presents the latter-day citizen of print with a host of questions, and opportunities. *If I give you a poem, is it still my poem? In a book, or on loose leaf—does that make a difference? Whether I signed my name to it or not? What if you copy it for yourself, onto a single sheet or into a commonplace book or a household miscellany? What if you alter it, adapting it to your own circumstances, or by your lights improving it? And does it matter what you do with it—if you pass it on to someone else afterwards? (Even to a printer?)* In the free and often unattributed circulation of lyrics at court, responsibility and credit could be distributed across a sometimes quite extensive network. Every time a poem found a new audience it was as part of some particular social transaction. Every time it was committed to paper, someone had written it again for him- or herself.

§220 Is That Your Coat?

You are wearing it; probably, you bought it. But is it yours? Did you make it? Does it look like you, or do you look like it? If so, how did that happen, that likeness—was it right away, as soon as you put it on, or did everybody have to get used to it? Did it only become yours once you broke it in? (Is use, the distress of daily wear, your title? Your look?) Is it really yours at all?—*I know you paid for it, and it hangs in your closet, but it's not really* you, *is it? Much more my style. May I?*

§221 Style as Gesture (2)

A thing, under the aspect of style, is a gesture.

§222 I Do This, I Do That

I do this, I do that.

> It's 5:03 a.m. on the 11th of July this morning
> and the day is bright gray turning green I can't stop
> loving you says Ray Charles and I know exactly
> what he means because the Swedish policeman in the
> next room is beating on my door demanding sleep
> and not Ray Charles and bluegrass

The *I* here is Frank O'Hara, obviously enough, with the in medias res time stamp, the casual enjambment, and such unexpected, vivifying particulars as the Swedish policeman. But then again— bluegrass? Taste-wise, that would make more sense coming from Ted Berrigan, late of Tulsa, Oklahoma, who sent a postcard to O'Hara out of the blue in 1961 and moved to New York soon after, along with his friends Ron Padgett, Dick Gallup, and Joe Brainard, and indeed, "Personal Poem," a title O'Hara used too, was published in Berrigan's book *Many Happy Returns*, in 1969. It does also sound like Berrigan, who dedicated that book to Frank, and there is every indication that Berrigan wrote it, if by writing we mean pushing the stylus or hitting the keys.

§223 Guessing Games (1)

The poet Anne Waldman would become one of the best-known members of the second-generation New York School, with Berrigan and company, but in the early 1960s she was a precocious teenager, excited and surprised and a little bemused to be in the company of O'Hara and his poet-friends. One night she had a dream—she doesn't say when; she recorded it in 1977—about playing a guessing game managed by O'Hara and Don Allen. Allen, in the dream, was an amateur artist, who made pastiche paintings in a variety of styles. (Larry Rivers enjoyed the same recreation in real life; Ashbery recalls that "he could do brilliant pastiches of classic styles of the past: Ingres and Rembrandt as well as the 'Dutch Masters' cigar labels derived from Rembrandt.") O'Hara revealed the paintings one by one in an elaborate easel-theater, and judged the answers. "Seems to be copies of Old Masters," Waldman recalls,

> plus Cubists, Abstract Impressionists, Joe Brainards & George Schneeman nudes. Frank has already compiled the list or "key" but we're all supposed to guess what the "source" of each one is like a parlour game. The panels are hinged & like a scroll covered with soft copper which peels back. I wonder what I am doing with this crowd of older men playing a guessing game! None of us are guessing properly the "sources," Kenneth the most agitated about this.

Waldman takes a certain pleasure in the confusion of her dream-friends. Why was the game so tricky for these men who spent so much time looking at paintings? Because the paintings were not all that good? Even the dream-Allen was no Larry Rivers. Or because the paintings were too good at disguising themselves, too clever, too oblique, too hard? Koch, who by the time of their acquaintance had been appointed to the faculty at Columbia, was particularly maddened. The stakes in such games are high, especially for professors, even in dreams. As D. W. Winnicott says, it is a joy to hide, but a disaster not to be found.

§224 Guessing Games (2)

Hyder Rollins, O'Hara's teacher, observes in his edition of Tottel that one of the poems first treated as Wyatt's was moved into the long section of "Uncertain Authors" in the second printing. (Only two months after the first; the book sold well.) Moving poems in and out of the Wyatt canon has been a sport ever since, sometimes a blood sport. Arguments about the diversity and reliability of manuscripts, the authority of marginal attribution, and the quality of the poems made for a contentious decade between the publication of Muir and Thomson's *Collected* in 1969 and Rebholz's *Complete* in 1978. What does Wyatt sound like? What would we have learned, if we could say? H. A. Mason laments that Richard Harrier, whose *Canon* treats everything in Egerton as Wyatt's, "does not consider the feelings of a reader who occasionally misses the Wyatt note as he goes through these Egerton poems." Joost Daalder protests any decisions made where "the only criterion we can generally invoke is style," a criterion he regards as "almost wholly without value from a scholarly point of view." A decade later Ellen Caldwell surveyed the still-smoking battlefield: "While they do seem to agree that the MSS need re-editing, they do not trust each other's ability to do so."

§225 Guessing Games (3)

A good game is one you can win, but not win always or easily. Strength, skill, and cunning are the usual ways of talking about what games measure and how you win them. A sociology of style might treat the subject differently, in terms of likeness and difference among the community of players. You want to be a winner, and therefore distinguished—but also a loser like everybody else, or at least someone who might lose and therefore shares the common jeopardy. So a good game generates both distinction and solidarity, and the prospect, through competition, of managing their balance. Guessing games work within such tolerances, as the tolerances are set by the larger culture in relation to its ideas of fame and privacy, attribution and anonymity, expression and censorship. It can be useful for identity to be difficult to establish—difficult, but not impossible. When the tolerances are set properly, they make for a good game, a good art history exam, even a worthy field of expertise, one in which objects and experts can both achieve distinction.

§226 Achieved Style

"So much of art is an exercising of an achieved style," James Schuyler wrote to Fairfield Porter in 1954, when Schuyler was sharing an apartment with O'Hara, on and off. "There are so many Monets I would like singularly and together, without finding a special uniqueness in any of them. The uniqueness seems to me between the total work and the rest of the world." The total work gathered under the signature of Monet, all his paintings together, is what is unique, over against everything else, and that difference is "achieved"—or accomplished, as the Roman rhetoricians might have put it, *disertus*, a result of training, time, and labor. Schuyler was readier to praise such attainment than his roommate O'Hara usually was. He wrote admiringly for *ARTnews* about Helen Frankenthaler's "achieved style," about how Elaine de Kooning "has developed this style over a long period of time," how Michael Goldberg "has evolved a style." Looking at Leland Bell, he was struck "by how formed his style already was." There is the phrase "formed style" again: the ideal of a total work, of the life-work-as-whole, which pushes the achievement of style toward aesthetics. It is as though in their totality all those paintings together might have a single form, and questions of their mere contingent and ever-subjective likeness might fall away.

§227 Style Is the Man

Not *the man is style*. In Georges-Louis Leclerc's 1753 *"Discours sur le Style,"* the phrase is *"le style c'est l'homme même"*: style is the man himself, the same man. It is as though the work of the famous aphorism were not so much to explain the man, as to defend the idea of style—to defend style by identifying it with identity itself, with the man who is not like others nor even like himself, but the same.

§228 Style and Likeness (3)

These two lines are like each other.

In frozen thought now and now it standeth in flame

I find no peace and all my war is done

The likeness is formal: both have the same chiastic arrangement, the form AB:BA. But something has happened in saying so, for the lines are no longer just like, but there is something identical about them, namely chiasmus. They are the same by abstraction, the immanent abstraction of form. Which is not to say that every likeness can be resolved to a formal identity, and even less, that identity is what likeness really is. But identity, sameness, is the only way of explaining likeness, of talking about likeness when, for whatever reason, asserting it and pointing are not enough. (*See, they are the same color*, or *look, they have the same proportions*.) Perhaps likeness itself hides, too, like style when you try to point it out.

§229 My Folly and Unthriftness

"And of my self, I may be a near example unto you of my folly and unthriftiness": so wrote Wyatt to his son Thomas, pausing in Paris on his way to take up his embassy to Charles V. It was April of 1537; he was out of prison and back in the king's good graces, back at work. Fortune and the king's needs and whims had raised him up again. His retrospect, however, was rueful. His follies had

> brought me into a thousand dangers and hazards, enmities, hatreds, prisonments, despites and indignations but that God hath of His goodness chastised me and not cast me clean out of His favor, which thing I can impute to no thing but to the goodness of my good father.

Young Thomas was just married, and Thomas the elder looks back not only on his own recent jeopardies, but on his failed marriage. What he presents his son instead of himself, instead of his example, is a litany of the proverbs so common in his poems. "He shall be sure of shame that feeleth no grief in other men's shames," "Have your friends in a reverence and think unkindness to be the greatest offense," and so on. In another letter, later that same year, he would urge young Wyatt "to gather a heap of good opinions and to get them perfectly as it were on your fingers' ends." Fearing he could never be the father to his son that his father was to him, he offers these principles rather than his likeness. "Think that I have herein printed a fatherly affection to you," he writes.

§230 Style and Likeness (4)

Is there any way to explain likeness, besides identity? One way out would be to say A is like B because they are both like C. Wyatt is like O'Hara because they are both like Petrarch. To say so would be to address the question of likeness within the idiom of style, on its plane or in its network, and not outside or above it.

§231 Style and Likeness (5)

These lines are alike, too.

and we drift into the clear sky enthralled by our disappointment

fragrant after-a-French-movie-rain is over
"and shine the stars"

What do they share, exactly? There is not a common form that it is easy to point to, but they both have—well, something; they seem to belong together. Their likeness, or their affinity, derives from another kind of association, a family resemblance, some relative that resembles both. Both of them sound like Frank O'Hara. (Is it the vigorous counter-intuition? The delicate mood-painting? The movies?) They come from the same world, the same place, the same mind; they are like by metonymy, the figure of adjacency, of association. They appeared together in the third issue of *Locus Solus*, the magazine edited by Koch, Ashbery, Schuyler, and Harry Mathews, on pages 96 and 101, respectively. The second was written in collaboration with Bill Berkson.

§232 How to Get There

Enthralled by what disappointment? O'Hara continues:

never to be alone again
never to be loved
sailing through space: didn't I have you once for my self?
West Side?
for a couple of hours, but I am not that person

O'Hara met Vincent Warren, a ballet dancer, in August 1959, and found in him a love he had longed for. The company of friends and lovers always modulated his style. "Unlike Larry Rivers who inspired poems of expressionist pain and dazzling surface," writes his biographer, "or Jane Freilicher and Grace Hartigan who inspired poems of almost weightless fondness and affection, Vincent Warren was the first muse to inspire O'Hara to openly gay love poems." The poem "How to Get There" already sounds like the end of an affair, but it was written in the middle. Warren traveled frequently to dance, and he was younger, twenty when O'Hara was thirty-three. "You never come when you say you'll come," O'Hara would write reproachfully, affectionately, in another of almost fifty poems to Warren, a few months later.

§233 Style and Likeness (6)

What goes next to what is the characteristic subject of the French sociologist Pierre Bourdieu. His book *Distinction*, which collates the sensibilities of French citizens of the 1960s according to social class, is a book about style. He and his researchers distributed 1,217 surveys, in Paris, Lille, and a provincial town, posing "twenty-five questions on tastes in interior decoration, clothing, singers, cooking, reading, cinema, painting, music, photography, radio, pastimes," and so on. The results discovered that taste for furniture (modern, antique, country-style) correlates reliably with a taste in music (*Concerto for the Left Hand*, *La Traviata*, *Rhapsody in Blue*); they predict one another, and much else about social situation, in fact almost everything. A particular *habitus*, in his term—one might say, lifestyle—"continuously generates practical metaphors [*métaphores pratiques*], that is to say, transfers . . . or, more precisely, systematic transpositions required by the particular conditions in which the habitus is 'put into practice.'" The Eames chair is a practical metaphor for the *Well-Tempered Clavier*, in the sense that where you find one, you will find the other. Metaphor may be the wrong trope here, or at least, Bourdieu's sense of transfer should be distinguished from the part-for-whole thinking of an Auerbach or a Spitzer. Bourdieu requires no such total implication, only lateral association. The fugue need not be implicit in the chair. The better figure for his social critique is metonymy, the figure of side-by-sideness, how things come to mean one another because they share space in the world, a space like a Parisian parlor or a book of poems.

§234 Imitation (2)

If likeness were an activity, the activity would be called imitation. It is this imitation-as-learning that Aristotle speaks of in his *Ethics*, an imitation "natural to man from childhood, one of his advantages over the lower animals being this, that he is the most imitative creature in the world, and learns first by imitation." Ethical imitation is different from pictorial imitation, from mimesis, getting the world onto the canvas. The word in Greek, however, is the same, and Aristotle allows that "it is also natural for all to delight in works of imitation," paintings and the like. There could be no style in a pure attempt to represent the world, what a modern would call realism. Style is at stake only when the realist imitates another realist. But then when does she not?

§235 No Man Is So Meet (1)

"Wyatt is in such credit with the emperor that no man is so meet to fill that room," wrote Edmund Bonner to Cromwell in October of 1538. "Yet if some things were reformed in him he could do better." Bonner, a fellow diplomat and a future bishop, had been sent to join Wyatt in Charles's court, perhaps to assist, perhaps to keep an eye on him, and he was impressed by how Wyatt had won the emperor's favor. Wyatt's brief was complex: to prevent the ever-threatening Imperial alliance with France, to monitor the troublemaking of English Catholic exiles, and to pursue the hopeless project of a marriage between the emperor and Henry's elder daughter Mary. He was to "fish out the bottom of his [Charles's] stomach and advertise his majesty [Henry] how he standeth disposed toward him." Charles's court was peripatetic, and Wyatt was forever riding in post from city to city. Still he was favored enough that it was observed in London how "the king looked upon master Huyet [Wyatt] more in the light of an Imperial ambassador than as one of his own." A month before, Bonner had written to Cromwell: "witty he is, and pleasant among company, contented to keep and make good cheer, but that he will either forget his imprisonment, or more regard the affairs of the king than his own glory . . . hitherto have I nothing seen to make me believe it."

§236 Imitation (3): Harmony

Imitation is basic to style. Why imitate? A first answer, and the grandest: the desire to imitate is the basic human experience of a universal, cosmic harmony, the original principle of our complicity with society and cosmos and of the two with each other. Dancing imitates the rounds of the seasons as the seasons imitate the circling sun and the sun the other stars. This homology might be a law, animating all of the local and the cosmic likenesses with a spark of emulation, of desire, or it might just be an archaic or an old-fashioned understanding. Walter Benjamin is of the latter disposition, but he mourns its loss all the same. Our ability to recognize style, he argues, is "nothing but a rudiment of the once powerful compulsion to become similar and to behave mimetically. There is perhaps not a single one of [man's] higher functions in which his mimetic faculty does not play a decisive role." The loss of these "magical correspondences and analogies," the dilapidation of this basic instinct, is the predicament of modernity, the reduction of a cosmologically integrative mimesis to mere style, with its passing social advantages and its adventitious continuities.

§237 Charisma

Frank O'Hara made a strong impression on Larry Rivers from the start. "He was thin and about five seven. He walked on his toes, stretched his neck, and angled his head, all to add an inch or two to his height. I never walked the same after I met him." Something about Frank made you want to imitate him. That invitation, or seduction, whatever it is that provokes imitation, might be called charisma. *I would like to walk, write, live like that.* The likeness of style is not just a neutral likeness, whether formal resemblance or metonymic association or both. Charisma captures the liking in it.

§238 The Anxiety of Assimilation

Wherever these people were born, or however they grew up, or whatever they have gone through—that's where their style comes from. There's no learning it now. It is already too late. They are always going to know I am pretending. Or lying—can a style be a lie? Their style is inside them, they know it in their bones, in their skin.

§239 Imitation (4): Assimilation

Imitation is basic to style. Why imitate? Another answer is the prospect of assimilation, or even dissolution, dissolving into a crowd or dissolving altogether. To imitate is to make yourself fit in, a promise of belonging, the solace of membership, the harbor of the familiar. Roger Caillois takes that allure to an uncanny limit. He is struck, in a famous essay on mimicry, by the fate of the phyllia moth: so good at resembling the leaf-forms around it, that it feeds indiscriminately on green pasture and on its fellows' wings. How could such cannibal camouflage be an evolutionary advantage? Caillois hypothesizes that the moth is instead subject to a biologically fundamental "temptation by space," the animal impulse to vanish into the environment, into the space around it. In such mimesis, he writes, "life seems to lose ground, blurring in its retreat the frontier between the organism and the milieu and *expanding to the same degree the limits within which*, according to Pythagoras, *we are allowed to know, as we should, that nature is everywhere the same.*" Caillois's idea of mimesis has been compared to Freud's constancy principle or death drive, un-selving by assimilation. To imitate is to lose yourself.

§240 The Fifth Limit of Style: Sameness

Everything has a style, but style's ease reaches a limit in easeful death, as our likeness to one another reaches its perfection in the ultimate peace of ashes and dust. One way to die of style is to follow it to the limit of sameness. Not identity *of*, but identity *with*, the sameness unto death.

§241 What Rage Is This?

> What rage is this? What furor of what kind?
> What pow'r, what plague doth weary thus my mind?
> Within my bones to rankle is assigned
>   What poison pleasant sweet?
>
> Lo, see mine eyes swell with continual tears.
> The body still away sleepless it wears.
> My food nothing my fainting strength repairs
>   Nor doth my limbs sustain.
>
> In deep wide wound the deadly stroke doth turn,
> To cured scar that never shall return.
> Go to, triumph, rejoice thy goodly turn.
>   Thy friend thou dost oppress.
>
> Oppress thou dost, and hast of him no cure,
> Nor yet my plaint no pity can procure.
> Fierce tiger fell, hard rock without recure,
>   Cruel rebel to love!
>
> Once may thou love, never be loved again:
> So love thou still and not thy love obtain.
> So wrathful Love with spites of just disdain
>   May threat thy cruel heart.

§242 Imitation (5): Knowing

Imitation is basic to style. Why do we imitate? Yet another answer is that it is a mode of knowing, the practical basis of what some philosophers, following Gilbert Ryle, call *knowing how*. In the classic example, you do not learn to ride a bicycle by studying the rules; you learn by watching others and by trying it yourself. Your knowledge consists not in propositions you can form about riding, but in your being able to do it. Making letters is like that, handling a stylus. Not only does the child have the example of an *A*, but she watches another hand make the three lines. At some point, the desire is not just to make an *A*, but to make an *A* like that, the way someone you like makes it, or the way they make them there, in some other place, or made them then, at some other time. Now the knowledge to be had is not limited to the action or capacity itself, how to write, but it promises to extend into the way that another writer, or even another time and place, thinks, feels, and lives. It is this territory that Wollheim describes as the explanation of style, the style's *why*, but the knowledge got by the writing hand does not necessarily take the form of explanation. If I can write like you, what do I not know about you? And yet however much I know, it may still be more than I could ever spell.

§243 You Have to Take Your Chances

But that's not why you fell in love in the first place, just to hang on to life.

§244 No Man Is So Meet

At what point does "What rage is this" become a love poem? Perhaps it is with the sweetness of the poison, already in the first stanza; perhaps when love is named, in the fourth. Perhaps never entirely. In Egerton the poem shows evidence of composition and correction at different times, in various inks and hands. Among the inks is the faded gray-brown, gall-poor ink, reconstituted from powder, that Wyatt made do with "running day and night / from realm to realm" on embassy in Spain. In the same ink he wrote to Cromwell, as he was becoming aware of growing suspicions at home, suspicions fueled partly, it would emerge, by Bonner: "But out of game I beseech your lordship humbly to help me. I need no long persuasions. Ye know what case I am in. I have written on this unto you. I am at the wall." "I never saw a man that had so many friends here," Cromwell warned, "leave so few perfect friends behind him."

§245 It Was Talked About for Weeks

"If you live in the studio next to Brancusi," wrote O'Hara, in "Larry Rivers: A Memoir," "you try to think about Poussin. If you drink with Kline you tend to do your black-and-whites in pencil on paper. The artists I knew at that time knew perfectly well who was Great and they weren't going to begin to imitate their works, only their spirit. When someone did a false Clyfford Still or Rothko, it was talked about for weeks. They hadn't read Sartre's *Being and Nothingness* for nothing."

§246 Imitation (6)

Recall Erasmus's charge to the student in *De Ratione Studii*:

> memorize the rules of poetry and all its patterns; have at your fingertips the chief points of rhetoric, namely propositions, the grounds of proof, figures of speech [*figurae*], amplifications, and the rules governing transitions. For these are conducive not only to criticism but to imitation.

His technical analyses are the basis of *imitatio* as a discipline, the rhetoricians' practice of learning to follow worthy models. Among the generations of schoolmasters who taught with the textbook he helped write, it was agreed that whatever the models, the practice was properly grounded in the parsing and construing of grammar and mastery of the tropes and schemes of rhetoric, the various parts of style. Wyatt rarely wrote without a model, but his versions are free to the point of perversity. He is an imitator, but he cannot be said to be a practitioner of what would soon be codified as the schoolmasters' *imitatio*, the function of which was to transform an instinct into a method, to translate hot charisma into cooler art.

§247 One Thing Is Needful

Says Nietzsche: "To 'give style' to one's character—a great and rare art!"

§248 Imitating Yourself (2)

"Later on, imitate yourself." This is the advice of O'Hara and Rivers, in an essay they wrote together in 1961 called "How to Proceed in the Arts." "After all, who do you love best? Don't be afraid of getting stuck in a style." (Recall Cicero: "*quis cuiusquam nisi sui similis?*") The practice of this self-resemblance, the activity of it, is imitation. The reflexivity may seem gratuitous. Why can't style simply arise from being yourself, doing what you do the way you do it, the purest version of the expressivist position? But to draft a sentence or apply a brushstroke is to make a representation of yourself, and with the next word, the next stoke, the question is immanent and inevitable, *will it be like the last, or different; like how, and different how? Do I like what I have done? Is it like me, like how I like to be, or want to become?* There is always some small surprise in what you actually make or do, if you are paying attention. That surprise asks for a reaction, an adjustment, and it is in such adjustments—conscious and unconscious, conformal or swerving—that the differences of style make their alliance with habit.

§249 Imitating Yourself (3)

Every made thing is a mirror for the maker: a mirror for what you are, and (like the morning mirror) for the as-you-go adjustments of becoming.

§250 The Fourth Limit of Style: Nature Again

Everything has a style, except nature. It is possible to imitate nature, obviously enough. But the continuities of the natural world, the likeness of tree to tree, and of tree to leaf to capillary system to branching estuary—these are not cases of imitation, certainly not in the sociable sense common with human beings. Nature does not imitate us the way we, as social animals, imitate each other, or the way we imitate nature. Nor does it imitate itself. Ergo, nature has no style.

§251 Camouflage

Do you imitate to blend in with the world? With the crowd? With yourself?

§252 Imitating Yourself (4)

Trying something yourself is always imitating yourself, at least if you try it more than once. The act is still indebted to others. You first got it somewhere else. Now that you've tried it, however, whom are you imitating exactly—your model, or your last attempt? If you keep your model steadily before you, the approximation of otherness may become more and more exact; if you rely upon an original impression, it will likely diverge, like a copy of a copy of a copy. The whole business operates at a higher level too, more deliberate, less immediately material, all the way up to the question of whether and how the next book or painting should be like the last one. Such self-imitation is what we recognize when we recognize a distinctive voice, an individual style. "Act as if there is continuity in your work," O'Hara and Rivers advise. That *act-as-if* is an exhortation to imitation and the recognition of imitative continuity, a kind of double imitation, in fact, for it presumably means to act like somebody whose work acts like itself. Then again: "if there isn't [continuity], it is because that position is truly greater."

§253 Almost

Cicero goes on, in the *De Oratore*: "the ideal types of oratory, different in form but each in its own kind praiseworthy, are almost [*paene*] countless in number." Quintilian follows him: "Looking now at the varieties of oratory, we can find almost [*paene*] as many sorts of talent as of physical appearance."

§254 Imitation (7): Alfred Leslie

"An orange sky, with a white band about its throat, and perhaps a sunken pool of black?" asks the Landscape Architect in O'Hara's play, *Awake in Spain*. "It's another case of nature imitating Alfred

Leslie!" proclaims the Tourist. The joke, as so often, proves the rule.

§255 Certain Cultural Proclivities

Is race a style?

> Wherever I go to claim
> my flesh, there are entrances
> of spirit. And even its comforts
> are hideous uses I strain
> to understand.

LeRoi Jones published those lines, from "The Liar," in his 1964 collection *The Dead Lecturer*. A race without styles, without ways of being in the world and with each other, would hardly matter to its members, at least could not commune or console. "As an African American I had a cultural history that should give me certain cultural proclivities," he wrote later, as Amiri Baraka. Those styles also make race available for imitation, for appropriation, by people of other races, however the differences are drawn; and those styles operate in a wide field of cultural charismas, alongside, say, the downtown canon of Williams and Whitman and Pound and Apollinaire in which the young Jones became so fluent. The year 1957 was the year of Norman Mailer's essay "The White Negro." Is race a style? Can it be imitated? Is that how anyone has it, inhabits it? What about race is beyond imitation? If anything? "In the US and the Western world generally," Jones continued, in his autobiography, "white supremacy can warp and muffle the full recognition by a black person of this history."

§256 Imitation (8): Liking

Imitation is basic to style. To harmonize, or fit in, or dissolve; to learn and to know; to befriend or possess. In every case, there is desire: desire in the subject, and charisma in the object. The sense of style makes a map that is not defined by neutral gradients of similarity and dissimilarity, but is instead a manifold of tropisms and aversions, the very opposite of the ideal of aesthetic indifference. To respond to something in terms of its style is to ask, always if not always explicitly, *would I want to do something like that, make something like that, live that way?* That is equally the case with styles to which one has no personal attraction, the candy-colored dropsy of the Saturday morning cartoons, for example, or the spit-shined dash of fascism. To recognize a style is to know that someone wants to be or make or live that way, to have at least a vicarious feeling for that desire. And so, to look or read that way is to look or read covetously, open to the idea not so much of possessing but of becoming like what you like. Once again, it is a special advantage of English that these questions revolve around the double meaning of that word *like*, the meanings of resemblance and affinity, for style is compound of both; it is the register of experience in which they cannot be separated.

§257 The Absolute Thing That Was Closest to Me

"I remember feeling a new freedom to do certain things when I read Frank's poems," recalled Kenneth Koch, forty years later. "When I read his poem 'Easter,' for instance. That was very inspiring. And I remember trying to do some of the things that Frank did, like writing a poem and somebody walks into the room and talks to you and you put what they say in the poem instead of getting irritated and stopping. Yes, there was a while when I wrote a little bit under the influence of Frank, and I think that John and Frank and I all influenced each other in a probably un-sort-outable way. I mean, we encouraged each other. We were so happy to be with each other. At least I was. It turned out that each of our poetry turned out to be rather different, but I know I got a lot out of their poetry. I never read anything by either of them that was boring during those days. That's the main thing. I was always fascinated to read what they wrote. It was primary stuff. It was really good and nobody else's poetry affected me that way. I could tell if something was written by John or Frank and that's the only kind of poetry that I really . . . Well, I felt equally inspired by certain French poets, I suppose, and by Williams and Stevens, but as far as the absolute thing that was closest to me, the thing that I felt was closest to me—it was John and Frank's poetry."

§258 An Experiment

A little experiment, requiring only the standard equipment. The next time you and I are talking, pay attention to the traffic in gesture and expression between us. You smile. I likely smile, too, at least a little. And if I don't? Even if I don't, I know that you did, and what it means, and the way I know has to do with my own smile. The twenty-first century's prophets of the mirror neuron are not the first to suggest that I cannot help but smile, even if I don't show it, just as, watching a dancer, my body dances even if I don't get up from my seat. (Nor were the anthropologists first: perhaps it was Aristotle, or Plato, as much as he feared it.) What we know of others, we know in the mirror of our own faces and bodies. Except it is not a mirror we look into, but the mirror we are. To understand the understanding of the world this way is to give fullest credence to our being as imitative animals, to take our knowledge of others to arise from our promptness to be like them. There is still the question of what to do about it. I may meet your smile with a smile. My smile may be broader, or narrower, or I may refuse the offer altogether, and for so many reasons. Too much mirroring is obsequious. Too little is uptight, or even cruel. The constant and the intimate nature of these solicitations is deranging to attend to, if you decide to monitor it in any given conversation. It is enabling of our social lives, indispensable, and uncomfortable to think about. Such solaces and anxieties are the crux of style.

§259 Imitation (9)

As *character* is the management of the self's constancy and change, as *form* is the management of the ideal in the actual, as *nature* is the management of the self's implication in and independence from the world, so *style* is the management of the predicament of our imitative essence. ("Imitative essence"?)

§260 The Third Irony of Style

The individual and the group define the third irony of style, the fundamental irony: how the word is used both to talk about what is common, or shared, and what is not. It is an irony because the alternatives so often evade or occlude one another.—It allows us to assume at some moments that style is so particular as to give any-one away.—At others it is a way of joining, or passing, and distributing identity across a multitude. The experience at either limit is uncomfortable, even intolerable, the exile of singularity, the self-dissolution of mere membership. The breadth of the territory in-between is what explains how and why the word works. Why else would we not have two words, or more? Style's tacit mobility makes social life possible, or at least, it is the best way we have of talking our way through the predicament of identity and difference.— Granted, all sorts of mischief can happen in that middle ground. Style's ironies are sometimes simply bewitchments, individuality sold to consumers in mass quantities, and common cause made against common interest. Sometimes a good synonym for style is *ideology.*—Practically speaking, however, *style*, the word, helps make it possible to live in that middle ground without having to declare oneself once and for all, helps make a human space in-between the stringency of our thinking categories.

STYLE V.
INTERPRETATION

§261 Style and Truth (5)

A philosophy that believes in changing minds by argument, once and for all, need not cultivate a style. (It may, but it need not.) A philosophy, or a theory, that understands itself as a therapy for intransigent habits of mind cannot do without style, may even consist in style.

§262 I Read What You Read

There is no writing a poem like "St. Paul and All That" without help from Thomas Wyatt, or some sonneteer:

I am alive with you
full of anxious pleasures and pleasurable anxiety
hardness and softness
listening while you talk and talking while you read
I read what you read
you do not read what I read
which is right, I am the one with the curiosity
you read for some mysterious reason
I read simply because I am a writer

the sun doesn't necessarily set, sometimes it just disappears
when you're not here someone walks in and says
"hey,
there's no dancer in that bed"

"Anxious pleasures and pleasurable anxiety" makes a neat Petrarchan chiasmus, and for several lines the poem is caught up in managing its parallelisms, listening while you talk and talking while you read and so on. There is no writing the poem, either, without Vincent Warren. (His middle name was Paul; not public about his sexuality, he wanted *Vincent* kept out of it.) The parallelisms, however, do begin to slip. Frank reads because he is a writer. That is how he read Wyatt, and everything else. Warren reads—for some mysterious reason. Is that concession a moment of wonder, or a flash of impatience, or a creeping indifference? The someone who walks in at the end, is he a sympathetic friend? Or an unexpected newcomer? The poise of equal affection between the lovers is delicate, but the poem reprises and transcends its habit of doubling in a beautiful final line: "you never come when you say you'll come," it concludes, "but on the other hand you do come."

§263 Simply Because I Am a Writer

The only thing to do is simply continue.

§264 Style and Irony

If style has its ironies, structural ironies, it could equally well be said that irony itself is stylish. The two concepts have affinities. Both could be said to be modes of knowingness, style a kind of already knowing how, and irony of knowing better. (Knowing better, that is, than to take a position, publicly or privately, without preserving some recourse to the alternative; knowing both sides; knowing better than the ideologues.) Style and irony are also both ways of continuing. All of style's ironies—part and whole, art and nature, individual and group, description and judgment—are aspects of a life-enabling double consciousness, a way of living with contradiction, carrying on in the face of a problem that cannot, on its own terms, be solved. The basic problem of style, once again, is the problem of our imitative natures, a problem that could only find a solution in an intolerable choice between impossible limits. So, instead, *style*, a word that allows, and has long allowed, for a certain tacit, ironical suspension of the alternatives.

§265 The Pillar Perished Is

The pillar perished is whereto I leant,
The strongest stay of mine unquiet mind;
The like of it no man again can find—
From east to west still seeking though he went—
To mine unhap, for hap away hath rent
Of all my joy the very bark and rind,
And I, alas, by chance am thus assigned
Dearly to mourn till death do it relent.
But since that thus it is by destiny,
What can I more but have a woeful heart,
My pen in plaint, my voice in woeful cry,
My mind in woe, my body full of smart,
And I myself myself always to hate
Till dreadful death do cease my doleful state?

§266 I Love Your Style

It is easy to say, *I love your style*, and easy to hear it. The sense of *love* is almost weightless. *I love you for your style* is a different matter, not quite right, not quite enough.

§267 Oh Gentle Wyatt

Wyatt was recalled from Spain in June 1539, and dispatched in November to France, where Charles was negotiating again with Francis. In May 1540, with prospects for an alliance between the two receding, he was called home once more, just as Cromwell's plans for Henry's marriage to the German Anne of Cleves were coming to grief. (The Protestant alliance that the marriage might secure now seemed less urgent, and though Henry had approved of the portrait he dispatched Hans Holbein to make, he found Anne, in person, not to his taste. "I am ashamed that men have so praised her as they have done, and I like her not.") The marriage was annulled on June 12, and on June 28 Cromwell, the pillar whereto Wyatt had leaned, was executed. "Oh, gentle Wyatt, good-bye, and pray to God for me," Cromwell is said to have said on the scaffold. A contemporary Spanish account embellishes: "Oh, Wyatt, do not weep, for if I were no more guilty than thou wert when they took thee, I should not be in this pass."

§268 Against Interpretation (1)

"I definitely don't believe that 'your idea is as good as anyone's about what it means,'" O'Hara wrote in 1961.

> But I don't want to make up a lot of prose about something that is perfectly clear in the poems. If you cover someone with earth and grass grows, you don't know what they looked like any more. Critical prose makes too much grass grow, and I don't want to help hide my own poems, much less kill them.

There are more hostile images for criticism: in spite of its smothering effects, the grass has a Whitmanian vitality. ("And now it seems to me the beautiful hair of graves.") Still O'Hara's wariness of the word *about* is obvious, and long-standing, already apparent in his reluctant commentary on "Second Avenue": "I hope the poem to *be* the subject, not just about it." That stance was more or less agreed upon among the loose fellowship of the New York School. Rivers reports that John Ashbery "rarely spoke about poetry and said nothing about his own. Even today he acts slightly miffed if I ask about the source of some line. This attitude predates Susan Sontag's 'Against Interpretation.'"

§269 About *About*

About is a word for a relation, and it makes a connection: x is about y. But it is also a word for detachment and distance. Its Middle

English root *bout* means *outside, without*, and that sense persists in *about*'s proximity to *around*, as one might gather about a fountain or a scaffold. *About* entertains any perspective, except from inside.

§270 About and Like

Is it possible to be both about and like? Yes: it is easy enough to imagine a study of Seneca in the style of Seneca, or of Gertrude Stein in the style of Stein. It is also easy to imagine the complaint that the likeness of style entails a compromise in the rigor of analysis. The scruple arises from the idea that any act of understanding is an act of translation, and the translation is a guarantee against merely repeating the object. Criticism wants distance; stylistic affinity can only distort the object under study, as though the imitative critic were suing for the object's approval. As one modern critic puts it: "cooptation must always be a process intolerable to critical consciousness, whose first obligation is to resist incorporation, and whose weapon is analysis." The *inter-* of interpretation falls properly between the painting and the looker, the reader and the text. (The Latin *interpres* was an intermediary, a go-between.) The word is reserved for an activity that in its strongest, allegorical versions displaces meaning to another plane, a transcendental sphere, and even in its weaker forms still describes talk at a certain wise remove. This separation of aboutness from likeness is the main spring of the tension between interpretation and style.

§271 Against Interpretation (2)

"God knoweth what restless torment it hath been to me since my hither coming to examine my self, perusing all my deeds to my remembrance whereby a malicious enemy might take advantage by evil interpretation." Wyatt spent the autumn after Cromwell's death at Allington Castle in Kent again, hunting and hawking and sitting, in foul weather, at his book; at least, there is little evidence of other activity. His mistress Elizabeth Darrell, once of Queen Katherine's retinue, was with him, and apparently pregnant. But without Cromwell to look out for his interests at court, Bonner's accusations resurfaced, and this time events moved swiftly. On the seventeenth of January he was transported in chains to the Tower. The French ambassador wrote, "Although he is more regretted than any man arrested in England these three years, both by Englishmen and foreigners, no man is bold enough to say a word for him, and by those fine laws he must be judged, without knowing why." His first statement of innocence shows the restless torment of a man ransacking his memory for possible cause. Soon after, the particulars of the case were made clear: he had been too familiar with Charles, to the point of treason; he had given aid to the recusant English cardinal Reginald Pole; and he had slandered the king's diplomacy, suggesting that Henry was likely be left out of a pact between Francis and Charles, and deserved it. "That same Wyatt, being also ambassador, maliciously, falsely and traitorously said that he feared that the king should be cast out of a cart's arse and that by God's blood if he were so, he were well served, and he would he were so."

§272 Style and Action (2)

Meaning is to *interpret* as *style* is to—what? *Imitate* may be the best answer, but it is hardly canonical, hardly inevitable. It says something about style's relation to action that it has no characteristic verb of its own.

§273 Against Interpretation (3)

If Wyatt can seem, in a poem, careless and unfocused, he could fight closely, syllable by syllable, when he was at the wall. Once he knew Bonner's accusations, he went after the damning language about the cart's arse. "For in this thing 'I fear,' or 'I trust,'" he wrote, "seemeth but one small syllable changed, and yet it maketh a great difference." How easily his fate could turn on such details: did he want Henry in or out of the Continental accords? "Again 'fall out,' 'cast out,' or 'left out' maketh difference. Yea, and the setting of the words one in an other's place may make great difference." He composed what has come to be called his "Defense" while waiting for a trial before the Privy Council, twenty dense manuscript pages in a surviving, nearly contemporary transcript. Surely he did not write everything, treatise, letter, poem—those volatile poems—with such intensity and grammatical precision after all?

§274 Against Interpretation (4)

One tactic against interpretation: disjunction, a sheer doggedness of self-difference and interruption. And then there always came a time when Happy Hooligan in his rusted green automobile came plowing down the course, just to make sure everything was OK. Disjunction takes aim at interpretation's ambition to unify, another valence of that prefix *inter-*, the effort to discover an economy of relation among the elements of a work, a relation that could be given independent statement.

> a long history of populations, though
> the phrase beginning with "Palms!" and quickly forgotten
> in the pit under the dark there were books

Try, Try!—as the title of one of O'Hara's plays would have it. But a passage like this one stands a chance of convincing the reader that interpretation is the wrong thing to do. The ingenuity that would be required for an efficient, inclusive paraphrase, let alone explanation, would be extreme, and alien to the cheerful sprezzatura of the object. The determined interpreter may be left with the discouraging, slightly embarrassing feeling of playing alone.

§275 And Suddenly

"Kenneth did it in this idealized way that seemed a little bit removed and extremely beautiful," said Bill Berkson, talking about the love poetry of his friends. "Frank had this other thing which was like you are walking down the street and you fall in love and suddenly you're in the bedroom and you're in bed, and the next thing you're reading and the next thing you're making coffee and the next thing somebody calls you and the next thing you don't love each other anymore. Anyway, I later learned to hear Frank's poetry and to know it."

§276 Against Interpretation (5)

The invitation is to play along: to act as if each leap were a sensible transition, to welcome Ashbery's Happy Hooligan as though you had been expecting him. If interpretation finds or puts meaning elsewhere, in another place, it also calls a halt, the arrest of a question that needs an answer. Interpretation is an interruption, just as an explanation is. But why not keep going—why not simply continue? Ashbery's characteristic disjunctions are the vagaries of thinking and of mood; Koch is a game player, setting up playful new rules for poems that parody the habits of ordinary speech. O'Hara lets the next thing spin the wheel of his attention, the next cocktail party, or headline, or friend in the street. "I do this, I do that." The taxonomy is crude, not least because the poets borrow so much from one another. But it does reflect a common interest in challenging poetic unity both as an aesthetic criterion and as an ideal for speech. The invitation is to read without furrowing the brow, taking the poem instead for whatever new pleasures it offers, letting anxiety about where things are going slide and enjoying not just the words but the very buoyancy of not worrying. What a pleasure to find you are the reader who already knew Happy was coming!—and to be part of a community of such readers. If disjunction can stymie interpretation, it can still be a style.

§277 Style and Scar (3)

Sighs are my food, drink are my tears;
Clinking of fetters such music would crave.
Stink and close air away my life wears.
Innocency is all the hope I have.
Rain, wind, or weather I judge by mine ears.
Malice assaulted that righteousness should save.
Sure I am, Brian, this wound shall heal again
But yet, alas, the scar shall still remain.

§278 Against Interpretation (6)

Another tactic against interpretation: speed. Style is fast; interpretation is slow. Consider what it is like to pick up a new poetry journal, and flip through its pages. (Say, the latest *New World Writing*, to see what the poets in Ghana are doing these days.) The poems flicker past under the flat of your thumb, their shape on the page, their diction, a line here and there. *What kind of poems are these?* you might ask. *Whom do their writers talk with? Drink with, sleep with? What do those people have on their minds? On their kitchen or coffee tables?* The experience is like walking into a new room, a new house, maybe in a new city or a new country. The question of whether to read any one of the poems there is open. This leafing, browsing, milling is not yet quite reading—better to say recognizing, situating, orienting. *Where does this fit? Where do I?* Something different begins to happen in pausing over a page, taking the lines one after another. Expectations are partly suspended. What becomes salient, even desirable, is idiosyncrasy, distinctiveness. The collating curiosity of stylistic attention contracts toward the boundary of the page, and the poem's relation to itself. The two states are not pure, but they are still different dispositions. Imagine them as postures: a tipped-back, free ambient curiosity, watching other lives flash by; or the subtle bowing over the codex, like a question mark. Their temporality is different. One passes the time; the other interrupts it, steps outside it.

§279 Recognition

Stylistic recognition is not anagnorisis, not the recognition that turns a plot for Aristotle, as when Oedipus all at once knows himself. Both happen fast, when they happen, but anagnorisis is not a matter of likeness; it is a matter of identity. The *Odyssey* would be a different poem if Penelope had been waiting for any man with Odysseus's sense of style. It is his scar that first reveals him to be the man himself.

§280 The Time of Style (4): Already

Style happens so fast, it has already happened.

§281 Style and Scar (4)

A scar is a sign. A sign of what? "For though he heal the wound yet the scar shall remain," Wyatt wrote in his defense, echoing, or anticipating, his poem to Francis Bryan, allowing himself for a moment to tell his persecutors the cost of his ordeal. The scar is a sign of a wound. It is paradigmatic of the idea of signification itself as a reckoning of loss. The recurrence of the image, however, may usher the scar into another register of experience, for recurrence is always an opening for style. It becomes possible to see the scar not just as an interpretable mark, but as a way that Wyatt has, even at a moment of carceral impasse, of keeping going, of keeping writing. It is the same scar, but its aspect has shifted from sign to style. Has the pain been eased? Perhaps a style can never hurt as much as a sign can.

§282 A Bad Sign

A bad sign: a stabbing pain. The wrong style: an ache.

§283 A Good Sign

at

a streetcorner I stop and a lamppost is
bending over the traffic pensively like a
praying mantis, not lighting anything,
just looking
      who dropped that empty carton
of cracker jacks I wonder I find the favor
that's a good sign

§284 Style and Sign (1)

An element of style is not a sign of that style. Take Wyatt's habitual "whoso," that bluff, fragile wager that begins many poems. It does not signify his style, simply because it *is* his style. The basic double structure of semiotics, a present signifier and an absent signified, does not apply to style; the style is already present in its elements and instances, insofar as they are elements or instances of that style. The style is already here. In the same way, style cannot be a sign of itself. A baroque ornament is not a sign of the baroque (or a symbol or a metaphor for it). It simply is baroque, simply and already. In this sense style cannot be said to refer. It is no language for absence; it lacks the pathos of the absent signified, and can't be said to mind that lack or be a way of minding it. A style is, in this sense, less serious than a sign, if not less important.

§285 Style and Scar (5)

When Surrey puts on Wyatt's scar, he makes a warning of it, admonishing his cousin Thomas Radcliffe to accept chastisement for the offenses of his "reckless youth."

> Yet Solomon said, the wronged shall recure,
> But Wyatt said true; "The scar doth aye endure."

The second line is a rebuke to the reassurance of the biblical Solomon. ("Recure" means "heal.") Proud Surrey, writing the poem in 1544, had already suffered many reversals in his own reckless youth: he had been suspected of treason, and imprisoned for dueling and again for vandalism; he was inconveniently zealous on behalf of the ancient liberties of his birth, and of the new religion. His military record was mixed, campaigning in the mostly stalemated sieges and countersieges around Calais, and when he wrote to Radcliffe his assault on Montreuil was soon to be abandoned. Still, in his admiration of Wyatt, his desire to make the elder poet an exemplar of Stoicism under pressure, and to cast himself as a kindred spirit, he too might be said to wear the scar as much as to suffer it.

§286 Style as Example (2)

What about style as the sign of where it comes from? Might one say that *whoso* is a sign of Wyatt, a signature, or more generally that, as a piece of archaic diction, it is a sign of its times? Here too there are reasons to say no. *Whoso* is not what Charles Sanders Peirce would call a symbol, a merely conventional sign arbitrarily associated with what it signified, as *jujube* is with the jujube. Nor is it a Peircian index, a sign that looks like its signifier, as a picture of a door stands for the exit. It might be better to think of it as an example, a piece of what it comes from. Gérard Genette gives such an account: "Style is the exemplificatory function of discourse, as opposed to its denotative function." His proposition captures two important aspects of style, the sense that any instance of it comes from someplace or sometime else, where there is or might be more of it; and that any instance can be a pattern for future instances, a way of carrying on, as we speak of following an example.

§287 The Time of Style (5): To Come

If recognition is basic to style, it cannot be only recognition of something familiar; it will also recognize a future possibility. *There might be more like this; this might continue.* The *re-* looks Janus-like in both directions. The future is already in the object when we encounter its style, even if other instances do not yet exist. This is why it is possible for something that has no precedent nonetheless to have a style.

§288 You Were Wearing (1)

"Oh dear I have such a frightful hangover and I just had a two-hour lunch with Helen Frankenthaler who is happy about getting her sojourn in France from the Paris Biennale," O'Hara wrote to Ashbery in 1959. "She was darling and looked very pretty in a red coat from Bordeaux, and carrying a beret from St. Jean de Luz. I was wearing my Bloomingdale silk tie and a dirty blue shirt. This sounds like one of Kenneth's cpoems [*sic*], cthonically speaking." As indeed it does, the poem "You Were Wearing," which Koch would publish three years later:

> Mother was walking in the living room, her Strauss Waltzes comb in her hair.

We waited for a time and then joined her, only to be served tea in cups
painted with
pictures of Herman Melville
As well as with illustrations from his book *Moby Dick* and from his
novella *Benito Cereno*.
Father came in wearing his Dick Tracy necktie: "How about a drink,
everyone?"

O'Hara catches the wave of Koch's poem, which he must have read in manuscript, and rides it for a couple of sentences. The typo "cpoems" allows him a deep joke about where the reflex comes from, subterranean, out of the earth. Or a superficial joke—but no more superficial than the Bloomingdale's tie and the dirty shirt. In time the curator O'Hara will be seen in photographs wearing a tux to an opening, but he still takes care, here, to rough up his work shirt.

§289 Style and Sign (2)

Style has no meaning; it needs no interpretation. A perfectly absurd claim: for as Nietzsche says, there are no facts, only interpretations. If we adopt a narrower account of interpretation, however, closer to what Susan Sontag is against, closer to what critics do professionally, the proposition becomes more intelligible. That essay "Against Interpretation," which came out in the *Evergreen Review* in 1964, treats the offending practice as a conscious act that implies a method and produces something that could be called an interpretation, something additional to the work, a screen or even a substitute. "The world, our world, is depleted, impoverished enough," Sontag protests. "Away with all duplicates of it, until we again experience more immediately what we have." If interpretation is like this, always a representation of the world, a duplicate, then style is different indeed. To encounter something in terms of style—to be moved into that register of experience—is to be activated as an imitative animal, whether in sympathy or aversion. Style is embodied in the simple capacity to be like what you see, or at least to recognize such likeness as a possibility, and to move or to feel your way toward or away. The features of that style may be subject to interpretation and explanation, but they need not be. It is not that style has no meaning. But it happens below the level of coding and decoding, below or before, even already—however ripe for reading the gestures of style may be. Style's likeness needs no aboutness to do its work.

§290 Style and Sign (3)

Imitation is not representation: that may be a better way of saying that style has no meaning. To adopt a style is not to make an image of it, but to instantiate it, exemplify it, incarnate it. The word *mimesis* is split down the middle, on one side the painter, on the other, the learning child. The two kinds are not only distinct, but mutually interfering. Just as interpretation might be compromised by imitation, by an entangling likeness, so the fluency and success and momentum of imitation might be compromised by the detachment (spatial) and interruption (temporal) of interpretation. Style *can* be interpreted, as interpretation *does* have style, but neither can be reduced to the other, and style, at least, can go it alone.

§291 You Were Wearing (2)

Wyatt feared that his accusers had him on his style, in particular his habit of salty language and strong oaths. Bonner's original complaint is heavy on those oaths: "he forbeareth not to make exclamations and after this sort, 'By God's blood, ye shall see the king our master last out of the cart's arse, and if he so be served, by God's body, he is well served.'" Lest Cromwell miss the point, he has Wyatt repeat: "By God's body, I would he might be so served." Bonner's Wyatt is profane and recklessly familiar at table, but even in the report's priggish tattling, the danger and the charm of Wyatt's confidences, his unpolitic freedoms, come through. Wyatt felt obliged to address the likeness. "But by cause I am wont some time to rap out an oath in an earnest talk," he wrote, "look how craftily they have put in an oath to the matter to make the matter seem mine."

> But let them be examined that have heard me talk of that matter, whereof they seem to tear a piece or two, and patch them together as if a man should take one of my doublet sleeves and one of my coat and sew

them together after a disguised fashion and then say "Look, I pray you what apparel Wyatt weareth."

Bonner's pastiche, Wyatt argues, is an unconvincing motley, not his style at all. The charge of treason was almost certainly a slander. Wyatt seems to have been a loyal man in an impossible job, whose liberties were inconvenient, but charismatic, and never not in Henry's service. Still it is easy enough to imagine him saying what Bonner says he said.

§292 Style and Truth (6)

Can a style be false? A lie? Forgery is the obvious case: *that looks like a Motherwell*, it has that "precise personal light," as O'Hara put it, but in fact, it was painted by someone else. And yet, if the proposition *that painting was made by Robert Motherwell* turns out to be false, still, for the question to have arisen, it must at least have been in the style of Robert Motherwell. That will be no less true when the fake is exposed. By the same token, if I convince you that a painting is not in the style of Motherwell after all, you are unlikely to maintain that it was pretending to be, but failed, much less that it lied or that its maker lied. It just isn't like a Motherwell, after all; you can see that now. Which is not to say that Motherwell didn't make it. A style in itself is never a fiction. As style, it simply is what it is, or rather, what it is like.

§293 The Third Antithesis of Style

The distinction between recognition and interpretation is not to be found in the object. Just as everything has a style, so everything is interpretable; the things that have style and the things that have meaning are not different things or different parts of things.— There are, of course, ways of talking that collapse the difference altogether, saying, for example, that reading a room for the style, feeling out the affinities and differences among the people there, the invitations and estrangements and origins and associations, is always an act of interpretation. Style's orientation is a kind of meaning. What is gained in saying so is another reminder, per

Nietzsche, that there are no facts but the facts we make.—But something is lost, too. What is lost is the felt difference between translation and participation, between standing invisibly at the window and walking in the door, making your way and your place. It is the difference, you could say, between objectivity and implication, between reading as a reader and reading as a writer.—The question becomes what kind of literary knowledge can be had only by entering the room and joining the party; by letting the distance go, the critical distance, if only for a time.

DESCRIPTION
AND JUDGMENT

§294 Make of It What You Will

"Frank's poetry undergoes a change that can be clearly perceived if we restrict ourselves to the love poems on the one hand and the Bill Berkson poems on the other." Joe LeSueur watched Vincent Warren fade from O'Hara's life with regret; it was with some resentment that he greeted Berkson, the handsome, straight, twenty-year-old son of the Upper East Side who soon became O'Hara's constant companion. "Bill Berkson all the way," as LeSueur put it forty years later.

In the former [poems], we are in the recognizable world of going to the movies and the ballet, drinking too much coffee and smoking too many cigarettes, sharing a coke with someone, eagerly awaiting the arrival of someone, deciding on a birthday present for someone, and, above all, having strong feelings about someone, while in the latter—well, make of it what you will, page after page of disparate thoughts, images, ideas, quoted remarks, antic wordplay, private jokes, and occasionally eccentric typography. I'm referring mainly to the work I have just now read through again, the ultimate Bill Berkson poem, "Biotherm," which I'm prepared to believe is terrific.

The poetry does change, if less categorically than LeSueur maintains. (Wyatt is still with O'Hara, and with Berkson: "That Muir volume was always handy in his house," Berkson recently recalled.) As it changes, so does LeSueur's description, from the recollection of events and feelings to a list of devices and techniques. He is prepared to believe in the value of the new poems but it seems he does not believe already.

§295 Personnage de Bon Esprit

Was it in prison that Wyatt began translating the penitential psalms? Or was it after? He did walk out of the Tower again in March of 1541. There is no evidence that he ever stood trial, or presented his case before a jury. The Privy Council recorded that "he confessed upon his examination all the things objected unto him, in a . . . lamentable and pitiful sort."

> O Lord, since in my mouth thy mighty name
> Suffer'th itself 'my Lord' to name and call,
> Here hath my heart hope taken by the same
> That the repentance which I have, and shall,
> May at thy hand seek mercy as the thing,
> Only comfort of wretched sinners all

The French ambassador wrote in a dispatch that he had been pardoned *"pour estre personnage de bon esprit,"* for being a good fellow.

> Whereby I dare with humble bemoaning,
> By thy goodness, of thee this thing require.
> Chastise me not for my deserving
> According to thy just conceived ire.

What was this life? So full of reversals as to lose any of its own integrity, save as the transcript of the exercise of someone else's arbitrary power, the negative image of a mercurial tyranny.

§296 Description Of (1)

If style, on style's own terms, is imitation, and if interpretation, by contrast, translates style out of itself, somewhere in-between the two is the act of description. The description of a style does not automatically assume or abjure the particular charisma of the style it describes. It is description not *like*, nor *about*, but *of*: the most spacious of prepositions, with much room to maneuver.

§297 How Do You Sound

"'HOW DO YOU SOUND??' is what we recent fellows are up to." That's how LeRoi Jones begins his "Statement on Poetics" for Allen's *New American Poetry*.

> How *we* sound; our peculiar grasp on, say: a. Melican speech, b. Poetries of the world, c. Our selves (which is attitudes, logics, theories, jumbles of our lives, & all that), d. And the final . . . The Totality of Mind: Spiritual . . . God?? (or you name it) : Social (zeitgeist) : or Heideggerian *umwelt*.

The description is cosmopolitan and perspectival. It hears its American speech through the ears of a Chinese immigrant (the transposition of *r* and *l* in "Melican"); it mixes up logic and lives, God and Heidegger. In 1959 Jones was still in the Village, still married to Hettie Cohen, still close friends with O'Hara. Again, it was "openness" that Baraka would later say he had most gotten from his friend and fellow-poet. They shared a commitment to live as variously as possible. "I CAN BE ANYTHING I CAN."

§298 Description Of (2)

In 1964, O'Hara wrote an essay about Franz Kline for a retrospective exhibition:

> The images have become hieratic and undeniable, composed of monumentally angular calligraphic strokes in constant tension with a rough

and awkward semigeometrical stubbornness, like a struggle between Picasso's *Guernica* and the Bauhaus.

This passage, about the painting *Cardinal*, makes an adventitious summa of descriptive technique. There is attention to the brushstrokes, to parts of the whole. Attached to them, some modestly technical, art-historical vocabulary, "composition" and "calligraphy." The idea of tension evokes the push-pull language given to the abstract expressionists by Hans Hofman at the academy, the Club, and the Cedar Tavern. There is a repertory of ordinary descriptive adjectives, like "rough" and "awkward." Other adjectives come from further away, and have almost the status of metaphor, like "hieratic"—as though there were a priestly authority in the images, as though they gestured from a height. (Unless this is the hieraticism of Egyptian art, in which case, more art-historical techne.) Then there is the *like* of comparison, the struggle evoked between the angular chaos of Picasso's *Guernica* and the rectilinear composure of Bauhaus architecture. Technical description, traces of origin, adjectives technical and impressionistic, comparison.

§299 Description Like

Like an interpretation, a description need not be like its object, but it can be: O'Hara's account of Kline has some of the free motion and fast pace often said to characterize action painting; it allows itself to be contagiously sympathetic with how Kline worked, or at least an idea of how he worked, the idea the paintings advertise. That kind of imitation is stylistic, not representational. O'Hara's description is in no sense a picture of Kline's painting, even if both happen to be black and white. Across their media, however, they somehow share a way of working.

§300 Sweet

From a half-century's distance, George Puttenham reads Wyatt and Surrey and declares, "I find very little difference." He has his story to tell about the continuity of style in English poetry across the reign of the Tudors. "I repute them (as before) for the two chief lanterns of light to all others that have since employed their pens upon English poesie. Their conceits were lofty, their styles stately, their conveyance cleanly, their terms proper, their meter sweet and well-proportioned." There is no hint of Wyatt's imprisonments here, of his precarious fortunes and erotic adventures. The dignity of English is Puttenham's subject, its capacity to rival the achievement of the classics. The rhetoric is highly patterned, full of civilizing parallelisms, but what does most of the assimilating work, assimilating each poet to the other and to himself, are the adjectives, *lofty, stately, cleanly, proper*, and *sweet*. *Sweet* above all; as Wyatt's elegist John Leland would put it, "sweet, and worthy of his mother tongue."

§301 Description Unlike

A description can equally well abstain from stylistic sympathy, can interrupt or slow down a sympathetic encounter, can be *of* without being *like*. Technical language will do the trick, partition, measurement, the identification of qualities with generic names and fixed criteria. Techne is a way of interdicting style. It is also possible simply to choose a different style, whether to strike sparks, or to accommodate a foreign object to a new context; you can give, for example, a surrealist description of Rachmaninoff.

§302 Style's Adjectives (1)

Some adjectives are particular to stylistic description, *classic, romantic, gothic, baroque, mannerist*, and so on: words identified with a period of history or a stage of artistic development or evolution, style going about its business of telling time. Gerundives have a special status, *flowing* or *curling*: they capture style as a way of carrying on, in motion. But any adjective can be made to serve.

> It's so
> original, hydrogenic, anthropomorphic, fiscal, post-anti-esthetic,
>   bland, unpicturesque, and WilliamCarlosWilliamsian!
> it's definitely not 19th Century, it's not even Partisan Review, it's
>   new, it must be vanguard!

Adjectives made from nouns are style words, especially the ones with suffixes like *-ian, -esque, -ish*, and so on. So, an arch in the Florentine manner, or a Fauvist painting. ("I'm getting rather Lorcaesque lately," O'Hara wrote in 1957, "and I don't like it.") The suffix isn't necessary; something can be *downtown*. Even a name can be an adjective, *Barthesian, Sidneian, very Frank*.

§303 Style and Names

A name is always an adjective. It only takes an act of stylistic appropriation, the discovery of someone's style somewhere else, to reveal its true grammar.

§304 Style and Synesthesia

Puttenham calls Wyatt's poetry *sweet* because that is what everyone called good poetry; it is the default word for poetic praise among the Elizabethans. No one instance of it is guaranteed to be all that interesting, but the habit is telling. It is a pleasure word, a pleasure that precedes the nourishment that humanist pedagogues promised good readers from their reading. Hence Philip Sidney's account of poetry as a "medicine of cherries." (*Taste* had not yet become a conventional word for stylistic preference, but it would not be long.) *Sweet* is somatic. It puts poetry in the mouth. It is also freely synesthetic, imparting a flavor to a sound. Synesthesia is a characteristic of many adjectives used to describe style, testimony to the way in which a particular style reaches out into the rest of life, proposes analogies, propagates likenesses. Something like this power is at work whenever a painter takes inspiration from a poem, a composer from a painting, and so on. In traversing the arts, a style also traverses the senses, and vice versa.

§305 Description Between

"Like a struggle between Picasso's *Guernica* and the Bauhaus": Kline's *Cardinal* bears the claim out, full of contending energy, locked into a form that is part structure, part skirmish. O'Hara's description is for a moment given over entirely to likenesses. The tactic has a kinship with the language of the Hollywood pitch, *Rebel without a Cause* meets *Dr. Zhivago*. ("Emotive Fruition / is wedding Poetic Insight perpetually," O'Hara might say.) There is no reduction of stylistic affinity to formal sameness. Nor is there any substitution of terms: *Guernica* is not a figure for the Bauhaus, nor the reverse. Their likeness is not a vector for travel from one to the other, but a possibility that arises from superimposing them in the imagination. There is something particularly stylish about such descriptions, perhaps because there is so much you already know when you recognize their fit.

§306 Style's Adjectives (2)

The analysis of style, separating and identifying its parts, re-inforces the distinction between analyzing subject and analyzed object. The impressionism of synesthetic description can undo the distinction, vesting style in the reaction of the perceiver, how it feels rather than what it is. We can argue about whether something is blue or it looks blue. But if it sounds blue, it sounds blue to you. "We don't even know what an impartial description of written discourse looks like," complains the critic Richard Lanham. There are technical remedies, and there is the word *stylistics* to cover them. But style has always functioned to blur boundaries between the objects you make and the objects you own, your prose and your bookshelf and that favorite coat.

§307 Style as Failure (3)

What is the difference between having bad style and having no style? They are both hard judgments, two varieties of social and artistic failure. The first allows you a style, even one successful on its own terms, affording a place in the world and a way of getting along there. The judgment is on the style's quality, and it might have a number of criteria, aesthetic (it is un-beautiful), pragmatic (it gets in your way), sociable (it puts you in with the wrong sort of people). The second judgment, no style, is more radical. It diagnoses a failure to hold together, a failure to live up to the demands of style for integration and fluency; a diagnosis of inconsistency, awkwardness, self-doubt or self-sabotage, an uneasy life or a blind or clumsy one. There is in such a judgment the fundamental implication that style is not everywhere, not in everyone, not evenly distributed through a world we can recognize. Instead it is an achievement, one that some people manage and that others do not. The real opposite of stylelessness is not having *a style*, but having *style*. Merely having *a style*, any style, is as good as having none at all, or even worse.

§308 Whoso List (2)

In 1959 H. A. Mason rendered a judgment on Wyatt's style famous among the poet's critics, one that he has never entirely escaped:

> By a little application we could compose a dictionary of conventional phrases which would show that many of these poems of Wyatt's are simply strung together from these phrases into set forms. There is not the slightest trace of poetic activity. The reason, I suggest, is that no poetic activity was attempted.

That dictionary would include such phrases as "stony heart," "'twixt hope and dread," "whoso list," and so on. It would serve as well for the Devonshire manuscript and the Arundel Harrington manuscript and the rest of Tottel: a period style, about which C. S. Lewis commented that it was not intended for reading. "It has little meaning until it is sung in a room with many ladies present. The whole scene comes before us. . . . We are having a little music after supper." There are, however, phrases in Wyatt that no dictionary will contain. "Wild for to hold." "I lay broad waking."

§309 Minor Style (1)

"I have been having a terribly spiritual morning bathing in Poulenc songs, 2 piano concertos and *Les Sécheresses* which I found here. (It is greater than *Tristan*, so there!)" That was the morning of February 11, 1956, as O'Hara recorded it in a letter to James Schuyler. The remark, however, was not a new one. John Ashbery remembers it as the first thing he heard O'Hara say at a cocktail party at Harvard in 1949, when they were students together. "Let's face it, *Les Sécheresses* is greater than *Tristan*." Ashbery described his reaction in a reminiscence from the 1970s.

> I know that *Les Sécheresses* was a vocal work by Poulenc which had been performed recently at Harvard; I also know, back in those dull and snobbish days, that nobody at Harvard took Poulenc or any other modern composer (except Hindemith, Piston, and Stravinsky), seriously, and that this assertion was in the way of a pleasant provocation. Also, I was somehow aware, it summed up a kind of aesthetic attitude which was very close to my own.

Poulenc is a modern composer; he is French, not German (nor on the Harvard faculty, as Walter Piston was), and, or perhaps therefore, minor. "I knew instinctively that Frank didn't really believe that *Les Sécheresses* was greater than *Tristan*," Ashbery continued: "but at the same time he felt it important to make that statement, possibly because he felt that art is already serious enough; there is no point in making it seem even more serious by taking it too seriously."

§310 The Sixth Limit of Style: Action

Everything has a style, except action. The phrase *I style* is idiomatic at the barbers and the posh boutique; *I style myself* is good usage too, but always has a light irony about it. Otherwise, to make *style* a verb is a transgression of its usual grammar. Style-words are modifiers, adjectives and adverbs, predications. The verb is the grammar of action. While an action may be performed in one style or another, the action qua action is not altered, insofar as it is defined in relation to its function. Whereas a gesture done in different styles is apt to be a different gesture.

§311 And So On (3)

O'Hara bathed regularly in French music. From another letter, to Kenneth Koch: "Jimmy and I are now listening to something of Lyon's which you simply must get ahold of and saturate yourself with—Milhaud's Poemes Juifs, ravishingly beautiful, perfect, sensitive, etc., etc." "Etc., etc.": and so on.

§312 Minor Style (2)

When critics trouble to define minor art, it is often as the negative image of what is major. "The diminution of letters is especially evident to those of us who write very seriously," wrote Paul Goodman, very seriously, for *Dissent* in 1958; those of us "who try for the classical literary functions of subtle ideas and accurate distinctions, ingenious and cogent reasoning, distilled learning, poetic expression." His essay, "Reflections on Literature as a Minor Art," is particularly concerned with the loss of literature's audience and influence, but implies an account of what minorness would be like in itself: un-classical, un-rigorous in its terms and its arguments, diffuse, above all un-serious. This is the same Paul Goodman, poet, social critic, gestalt therapist, whose "Advance-Guard Writing" so galvanized O'Hara in 1951. By 1957, they were acquainted well enough for O'Hara to be disenchanted. "I liked him better when I didn't know him," he told Joe LeSueur. LeSueur recalls an argument at the intermission of a concert at Town Hall: "as we got into a discussion of a piece by Prokofiev—was it on the program?—[Frank] went out of his way to disagree with Paul, who naturally wrote off the flashy Russian as a lightweight."

§313 Penitential Psalms (1)

In the days before his execution in 1535, Thomas More, who had refused to condone Henry's break with Rome, undertook the spiritual exercise of paraphrasing the penitential psalms, the seven psalms traditionally identified with the sorrows of King David. Eleven years later Surrey would do the same in his own last imprisonment. Surrey's career of overreaching had caught up with him: he was accused of using the royal arms to ornament the great house he was building at Kenninghall, a symbolic but unpardonable usurpation. He was executed just nine days before the death of the king he served and so resented. Once again, and for the last time, Wyatt was among the models he chose to follow.

§314 Style and Belief (1)

Style is not something you believe. You may say, *I believe his style*, but it has the sound of a category mistake—resistance, the spring-back of an idiom bent out of shape. Still less is style something to believe *in*. It is more like an alternative to belief, another way of holding on to the world you are in. Style in this sense is an anti-dote to skepticism, not because it proves anything, but because it doesn't need to. It discourages questions about what is really be-hind, or underneath. It has little interest in epistemology (unless it is in the conversations and the cafés talk about epistemology might get you into). Even more, style relaxes that temporalized form of skepticism that frets the problem of action, of cause and effect, of what is next and how it follows. The continuity of style is obvious and might suffice. "I am always impressed by how difficult and yet how easy it is to get from one moment to the next of one's life," Ash-bery would muse, some years later. The easy part is style.

§315 His Harp He Taketh

His harp he taketh in hand to be his guide
Wherewith he offer'th his plaints, his soul to save,
That from his heart distils on every side,
Withdrawing him into a dark cave
Within the ground, wherein he might him hide,
Fleeing the light as in prison or grave,
In which as soon as David entered had,
The dark horror did make his fault adrad.

§316 Penitential Psalms (2)

The principal model for Wyatt's psalms was the paraphrase made by the Italian poet Pietro Aretino, who stitched together the seven penitential psalms with his own narrative of King David's struggle toward repentance. The story comes from 2 Samuel. Overcome with desire for the beautiful Bathsheba, David sends her husband Uriah to die in the vanguard of battle; when he marries the widow, he is punished by the death of their first child. The free translation

Wyatt makes from Aretino and from a bookshelf of other sources sounds like Wyatt all the same. It studiously forgoes the romance vocabulary of its original; it is fractured in its grammar, awkward in its conceits; its demotic urgency sounds, as the lyrics often do, lost and godless. Its David sounds like Henry VIII, whose crimes against marriage were still reverberating in England.

§317 The San Remo and the Cedar Tavern

"John Ashbery, Barbara Guest, Kenneth Koch and I," reported O'Hara, "being poets, divided our time between the literary bar, the San Remo, and the artists' bar, the Cedar Tavern." The major major art for O'Hara and friends was painting, especially the macho, hard-drinking action painting of Pollock and the first-generation abstract expressionists. Those brash canvases were the shelter behind which they could develop their minor major art, or major minor art, or whatever it was. "In the San Remo we argued and gossiped: in the Cedar we often wrote poems while listening to the painters argue and gossip. So far as I know nobody painted in the San Remo while they listened to the writers argue." Painting gave O'Hara someplace to project his own seriousness: "Abstract Expressionism is the art of serious men," he wrote a decade after Rosenberg's action painting essay; serious men who make "brilliant, uncomfortable works, works that don't reflect you or your life, though you can know them. Art is not *your* life, it is someone else's."

§318 Minor Style (3)

A dozen years before Goodman, T. S. Eliot had made an attempt at a definition in his essay "What Is Minor Poetry?" Major poetry, Eliot argues, obliges us to read everything: "the whole is more than the sum of the parts." When he thinks of the major poet, "it is not of a few favourite poems that I am reminded . . . but of the whole work." Minor poetry, meanwhile, circulates among the young poets and the little journals, suits private needs, and can be taken in small doses. Eliot is sympathetic to minorness, and cautious about deciding what works fall on which side; nonetheless he depends upon the contrast. One might say that underneath this attitude lies the hope that major poetry could be an alternative to life; that in its wholeness, it might be another plenum, a replacement for the world that we live in, a "second nature," as Philip Sidney would say. Whereas minor poetry is not whole, not complete, but merely continuous, with itself and with the rest of life; it fits in with the rest of our tastes, "second nature" in the more colloquial, present-day sense. It continues the way that style continues, in an ironical adaptation that asks no radical change of the reader, and is basically tolerant of the circumstances in which it is read.

§319 The Judgment of Style

If we see style—if style is what we see, how we see—it is because the object of our attention has made a claim neither for beauty nor for usefulness; or at least, neither claim is pressing; or if they are, we have chosen not to answer. As a mode of attention, style is minor, if it requires attention at all.

§320 Judgment of His Ear

At the beginning of the paraphrase, Wyatt's David searches for the sound of penitence:

> Gathering his sprites that were dismayed for fear,
> His harp again into his hand he rought.
> Tuning accord by judgement of his ear,
> His heart's bottom for a sigh he sought

Then the sound is gone.

> On sonour chords his fingers he extends
> Without hearing or judgement of the sound.
> Down from his eyes a storm of tears descends,
> Without feeling, that trickle on the ground,
> As he that bleeds in bain right so intends
> Th'altered senses to that that they are bound.
> But sigh and weep he can none other thing
> And look up still unto the heaven's king.

He is left only with his sight, and not even sight to see with, but only to point with, upward.

§321 The Seventh Limit of Style: Passion

Everything has a style, except passion. Passion's extremity is another limit of style, how it feels wrong to speak of a style of rage or a style of grief. From an anthropological distance, perhaps, a culture might be said to have such styles, relative to other cultures. But at anything like close range, to adopt a style of rage implies something less than rage. Rage and grief are the thorough passions, as Philip Fisher puts it: they cannot be mixed, as styles can; their focus on their object, present or absent, is singular. They refuse awareness of the plane of collation and comparison that style requires. Style, by contrast, is a matter of emotions, or of moods.

§322 Essay on Style

O'Hara wrote his essay on style as a poem:

> Someone else's Leica sitting on the table
> the black kitchen table I am painting
> the floor yellow, Bill is painting it
> wouldn't you know my mother would call
> up
>   and complain?
>   my sister's pregnant and
> went to the country for the weekend without
> telling her
>   in point of fact why don't I
> go out to have dinner with her or "let her"
> come in?

Frank and Bill are in Frank's apartment, painting the floor yellow, a free whimsical domesticity, when the past breaks in—his mother calls, a voice from the ancient drama of the nuclear family, intent on staking her claim upon her son. She imposes her language, too, the passive aggressive "let her" and, one suspects, the acerbic "in point of fact."

> drinking a cognac while Edwin
> read my new poem it occurred to me how impossible
> it is to fool Edwin not that I don't know as
> much as the next about obscurity in modern verse
> but he
>   always knows what it's about as well
> as what it is do you think we can ever
> strike *as* and *but*, too, out of the language
> then we can attack *well* since it has no
> application whatsoever neither as a state
> of being or a rest for the mind no such
> things available.

In the poem's middle movement, Frank is at a bar with Edwin Denby, an older friend who was the elegant and exacting dance critic for the *Times*. Here is another way to live, drinking cognac, quite grown up, knowing what things are about as well as what they are, as though interpretation were something you might mature into. Frank's mind leaps back to conversation with Bill all the same. *Do you think we could strip our language of all its qualifications and hesitations*, he asks, *just keep going, since anyway there is no place to rest?*

>   do you think
> ,Bill, we can get rid of *though* also, and *also*?
> maybe your
>   lettrism is the only answer treating
> the typewriter as an intimate organ why not?
> nothing else is (intimate)
>   no I am not going
> to have you "in" for dinner nor am I going "out"
> I am going to eat alone for the rest of my life

Now, more games with Bill (of the sort Joe hated), and the avant-garde gesture of lettrism, an experiment that tends away from the family drama and the meaningful poem both, toward the mediated intimacies of the typewriter. Why not, since they would never sleep together, Frank and Bill? But then the poem is back on the phone with his mother, or pretending to be, and it ends by opting out of everything. How is this poem an essay on style, as the title has it? Perhaps because there are so many people to be with and so many ways to sound and the question finally arises whether it is a good idea to sound like any of them. The other enemy: style. In the meantime, he does still sound like Frank, and it is not clear that he could help that.

§323 Minor Style (4)

Another definition, from Gilles Deleuze and Félix Guattari, in their study of Franz Kafka. Minor literature is written in a minor language, a local dialect carved out from a national standard; it is everywhere political, written in such a "cramped space" that there is no escape from social meaning; and, because of the small size of the community and the shared political predicament, "everything takes on a collective value." Their definition can readily be rewritten in terms of style, its capacity to rebuke the universal and to insist upon locality, its situation among its speakers and writers. Minor art is the art of mere style, nothing more or less. Deleuze and Guattari conclude: "There is nothing that is major or revolutionary except the minor." Is their transvaluation style's secret wager? The wager that major art, in its ideal exemption, will leave life untouched; that it is only the tacit collaborations of ways of life and of writing that ever truly move history, or bear witness to its motion?

§324 Quiet of Mind (6)

Happiness: a minor art, a quiet of mind. It exists as much in prospect as it does in the present, a promise of continuing. Is likeness its principle? That things will keep being like they are now?

§325 The Fourth Irony of Style

Style is everywhere, in everything, the texture of being in the world; everyone and everything has a style, an acknowledgment that frees us from our values, and opens onto a scientific stylistics and a liberal tolerance.—Then again, there is good style and bad style; or even, style and no style. Once again, the word affords a freedom of movement across some otherwise treacherous human terrain. A judgment on style itself broods over such maneuvers, the judgment that style is minor, that it falls ineffectually somewhere between action and passion.—But there is also the possibility that the only real change, in the world, in the self, is a change of style, from which the interruption of event could only be a distraction. Are we not ourselves minor, most of the time?—The terms allow for that tacit movement, the passing off of one as the other. The freedom to treat a judgment as a description, a description as a judgment, is the fourth irony of style.

STYLE V. NARRATIVE

§326 Periods of Style (1)

"His sentence / is an image of the times," says O'Hara about Bertolt Brecht's Mackie, in a poem called "The Threepenny Opera" that he wrote back when he was at Michigan. Rhetoric calls a sentence a *period*, which is also the unit of historical style; the word comes to English from the Latin *periodus*, a complete utterance. (For Aristotle, it is complete thought; for modern grammar, the domain of a finite verb.) As a piece of its place and time, the sentence will do as well as any other part to represent the whole. In its particular self-sufficiency, however, it is not only a mark but a possible model of the wholeness of its origin.

§327 The Anxiety of Appropriation (3)

Am I getting my style on the cheap? The thought crossed Larry Rivers's mind, especially back in his jazz days: his mother and sister accused the former Irving Grossberg of taking the name of a black judge "in order to give myself black airs that might boost my jazz standing." *Am I really getting it right? Am I making myself ridiculous?* Ridiculous to the community from which I borrowed that style, or to my own, if they'll still have me? *Will the style work for me?* If it is cut off from its original, dissident energies? *Will it work for anyone anymore? What have I done?* And then, *What if that's all there is?* Style is not an expression of experience (*Was that why I wanted it, to take on, to understand something of that experience?*)—but a set of gestures that can be got by study and practice. It's not even a style, really, or not anymore, but a genre or a method or a mere skill or something like that. *Or that's what it has become in my hands.*

§328 To the Film Industry in Crisis (2)

In times of crisis, how do you get from one period to the next? Or at any time, for that matter? How do you get from one sentence to the next? Do you have to start all over again? "In times of crisis," O'Hara tells the movies, "we must all decide again and again whom we love." Is that what freedom is? The freedom of choice, the freedom to decide each time?

§329 Periods of Style (2)

Some periods: songs and sonnets, satires, psalms (Thomas Wyatt, ca. 1520–42); Trecento, Quattrocento, Cinquecento (Vasari, *The Lives of the Most Excellent Painters, Sculptors, and Architects*, 1550); Archaic, Sublime, Beautiful (Johann Joachim Winckelmann, *History of the Art of Antiquity*, 1764); Symbolic, Classical, Romantic (Georg Wilhelm Friedrich Hegel, *Lectures on Aesthetics*, 1835); Experimental, Classic, Baroque (Henri Focillon, *The Life of Forms*, 1934); Archaic, Classic, Baroque, Impressionist, Archaistic (Meyer Schapiro, "Style," 1961); Surrealism, I-do-this, I-do-that, Vincent Warren, Bill Berkson (Frank O'Hara, ca. 1950–66).

§330 The Donation of Constantine

While still on his Spanish embassy, Wyatt found himself rehearsing, for the emperor, the old argument that the Donation of Constantine was a forgery. The Donation supposedly recorded the Emperor Constantine's fourth-century gift of the western Roman Empire to the papacy. Lorenzo Valla's analysis of its style, in his

1440 *De Falso Credita et Ementita Constantini Donatione Declamatio*, had shown by close philological analysis that it was in fact a product of the eighth century. Valla's work is an undisputed landmark in the development of Western historical consciousness, but more to the point, in the winter of 1538, it would have meant that the pope could not rely on any ancient right to call a general council of the church. Such councils, bringing Germany, France, and Spain to the table together, were ever a terror for the ever more paranoid Henry. Charles was unconvinced by the ambassador's stylistic scrupling. "Whatever Constantine's donation might have been," he recorded afterward, "We were unwilling to introduce novelties in such matters." Wyatt was persistent; he attempted to read "certain allegations in writing," but again, "We declined to hear them," though "no doubt they were scholastic [scholarly] compositions." More than ten years later Charles still recalled the episode with irritation: how Wyatt had come to him "with dishonorable words . . . urging many to study certain pamphlets of his, full of heresies."

§331 Periods of Style (3)

How do you get from one period to the next? How, if a period is a unified complex of syntax and pigment and accent and gesture, "whose character," to return to Auerbach, "is reflected in each of its manifestations"? How do you move from one whole to another? It is a good question for any vision of the past that does its seeing with style, under the aspect of style's continuing. To speak of the style of a whole period is to speak of the experience of it, participation in a history that is complete and immersive to the imagination, the feeling of everything about being alive then. Nostalgia is one mode of such retrospective holism. Is it possible to be similarly aware of the style of the present, its characteristic weather—to treat the present as a period? One way would be to be afraid that it is already disappearing.

§332 The Time of Style (6): Past

We know style best not when it is already here, but when it is already gone.

§333 Early on Sunday (1)

It's eight in the morning
everyone has left
the *New York Times* had put itself to bed on Wednesday
or Thursday and arrived
this morning I feel pale
and read the difference between the Masai and the Kikuyu
one keeps and identifies
the other keeps and learns
"newfangleness" in Wyatt's time was not a virtue was it
or should I get up
go out into the Polish sunlight
and riot in Washington Square with Joan with the "folk"
if you like singing
what happened to the clavichord

§334 What Happened to the Clavichord

Early on Sunday, April 30, 1961, and it's already late: last night's
friends are gone; most of the *Times* was printed days ago; the Beatniks' Riot, with the folk in Washington Square Park, had happened
three Sundays before. Elspeth Huxley's article "Two Tribes Tell Africa's Story" depicts a continent out of sync with itself, the Masai
who have "resisted change deliberately," the Kikuyu who have "em-
braced Westernism with both hands." The poem's disjunctions are
both a symptom of historical dissonance and a way, a familiar way,
for O'Hara to make something of his own out of a broken-up day. It
is being weary that makes him reach for Thomas Wyatt, a moment
of unreadiness for what is next, a shadow of erotic disappointment
in his waking up alone. There is a note of self-mockery, too, from
the son of the 1950s, aficionado of action painting and French music. The clavichord was not an instrument of the folk in any age.

§335 My Heart (3)

He, then inflamed with far more hot affect
Of God than he was erst of Barsabe,

His left foot did on the earth erect,
And just thereby remain'th the t'other knee.
To his left side his weight he doth direct—
Sure hope of health—and harp again tak'th he.
His hand his tune, his mind sought his lay
Which to the Lord with sober voice did say.

§336 The New World

"The sun is folding," writes LeRoi Jones; his is an evening poem, also at the window, watching the street. The milieu is his Village life, workmen and bums and painters' wives pushing their babies home,

> All
> My doubles, and friends, whose mistakes cannot
> be duplicated by machines, and this is all of our
> arrogance.

"The New World" was published in his third book of poems, *Black Magic*, in 1969. By that time, he had left the Village for Harlem, then Harlem for Newark, where he had grown up. "Beatniks," the poem continues, "like Bohemians, go calmly out of style." The poem is almost fond in its tone, fond of the people and its own observant posture, but it is definitely elegiac. He maintained few ties with the white poets and painters who had been his company in the late 1950s, reading Whitman and Williams and Pound and Apollinaire: "you part of the dying shit just like them!" he said to Larry Rivers one night at a forum at the Village Vanguard, in the days when he was approaching his escape velocity. He left New York, as his autobiography has it, "Seeking revolution!"

§337 Style and Action (3)

An action with a style has already happened.

§338 Style and Action (4)

It is still possible to speak of a style of action. But if you find yourself noticing that an action has a style, the emphasis has already been displaced from its aim or effect to its manner. Has the action lost its focus? Even purpose? Become a performance? For someone to have a style of action, the action has to be familiar enough for the association between person and action to form. *That's the sort of thing he always does.* A familiar action will lose some of the word's strong sense of intention or agency, just because it is done from habit, because it is someone's style. The decisive *I* recedes, and the pattern (of action, or, one might start to say, of behavior) comes forward. Harold Rosenberg again: "An action is not a matter of taste. You don't let taste decide the firing of a pistol." If the action is many times repeated, it is proportionately less consequential, or at least any given instance is less consequential. It is no climax, no turning point, not in a life nor a history nor any other story.

§339 What He Hath Deserved

"Let me again consider and repeat," says Wyatt's David:

> And so he doth, but not expressed by word.
> But in his heart he turneth and poiseth
> Each word that erst his lips might forth afford.
> He points, he pauseth, he wonders, he praiseth
> The mercy that hides of justice the sword

"And so he doth": the lines still sound like Wyatt; one could pick out the rhyming on -*eth* or the free placement of prepositional phrases. David's penitence, however, has become silent, abjuring speech and song as he has abjured action, casting himself upon God's mercy. Here is the Wyatt who is identified by Leland, Surrey, and Puttenham, and by Mason and Greenblatt, as a reformer not only of verse but of religion; whose paraphrase is shot through with the Protestant doctrine of justification by faith alone, not works, not action.

The justice that so his promise complisheth
For his words' sake to worthless desert
That gratis his graces to men doth depart.

David's acknowledgment of God's grace and of his powerlessness to deserve it lets go of the debilitating question that ends "They flee from me." We all of us deserve nothing. The David story allowed Wyatt to forgo Bathsheba, the beautiful beloved, and to bury Uriah, the courtly competitor, and to turn toward God. The claustrophobic court society of his sonnets is reorganized to turn the passivity of erotic impasse into the passivity of religious submission.

§340 Style and Belief (2)

If style is unsayable, it is not because it is sacred, unknowable. On the contrary, it is because it is already here and saying cannot bring it closer, can only push it away.

§341 Style and Narrative (1)

How do you get from one period to another? Recall the method of the hermeneutic circle, which allows for the period to be dilated and integrated with itself. It revolves, however, without revolution. As Gadamer puts it: "Transferring the concept of style from the history of art to history in general involves viewing historical events not in their own significance but in relation to a totality of forms of expression characteristic of their time." Events, that is, are not links in a causal chain, but instances typical of where and when they happen. Events are examples. So, the Beatniks' Riot as a symptom of the 1960s, or the Field of the Cloth of Gold as a specimen of Tudor pageantry. A history of style may be able to place them, but its explanations for their occurrence will tend toward the unfolding of large schemes and the unspooling of cycles, analogies to other careers, life courses of the individual or even the organism.

§342 Style and Distance (2)

If you step back far enough, any conversation of styles, even any succession of styles, will resolve to a single style. This distance is not analytic, not critical; it is more like the moody remove of nostalgia.

§343 Style and Narrative (2)

Style has long been described as having a natural life. The model is the biological arc, from juvenilia to maturity to decline; it is rewritten for culture as primitivism, classicism, and decadence. (Sometimes the last is dignified, elevated, by the category of late style.) Johann Joachim Winckelmann deserves credit for fixing the idea in the canons of art history, in his 1764 *History of the Art of Antiquity*. Hegel contributes a grand narrative of the symbolic (the young idea cowed by its forms), the classical (their perfect harmony), and the romantic (when the idea, coming into its own, shatters forms to fragments). Such conceptions of style's intrinsic development or cyclicality have had their critics, but they remain commonplace at all scales of stylistic description: a phase of a career or a total career; a period or a succession of periods; an artistic movement or a civilization. Consistent if not quite inevitable is their threeness, a fundamental affinity with Aristotle's ancient, tripartite division of narrative itself into beginning, middle, and end.

§344 The Past Is Really Something (1)

"now the past is something else," O'Hara writes, in "Biotherm": "the past is like a future that came through you can remember everything accurately and be proud of your honesty you can lie about everything that happened and be happily reminiscent you can alter here and there for increased values you can truly misremember and have it both ways or you can forget everything completely the past is really something"

§345 Ending Faithfully

What may I do when my master feareth,
But in the field with him to live and die?
For good is the life ending faithfully.

§346 The Past Is Really Something

In the "bohemian artworld of 1950s Manhattan"—Brad Gooch's
phrase—people didn't want to talk about where they came from.
"I didn't want [Frank] to meet my parents," said Grace Hartigan,
who was so close to O'Hara then. "You leave that." Back at the start
of the decade O'Hara's "Autobiographia Literaria" had declared, "I
am / an orphan." What comes across in "Biotherm," a dozen years
later, is the past's malleability; if it is, or was, really something,
still what you do with it is pretty much up to you. That attitude was
useful, because relatively few of O'Hara's friends' lives were likely
to find one of the conventional shapes that the 1950s canonized,
marriage and children and the children's children, the steady rise
up the organization chart of a successful career. That was particularly true for O'Hara, Ashbery, Schuyler, and so many of the other
gay men who had come to New York to find a new community; as
it was perhaps for Hartigan, who left an early marriage and a son
behind to make her way as a painter. There was not much for them
in the received narratives, and perhaps not even in narrative itself.

§347 Style and Narrative (3)

Good is the life that makes a good story: a story with a beginning,
a middle, and an end to aim at; a story, inevitably, with reversals,
but also with an arc; a story that leaves nothing out. This narrative
conception of the healthy self is a commonplace of the present-
day humanities. It is also quite fragile, for it depends on a strong
measure of authorial agency in the protagonist. It might not work
if you do not have a reliable hand in the writing, or if there is no
good shape that fits the facts or the desires behind them. It might
not work for an ambassador cast about the continent by his king's

shifting policy, cast into and out of prison by his paranoia. It might not work, or much appeal, for a gay man in 1950s Manhattan, who found community and household outside of the conventional shapes of midcentury kinship. The story, or at least the stories available, might not hold together all that needs holding together, or leave out what needs leaving out. If you don't have a story, however, you can still have a style.

§348 Style and Truth (7)

Is style a fiction? To give style to a world is a necessity for the novelist. But the heightening, or, you might say, the stylizing of that style comes at a cost, if it keeps reminding the reader of the place the writing has among past novels, or possible novels, including, or especially, the reader's own. Stylistic awareness—at least, conscious awareness—and fictional immersion, immersion in the book's other world, keep an inverse proportion.

§349 Style and Narrative (4)

If you don't have a story, you can still have a style. It will not always be yours to choose whether you go to the office or to Barcelona on embassy or to the opera or to the scaffold. There may be no room in these fates for your action, for your agency. But then, style is not an action. Wherever you go, wherever you are, you can go and you can be there in your style. They can't take that away from you—or at least, it's much harder for them. Style is subtler than agency. It is less vulnerable, surviving as it can in inflections and innuendos. It may still serve as well, at least as well, for recognizing yourself, having your way about you, continuing in and as you do. The capacity of style to hold you together, in spite of the deeds and the sufferings of fortune, is among the basic reasons to have one.

§350 Changes in Style

At his desk at MoMA, O'Hara jotted notes on some painters' careers under the heading "Changes in Style."

Blaine (ab + fig)
Ossorio (sur + ab)
Vicente (allover + neo p)
Pearlstein (ab + fig)
Reinhardt (lyr + geo)
Grillo (neo + ab)
Rothko (symb + ab)
Guston (fig + ab)
Hartigan (ab + fig)
Ferrer (3: ab, fig, ab)

Were these notes made for an exhibition? Would it have told a story about the direction and momentum of art history, or an opposite story, if a story at all, about individual versatility? The three styles of Ferrer, abstract to figurative to abstract again, suggest that O'Hara's abbreviations take the painter's modes in the order of their influence on his practice, and that he returns to where he started. If that is so, there is little to read by way of a larger historical narrative here. Abstraction is as likely to lead to figuration as the reverse, or elsewhere.

§351 Style and Narrative (5)

If you don't have a story, you can still have a style. This principle can explain the formation of many of style's communities: the communities where style, or fashion, becomes a central and self-conscious mode of social organization and mutual recognition. Style may be everywhere, but power tends to represent itself in terms of its functions, whether the heroic self-assertion of an aristocrat or the discreet, essential service of a bureaucrat. The right suit, the right doublet may be indispensable, but authority's styles are tacit and often conformist. (Displays of aristocratic peacockery were common in the Tudor court, but no true index of power. Frustrated Surrey was grand; effectual Cromwell was plain.) Communities that do not easily lay their hands on the levers of power, by contrast, cultivate style as an open interest. Subcultures flaunt style, in its differences from the larger culture and in its internal variety; youth movements, for example, or queer communities,

communities of gendered difference where there is a premium on mutual recognition under burdens of censorship and oppression. This dynamic helps explain style's persistent feminization. In cultures where women's latitude of action is restricted men often cede style. Style functions no less importantly for the first sex, to co-opt de Beauvoir's phrase; but its explicit cultivation is treated as though it belonged to the second.

§352 In Memory of My Feelings (2)

> For we have advanced, France,
> together into a new land, like the Greeks, where one feels nostalgic
> for mere ideas, where truth lies on its deathbed like an uncle
> and one of me has a sentimental longing for number,
> as has another for the ball gowns of the Directoire

§353 Style as History (2)

Style is undoubtedly historical, but it is not narrative. It has no native grammar of cause and effect. It cannot explain. What then is left of history for style to claim? One might answer, *experience*, the feeling of being in a time and a place. The Dutch historian Johan Huizinga says that "historical sensation does not present itself to us as a re-living, but as an understanding that is closely akin to the understanding of music, or, rather of the world by music." History is made up of perceptions and moods, the weather of the past, inner and outer; a surround constructed from reading and looking at and listening to artifacts, filled in with half-conscious assumptions and borrowed impressions of how it was. (*How*: a style word.) Gadamer asserts that "the concept of style is one of the undiscussed assumptions on which historical consciousness lives," and his word "consciousness," *Bewüßtsein*, is just capacious enough.

§354 Style as Structure (3)

Experience and *structure* are opposites, one intimate, one abstract. But they can also collaborate, as when the idea of structure is used to stabilize a culture, a particular time and place, to shelter it from history by defining its recurrent patterns and habits; ordinary experience may be safe in such a structure, safe from history. Style makes alliances with both terms, especially when they are allied with each other.

§355 Insight

In 1959, O'Hara was invited to write a short monograph on the work of Jackson Pollock for the publisher George Braziller's *Great American Artists* series.

> If there is unity in the total *oeuvre* of Pollock, it is formed by a drastic self-knowledge which permeates each of his periods and underlines each change of interest, each search. In considering the work as a whole one finds the ego totally absorbed in the work. By being "in" the specific painting, as he himself put it, he gave himself over to cultural necessities which, in turn, freed him from the external encumbrances which surround art as an occasion of extreme cultural concern, encumbrances external to the act of applying a specific truth to the specific cultural event for which it has been waiting in order to be fully revealed. This is not automatism or self-expression, but insight.

His analysis moves across the large questions about style and history: ego and culture, consistency and change, necessity and freedom. Its rhetoric is decisive, full of consequence ("in turn") and discrimination ("not . . . or . . . but"). To offer a paraphrase of his argument, however, one that could fix the terms in a perspicuous order, could only undermine it, missing the nimble energy that makes the passage accountable to the difficulty of its subject. More than having an argument, it has a style, a way of moving that incorporates Marxist impulses; a syntax Lionel Trilling might approve, stretched almost to the end of the breath; and a soupçon of camp exaggeration. The unity of Pollock's work arises out of this energetic matrix, and what the passage mostly achieves is a certain freedom for both parties, for Pollock and O'Hara. Neither cultural determinism ("automatism"), nor the determinism of personality ("self-expression"), is given final say. The third term is "insight," or drastic self-knowledge. It is not clear exactly what that means, except that it is not the others. Perhaps one should just look at the paintings again?

§356 Style as History (3)

If history-as-experience has a method, it is the hermeneutic circle again, the stylistic unity of time and place achieved by making the rounds, discovering the implication of everything in everything. There is a sense, however, in which that procedure is only an attempt to bring into focus a unity of the past that the present always already supplies for itself, the ordinary fact of the unity of apperception, as Kant might say, how everything that is now goes together. Still, the past as experience is *now* with a difference: having that unity not as a matter of background, but as a possible object of a total attention, with the special alertness of the foreign traveler. In this sense historical experience offers the simple, radical freedom of an other whole, one that cannot be mistaken for the whole you are already in; another style as another world.

§357 The Eighth Limit of Style: God

Everything has a style, but does Everything? Does God? The Protestant God, yes, compared to the Catholic God; every faith offers its followers a way of life. But those are styles of worship, of church architecture, of scripture. What about God himself? *Imitatio Christi*: did Christ's incarnation propose a style for us? Or does God, at least the one true God (or any one true God), define a limit to style, since He is creator of all the styles, and they are all His, and moreover, there is no other God to compare Him with? Truly He resembles no one but Himself. A moment to ask again, is there a style of Truth?

§358 Style as History (4)

But then what if history is what hurts, as Fredric Jameson has it; or even, if history is what happens? "Happens" in its full, old sense of contingency; history as disruption, or the potential for disruption, for change. Style is the medium of historicism, the past in its developmental continuity and under the aspect of its necessity. It always offers the aspect of its own unbrokenness. But what if "articulating the past historically does not mean recognizing it 'the way it really was,'" as Walter Benjamin asks; what if "it means appropriating a memory as it flashes up in a moment of danger"? History so understood is an active force and the past is a resource for changing the present, by recovering a fragment to make a new beginning.

§359 Style and Explanation (5)

It's like that. Is that an explanation? We sometimes act that way; sometimes it is enough to quiet a *why*, to displace cause into context. But style never explains, really—never explains itself, nor anything else.

§360 He Will Now Be Obliged to Receive Her

When Wyatt was pardoned, in 1541, he was quickly back to work, captaining three hundred of the king's cavalry in Calais a few months later. His life, however, was not unchanged, for the pardon seems to have come with two conditions. The first was that he confess his guilt. The second was that he should take back Elizabeth Brooke, the wife from whom he had separated fifteen years before. "Wyatt had cast her away on account of adultery, and had not seen her for many years," reported the Spanish ambassador. "He will now be obliged to receive her and should he not do so, and not lead a conjugal life with her, or should he be found to keep up adulterous relations with one or two other ladies that he has since loved, he is to suffer pain of death and confiscation of property." The Brooke family may have pressed for the rehabilitation of Elizabeth that year; they had leverage, for the gouty, paranoid Henry had taken an interest in her beautiful niece as a possible sixth wife. Wyatt's mistress Elizabeth Darrell had been living at Allington for at least three years when he left the Tower. Their son was born soon after. There is no record that shows, one way or another, whether the conditions of the pardon were kept; whether his life looped back those fifteen years, or went on, and what he might have thought about it.

§361 Radical Style

There is no social movement without a style, no subculture without a signature. It is the dissident style itself that intervenes in the larger social consonance, striking the dissonant note. (Of the Beatniks' Riot, where O'Hara was not, the *Times* observed that "at the height of the battle, hundreds of young people, many of the boys with beards or banjos and many of the girls with long hair or guitars, fought with fifty policemen in clashes across the square"—as though banjos and long hair were their weapons.) The radical style is a new way, even an aesthetic event, a stimulating frustration to the concepts that would receive it. Could one not say, however, that the more it is a style, the less it is radical? Some of the energy of the phrase *radical style* comes from its self-contradiction. The *radix* is a root, while style is a lateral glance. Perhaps style is a social necessity of any movement, the mode of its self-recognition and its solidarity—the way you get people together and get them out on the streets—but it will always be recognized in the language of its assimilation. Then again, when Benjamin considers what can break the hold of historicism, and reach across time to open up the present, he turns to style. "The French Revolution . . . cited ancient Rome exactly the way fashion cites a bygone mode of dress."

§362 Style as History (5)

Style is what history leaves behind. Events move on, remorselessly; style tries to smooth over the aftermath. If style could prevent history, it would.

§363 Early on Sunday (2)

with hot dogs peanuts and pigeons where's the clavichord
though it's raining
I'm not afraid for the string
they have their hats on across the street in the dirty window
leaning on elbows
without any pillows
how sad the lower East side is on Sunday morning in May

eating yellow eggs
eating St. Bridget's benediction
washing the world down with rye and Coca-Cola and the news
Joe stumbles home
pots and pans crash to the floor
everyone's happy again

§364 Style as History (6)

Style is what history leaves behind. Events move on, remorselessly; what stays, in the way we treat one another, the limits and the potentials of what we can recognize, the texture of social and political life—what stays is style, the history we live in.

§365 Happiness (3)

The clavichord in the rain. O'Hara looks out the window and across the street at his fellow East Villagers; suspended between physical sympathy and disdain, he sees them leaning their bare arms on the hard sills. It is an obscurely depressing spectacle. Are the yellow eggs their dull breakfast, or his, or worse, both? With Saint Bridget's benediction, the poem is at risk of lapsing into an ethnic despond, the morning-after revenge of his Irish Catholic upbringing. Rye and Coca-Cola make a poor antidote. The restless movement of history is palpable in the morning's repertoire of styles, the mutual abrasion of so many ways of living, old and new, foreign and domestic. It can only be stilled by a style that could contain it all. The catastrophe of the final lines is the reassertion of a familiar, not-yet-exhausted glad parataxis: Joe LeSueur comes home and everyone's already happy again.

§366 Again to Such a Fall

A Wyatt sonnet might begin:

> By nightly plaints instead of pleasures old
> I wash my bed with tears continual
> To dull my sight that it be never bold
> To stir my heart again to such a fall.

The chiastic structure, "nightly plaints" and "pleasures old"; the distribution of agency among dissociated parts of the body, sight stirring the heart; the plain diction and the preference for monosyllables: all keep decorum with Wyatt's Petrarch. They could, at a stretch, even be read as a free imitation of *Rime* 226, where Petrarch weeps in a hard bed (*"et duro campo di battaglia il letto"*). But the rhymes are interlocking, ABAB rather than the sonnets' ABBA. In fact, they are excerpted from the terza rima of the psalms. The psalms make a double reckoning, Wyatt facing his own sins and his king's. They mark the final station of a progress that leads from the courtly lyrics and songs through the satires to these penitent meditations. Readers have long been so persuaded; they make for a satisfying last act. But Jason Powell, Wyatt's most recent, most thorough editor, identifies the hand in which the psalms are first entered into Egerton as that of Wyatt's secretary John Brereton, who accompanied him in Spain; the ink is the light brown color of their traveling supply. So Wyatt actually began the psalms in 1538 or 1539, Powell sensibly concludes. So much for that story, the story about writing them in prison.

§367 The Fourth Antithesis of Style

Style is not narrative. It may be useful for storytelling, but the structure of the story, and the causal forces that drive it, will have to be imported from elsewhere. That makes style good for the sort of history that puts us in the past, bad for the sort that would explain how the past happened, or how we got here from there, or where we're going and how we might change course. —Then again, that independence makes style good for holding yourself together so long as history, the history of events, denies you rest, denies you quietness of mind or happiness.

CONTINUING

---

§368 We Will Begin Again (2)

"But we will begin again, won't we." Freedom is a matter of action, and free action is a new beginning, unconditioned, self-original. You could get that idea from Sartre, the 1950s' most prominent philosopher. ("They hadn't read Sartre's *Being and Nothingness* for nothing," said O'Hara of the downtown artists.) You could also get it from Hannah Arendt, whose essay "What Is Freedom" was published in 1961, the same year that O'Hara was writing "Biotherm." She argues for an idea of freedom that requires a public space, and presumes the possibility of a new beginning, "the freedom to call into being something which did not exist before, which was not given, not even as an object of cognition or imagination, and which therefore, strictly speaking, could not be known." No antecedent, no habit; the exercise, instead, of a principle, intervening from outside in what was already there. It is a conception of freedom that she associates with the arts. Her favored model for the free political act is improvisatory aesthetic virtuosity. Such freedom, however, will always be a challenge to narrative insofar as it refutes ordinary cause and effect. It could only interrupt a story, if the story follows from itself. So much more is it a challenge to style, if style is a continuing. "Continuez, même stupide garçon."

§369 We Think by Feeling

We think by feeling. What is there to know?
Bouncing a red rubber ball in the veins
Though my ship was on the way it got caught in some moorings
Melodic sighs of an Arabic adventure
Darting into a tender fracas leeward and lee

§370 Style and Making (1)

Ted Berrigan again. Or, again, is it? To be sure, the poem is published in his volume *Nothing for You*, in 1977, and again in his *Collected* in 2005; but the ship is O'Hara's, or if not O'Hara's, Wyatt's, or if not Wyatt's, then Petrarch's. The line about the tender fracas comes from O'Hara, too, and the question is Theodore Roethke's, and the melodic sighs had transpired thirteen years before in Berrigan's own *Sonnets*, wherever those sonnets came from. (There already his borrowings from O'Hara were free.) The title confesses the poem's generic indebtedness: "Cento: A Note on Philosophy." The cento is a traditional form, always cobbled together with other peoples' lines. There is plenty of latitude in the fit and misfit of its joinery, and something of O'Hara's offhanded way with a non sequitur marks Berrigan's poem, even though the syntactic independence of the lines preempts his free enjambment. Does the poem formalize the allusive bricolage of "Biotherm"? It had been nearly two decades since Berrigan sent O'Hara a postcard from Tulsa; he was the one who would recall that "a particular poem of Wyatt's, one particular poem, will lead Frank to writing a number of different poems."

§371 Style and Making (2)

Back in 1952, when O'Hara was still working the desk at MoMA, he sometimes painted on his day off. He wrote to Jane Freilicher:

I've been painting all day and reading Tom Hess' *Abstract Painting* which I find mightily diverting what with all the lovely Things he Says. I've been working on these two pictures, one is a collage featuring the dripping face of Greta Keller about the size of a postage stamp and the postcard Penny sent us inviting us out to Genius Acres, the latter torn in two. The other is a man who had a beautiful button on light cadmium yellow surrounded by medium cadmium yellow (both courtesy of Al Kresch), but it had to be smudged up to Save The Picture as they say, don't they.

O'Hara doesn't seem to have kept up the habit in later years, though his job as curator called on some pragmatic sketch-work from time to time. (His papers at MoMA contain several swift, vivid pencil précis of Pollock drawings for the São Paulo biennial, for example.) His letter to Jane shows him trying lots of things, collage and oils, happily derivative of Albert Kresch's yellow and the argot of the painters, "Save the Picture as they say." He was a pianist and a composer in college too. There wasn't much he liked he didn't try.

§372 Style and Freedom (6)

Is the freedom of style a freedom to imitate? Is imitation ever free? It is not a new beginning—just the opposite—and its poise between active and passive, between forging and following, seems to tip to the latter, at least when it is obliged to confront the question of freedom. Is style obliged to confront the question of freedom?

§373 Allusion (1)

Like Ted Berrigan, Surrey too took up Wyatt's "My galley"; he wrote a response three years before his death. The poem is changed in many ways, becoming the lament of a woman whose beloved husband is at sea. It is written in six seven-line stanzas, of which this is the second:

> In ship, freight with rememberance
> Of thoughts and pleasures past,
> He sails that hath in governance
> My life, while it will last;
> With scalding sighs, for lack of gale,

Furthering his hope, that is his sail
Toward me, the sweet port of his avail.

The ship is not the lover, but the vessel that carries him; the sighs, whether his or hers, do not tear the rigging, but push him home. Wyatt's paradoxical cargo of forgetfulness becomes loyal memory instead. There are not many courtier's lyrics written in a woman's voice. Surrey's change of vantage is radical in its own way, and since modernity does tend to make him Wyatt's straight man, let this poem stand for how far he could stray from the persona of proud humanist aristocrat. Here however his ambition does seem to be to reform Wyatt and Petrarch, to rewrite their nearly autonomous agonies as the sufferings of true love under conditions of separation. The allusion to Wyatt is unmistakable, but it is only an allusion; the broken conceits, the prison of paradox, the unsalvageable syntax are gone. The poem declines to be like Wyatt, and it is hard to say that Wyatt survives in it, even if he is remembered there.

§374 Style and Making (3)

The only way to know a style is by making it. The claim is descriptive: style is an imitative knowledge; knowing it is having a feeling for its likenesses, trying them on whether or not you act them out. But it is also normative: a discipline, a pedagogy, close to humanist *imitatio*. To know a style, try it; to know a maker, imitate her. An encounter with style is always with a *how*, and knowing is know-how. The knowledge of style is in the painter's practiced wrist, the tailor's fingers and the model's shoulders, even in the nervous, sinewy circuit from mind to hand that transmits the habit of sentences. Such knowledge could be a matter of exercise, of a capacity developed in a studio or a classroom, through the study of models. It could also compass the wider knowing of carrying on into the world, how to wear that coat out the door and into company. As ever, *knowledge* is a tricky word. There is no requirement to be able to say what you are doing. Whatever it gets called, style's knowledge is the kind that Terence Cave means when he says of Renaissance rhetoric, "In imitation . . . the activities of reading and writing become virtually identified." Or when Frank O'Hara says: "I read simply because I am a writer."

§375 Allusion (2)

An allusion is a point of contact, and a call for interpretation, but not, in itself, a way of continuing; it need not have anything to do with style.

§376 My Galley (1)

> My galley charged with forgetfulness
> Thorough sharp seas in winter nights doth pass
> 'Tween rock and rock; and eke mine enemy, alas,
> That is my lord, steereth with cruelness

§377 'Tween Rock and Rock

Wyatt spent the year after his release from the Tower about the king's business again, at Calais (where he entertained a visit from Surrey), and in various offices at court and in his native Kent. On October 3, 1542, he was dispatched to greet the Spanish envoy Montmorency de Courrières, who had arrived ahead of expectation at Falmouth. He set out, his friend Mason reported, with "more regard for the royal mandate than for his own health." He rode hard, on the move yet again, through heat and stink as he had on embassy; the day was, according to Mason, unseasonably warm. He went through many horses. By the time he reached Sherborne he had a fever, and he stopped there to recover.

§378 The Ninth Limit of Style: Death

Everything has a style, except death. Death, in its indifference, is style's last limit. It is the end of imitation, the end of the vital accommodations between the self and its communities, the end of that lifelong negotiation of likeness and difference. The likeness of death is undialectical, pure assimilation, the likeness of dust to dust.

§379 To the Harbormaster (1)

I wanted to be sure to reach you;
though my ship was on the way it got caught
in some moorings. I am always tying up
and then deciding to depart.

§380 Always Coming Back

John Ashbery, Kenneth Koch, Barbara Guest, Bill and Elaine de
Kooning, and Bill Berkson all gathered in Springs, Long Island,
on the afternoon of July 28, 1966, for Frank O'Hara's funeral. They
were joined by about two hundred other mourners, from the mixed
company of poets and artists O'Hara kept in New York, and his
mother and sister and brother, and Sir Thomas Wyatt. Wyatt was
the guest of John Ashbery, who read "To the Harbormaster" as a
eulogy. "Harbormaster" is a poem of habit, not to say compulsion,
a poem about what I am always doing. Ashbery knew its genealogy
as surely as Berrigan did, and it would come back to him in his
"Soonest Mended," of 1969, which ends with "always coming back /
To the mooring of starting out, that day so long ago." The beginning
always comes in the middle of something, and when it comes back
again it comes back as a style.

§381 The Life of Style (1)

The canonical ideal of literary survival is the persistence of the
poem itself: the powerful rhyme that will outlive marble and the
gilded monuments of princes. The continued life of the author is
guaranteed by the accuracy of the text as it is transmitted through
time. Such is the apparent fate of Virgil, even of the Bible, the
reverent preservation of the words in their right order under the
perpetual, tender ministrations of the editors. Such an idea of survival, however, is only as durable as writing itself. Writing, moreover, is capable only of endless repetition, saying the same thing
over and over again in perpetuity, no matter whom it is talking to.
What kind of a life is that?

§382 To the Harbormaster (2)

In storms and
at sunset, with the metallic coils of the tide
around my fathomless arms, I am unable
to understand the forms of my vanity
or I am hard alee with my Polish rudder
in my hand and the sun sinking.

§383 We'll Tell Her What to Wear

Frank O'Hara was on Fire Island the night of July 23, 1966, returning from a party with his friend J. J. Mitchell. At around 3:00 a.m.,
the beach taxi they were riding in lost a tire in the sand; while they
were waiting for another ride, a jeep came on them in the darkness,
swerved to avoid the disabled taxi, and struck O'Hara. He was carried to a Long Island hospital, where he lay for two days as the word
of his injuries spread. His liver, already scarred by years of vigorous
drinking, was badly damaged. A few visitors were given a few min-
utes with him. Kenneth Koch was half convinced by his dogged optimism. Larry Rivers found him delirious, talking nonstop: "'I think
that Norman Bluhm should give a cocktail party and we'll invite
Joan but we'll tell her what to wear . . .' It was like that." Like that.

§384 The Life of Style (2)

Style is genetic; or at least, it is an inheritance best understood on
the analogy of biological inheritance. Certainly it is not a matter
of mechanical reproduction. It is less like book printing, or mon-
ument making, and more like having children. There is some necessary hybridizing in any new style, a mixing of genetic materials,
and yet the parent's voice persists, expressed as a strain that someone listening closely could follow, even many generations on. In
the case of style, there is no limit to the number or the combination
of parents, who themselves need never have met, nor even to have
been contemporaries; that much is different. But the idea of genetic material—material with a capacity to replicate, not so much
a selfish as a charismatic gene; material that will be combined

and recombined over successive encounters—this idea suits the case relatively well, making genetics a better model for the continuation of style, or a better projection of hopes for that continuation, than any inscription on a tomb. As a model it also captures, more generously than style-as-disease, the sense that style moves through us, passing from parent to child, student to teacher. Someone after you will sound like you. She will not repeat your words, but your voice will be audible in hers. At the same time, her voice—and yours—will continue to answer the world, adaptable, alive.

§385 My Galley (2)

And every oar a thought in readiness,
As though that death were light in such a case.
An endless wind doth tear the sail apace
Of forced sighs and trusty fearfulness.

§386 As Though That Death Were Light

Reading for the style is not just reading for the time and the place and the company the text finds or makes around itself. It is reading for the feeling of making it, because you might want the feeling for yourself. It could not be wrong to say that "My galley" is a mimesis of helpless suffering. But it is also a record of intense exhilaration, the alertness, responsiveness, of a writer immersed in his writing, the momentum of style even across the fissures of the made thing. The exhilaration, that is, of being inside a form of life, a form you have made, which is always better than being cast or left out, exiled or blocked. It is as though there were two parallel streams of feeling, the pain of what the poem is about, and the pleasure of carrying on. Wyatt's wind is endless, and it tears the sails apace, not apart. Death is light in such a case. Even if the poem is about death, it is hard to imagine death befalling a man in such full career.

§387 Styles of Dying (1)

Death has no style. What about dying? There is a tradition of last words to answer that it does. O'Hara's divine Oscar makes a famous contribution to the literature, from the hotel room in France where he spent his final days: "My wallpaper and I are fighting a duel to the death. One or the other of us has to go." There is a particular kind of triumph in making such an exit, on account of the continuing that is native to style; as though one might carry on through death's period, into the next sentence and the next. Such continuing is another defiance of the authority of narrative, defying not its disruptive reversals, its events, but its telos and its closure. Style's continuity is undefeated by the end of the story.

§388 Style and Making (4)

When we consider a work of art, or any practical object, some feel for the *how* of its making is always potential in us, a sense of the action of the brushstrokes or the balancing of the clauses. To see something in terms of its style, then, is to see it with sympathy—in a strong sense, feeling-with, a sympathy for how it was made and for the world of things made that way. That style-aspect can also involve a more general sense of the thing's uses, as long as it is the *how* of that use, rather than its *what* or *what-for*. It is enough for style to recognize any object in terms of who wears it or hangs it on the wall or reads it in the bath, the object inseparable from a web of activity around it. Stylistic fluency of one kind is got by craft, but another by consumption. Both open onto a form of life. Style cannot simply be bought—at least, owning a coat does not guarantee that you can really wear it, *really* wear it—but buying, for better or worse, can be style.

§389 Styles of Dying (2)

Then again, Oscar Wilde, who was as fastidious in preparation as he was brilliant at improvising, spoke those last words some weeks before his last breath. The true end was not an aphoristic sigh, but a grimmer, sadder business, and his signature is hard to read in his final suffering. What about Wyatt? Did he die in his style, on horseback, in service? Did O'Hara, coming back late from a party? Even if you could say yes, the emblematic moment was not quite the last. Again, there is the sense that style is not the proper language of last things, nor of pain, that its interest in continuity makes a posture out of loss, and a mere mood out of grief.

§390 To the Harbormaster (3)

To
you I offer my hull and the tattered cordage
of my will. The terrible channels where
the wind drives me against the brown lips
of the reeds are not all behind me. Yet
I trust the sanity of my vessel; and
if it sinks, it may well be in answer
to the reasoning of the eternal voices,
the waves which have kept me from reaching you.

§391 Reaching You

Ashbery might have chosen "To the Harbormaster," the day of the funeral, as a kind of cento of O'Hara's influences. The poem certainly represents his friend's range. There is Wyatt, his wearied cords in that tattered cordage, and the allusion turns the poem away from the playful bawdry of the Polish rudder, bringing things to a momentary halt, almost giving up. The surrealist swerve that follows is both a fresh start and an evasion, a moment when the poem all but says, *don't take me at my word*; a swerve, or even a flinch. Such swerves too are like O'Hara. Then come the final lines, which have a discursive lucidity that does not belong to either idiom. The deference to reason is unexpected, as is the advice against consummation and against harbor. The eternal voices lift the poem into a diction almost without adjectives. The gesture is no more styleless than any other, but it may be possible to recognize it as nonetheless against style, reaching toward the plainness of the last line. Love is a serious subject after all.

§392 Periods of Style (4)

May Natalie Tabak was at O'Hara's funeral; she was a writer, married to Harold Rosenberg. The next day she wrote to Grace

Hartigan. She had tried to call, and failed to get through. "I finally cried by myself with misery for the death of a period to which Frank belonged."

§393 Style and Freedom (7)

The final irony of style is the irony of freedom itself. Style and freedom: on the one side, there is the autonomy of Nietzschean self-creation, style as a successful performance of self-imitation; on the other, style as predetermination, mere following or going along, as what is already decided, the surrender of action to a more or less charismatic field of solidarity, convention, habit. The other ironies can be aligned with these poles. On the side of autonomy, there is the independent part, the liberties and the leverage of an accomplished art, the unbeholden individual, and the clarity of judgment; on the side of the already, there is the whole, nature, the group, the description of what already is, style as what you have whether you like it or not.

§394 Style and Freedom (8)

Part, art, individual, judgment: freedom. Whole, nature, group, description: necessity. Then again, with a modicum of ingenuity, most of those terms could be made to change places. Is it not the rules of art that bind, the expression of nature that liberates? And so on. If such questions do not admit of final answers, that is because freedom, at least the kind of freedom style offers, does not lie at one limit or other of a problem defined by the opposition of freedom and bondage. Freedom is no freedom, by style's lights. What style offers instead is the tacit freedom of the problem itself, or better, of the problematic word. As with the ironies of *style*, *freedom* is functional because it gives recourse at need to both of its limits, to the freedom of the law and the freedom of anarchy, and to the space in-between. And indeed, we freely interchange the idioms of will and determinism from moment to moment of an ordinary day. So much more with the ironies of *style*. That interchange is style's freedom, freedom as an irony, and nothing else, and nothing less—the irony that has sustained the word *style* in its contradictions since it entered the language. I am like you but not, and then again. It is a freedom not of founding nor of starting over, but a freedom to keep going, the freedom we already have.

§395 My Galley (3)

A rain of tears, a cloud of dark disdain
Hath done the wearied cords great hindrance,
Wreathed with error and eke with ignorance.
The stars be hid that led me to this pain.
Drowned is reason that should me comfort
And I remain despairing of the port.

§396 I Remain

There is a strain of surrealism in Wyatt, is there not? Every oar a thought in readiness, for example; he might have gotten that from Mayakovsky. His proverbs and clichés threaten to subdue the sensory intelligence, but an obdurate strangeness keeps the poem quick: a rain of tears can still be salt to taste; there is something Laocoön-like about the coils of error and ignorance that wreathe the tattered cordage. The mood-making is palpable, the feel of not wanting to let go of a feeling, which must have quickened Wyatt as he sat at his typewriter. One can imagine him groping for a cigarette in his jacket pocket, without taking his eyes off the page. Whether or not he knew he was imitating Frank O'Hara, it is obvious enough now.

ACKNOWLEDGMENTS

It runs counter to the spirit of this book to try to say where it began: it was already underway, no matter how far back I look. Somewhere near the start, though, is the experience of listening to music with my parents. I remember guessing that the symphony on the radio one afternoon in the late 1970s was by Brahms. (I had followed the *Star Wars* soundtrack into concert music, and I knew his fourth well.) "Right," said my dad. "Now what makes you say so?" That question has stayed with me.

I first tried to write something about style in response to Oren Izenberg's invitation to participate in a conference at the University of Chicago, "How to Read. What to Do." His response and the good questions of that audience convinced me that I had something to say on the subject. Many people have helped me think things through since then, and helped to orient me in a new field, my graduate training having been closer to Wyatt than to O'Hara. Sometimes that help took the form of an impromptu tutorial or an invitation to a seminar. Sometimes I spent months mulling a passing remark, one barely noticed or quickly forgotten by the friend who made it. I am sure I am leaving out vital contributions, of all kinds, when I name Gavin Alexander, Nuar Alsadir, Leonard Barkan, Bill Berkson, Lila Cecil, Andrew Cole, Joy Connolly, Bill

Corbett, Elizabeth Demaray, Kathy Eden, Andrew Escobedo, Matthew Harrison, David Hillman, Wayne Koestenbaum, John Koethe, Abigail Levine, Maureen McLane, Joe Moshenska, Alex Nagel, Erika Naginski, Jim Richardson, Daniel Shore, Nigel Smith, Michael Strevens, Meredith TenHoor, Henry Turner, Emily Vasiliauskas, Chris Warley, Will West, Christopher Wood, and Michael Wood. Karen Koch and Ron Padgett generously granted me permissions for the frontispiece. My friend Josh Katz and the students in our co-taught graduate seminar "Style and Rule" are plagiarized freely throughout. I would like to have given a copy to Charlie Williams, who took a warm interest, and to my *Doktorvater* John Hollander. I miss them both.

I have been lucky in my association with *Cabinet*, and it is hard to imagine writing this book without the sense of possibility and permission that Sina Najafi communicates to the magazine's writers and readers. I could say the same of Asad Raza, who introduced me to the work of Tino Sehgal, and of my colleagues in the research collaborative ESTAR(SER), for their help thinking about, and practicing, sustained attention. Conversations and experiments with my great good friend and chronic collaborator Graham Burnett have been sustaining throughout.

Several friends made their way through the manuscript, in part or, bless them, in whole, and gave me valuable comments: Hal Foster, Ben Lerner, Len Nalensz, Cathy Nicholson, Elaine Scarry, Lytle Shaw, and Lorin Stein (who marked up a copy while waiting to be called for jury duty). Sal Randolph read the first fifty pages back to me, aloud, at a moment of doubt, and her wise enthusiasm gave me courage. Dorothea von Moltke read fragments all the way along, then the whole thing end to end. I am grateful for her clear judgment, strong imagination, and friendship. Aaron Hirsh came away from a thorough reading convinced that we had been writing the same book all along, and I can only hope so. Truly none of them is to blame for the errors and blind spots here. All however are responsible for buoying my spirits as I worked.

Thanks go to many institutions, too: audiences at Berkeley, Cambridge, Columbia, NYU, Northwestern, Oxford, Rutgers, Stanford, and the English Institute, as well as several conferences along the way. It has been a great pleasure to work again with everyone

at the University of Chicago Press, and I have appreciated particularly Randy Petilos's practical wisdom, Dawn Hall's eagle eye, and
Alan Thomas's faith and judgment; also, the acute and thorough
reports from the book's anonymous readers. Andrew Miller read
proofs with exemplary and characteristic care. Resources, support, and camaraderie at Princeton have been unflagging, in the
English Department and in IHUM, the Interdisciplinary Doctoral
Program in the Humanities. The American Philosophical Society
helped with a gift of time at the beginning, and the Guggenheim
Foundation and Trinity College, Cambridge, helped at the end.

NOTES

Quotations from the main text are identified by their **first three words** in bold.

§2: "**The first step**" (Kubler 1987, 163). In an earlier book, *The Shape of Time* (first published in 1962), George Kubler declared that "In practice certain words, when they are abused by too common use, suffer in their meaning as if with cancer or inflation. Style is one of these" (Kubler 2008, 2). An art historian with a specialty in pre-Columbian art, Kubler set out to rewrite the history of forms without depending on the notion of style, a notion corrupt, to his mind, for its promiscuous generalizations. The critic Richard Ohmann makes a similar point about the term's erosion: "the theorist of style is confronted by a kind of task that is commonplace enough in most fields: the task of explicating and toughening up for rigorous use a notion already familiar to the layman" (Ohmann 1964, 423). The project in the present book is opposite: to consider the meanings of the word at three moments in its history, two thens and a now, and to try to explain what is durable and what has changed in the matrix of its contradictions.

§3: "**I've been going**" (letter to Donald Allen, September 20, 1961). A portion of the letter is quoted in Allen's note to "Biotherm" (O'Hara 1995, 553–54). "**I don't believe**" (O'Hara 1983, 21). "**What's so great**" (Berkson and LeSueur 1988, 198). "**Life and art**" (LeSueur 2003, xx). The first remark (promptly qualified with a second thought: "—too much") and the second are both O'Hara's, in a 1965 interview with Edward Lucie-Smith and as recalled by Bill Berkson, respectively; the third is LeSueur's about his friend: "He didn't make distinctions, he mixed everything up: life and art, friends and lovers—what was the difference between them?" **"The only thing"** (O'Hara 1995, 329). Helen Vendler is among the critics who finds this continuing to be basic to O'Hara's poetry: "there is no reason why a poem of this sort should ever stop" (Vendler 1972, 6).

§5: **"MLFY, I hasten"** (letter to Donald Allen, September 20, 1961). MLFY: perhaps My Love For You?

§6: **"Marvelous sunburn preparation"** (letter to Donald Allen, September 20, 1961). **"But we will"** (O'Hara 1995, 438–39). Of O'Hara's use of Wyatt here, Ben Hickman observes that he "does not 'absorb' Wyatt as Lowell would, nor does he become absorbed into Wyatt, as Eliot or Pound's notion of *personae* requires. Wyatt is made part of a conversation" (Hickman 2013, 26).

§7: **"I don't wear"** (O'Hara 1995, 231).

§9: **"My ship is"** (O'Hara 1995, 76). The sequence of sonnets "A City Winter" is from the chapbook of the same name. Allen's note cites James Schuyler in estimating that they were complete before early 1952. See also Gooch 1993, 213–14. In 1983 Schuyler recalled that Ashbery was put off by the sequence's strict form: "I know that he was very mad at Frank O'Hara for writing the sonnet 'A City Winter' and using the conventional form of the sonnet" (Schuyler 1983, 36). John Berryman wrote a version of "My galley" in 1947, "What was ashore, then?" (Berryman 1989, 78). It was published in *Sonnets to Chris* in 1966.

§11: **"All of the past"** (Allen 1999, 420).

§12: Chaucer adapts one of Petrarch's sonnets into three stanzas of rhyme royale in *Troilus and Criseyde*; later in *Troilus*, Troilus's song "O sterre, of which I lost have al the light" has sometimes been thought to be an adaptation of "*Passa la nave*" (see Gray 2003, 376). Wyatt has long been taken to be the first to translate Petrarch's sonnets as English sonnets, though Jason Powell recommends some caution, arguing that some of the Petrarchan sonnets attributed to Wyatt are of uncertain authorship, as Muir and Thomson already recognized: "we can no longer say in complete confidence that Wyatt or Surrey first imported these forms" (Powell 2009a, 102). **"I was content"** (Wyatt 1978, 78). **"I your thrall"** (ibid., 141). **"My hope, alas"** (ibid., 123). **"Yet I remain"** (ibid., 123). **"But yet, alas"** (ibid., 99). **"Restless to remain"** (Surrey 1964, 6).

§14: **"The stars be"** (Wyatt 1978, 81). **"I begin to"** (Petrarch 1976, 334).

§15: Wyatt may well have been on the syllabus of James Munn's English 1a, "History and Development of English Literature from the Beginning to 1700," which O'Hara took fall and spring in 1947–48; he was certainly taught in the fall of 1948 by Rollins, in English 120, "English Literature from 1500 to 1603." See the list of O'Hara's coursework compiled by Donald Allen in *Early Writing* (O'Hara 1977, 149–51). **"Models are impeccable,"** from an interview with the poet Simon Schuchat in 1977 (Berkson and LeSueur 1988, 210).

§16: **"I trust the"** (O'Hara 1995, 217).

§18: **"I must take"** (O'Hara 1977, 103). The most sustained reading in the criticism of O'Hara's ambivalent agon with style is Oren Izenberg's, in *Being Numerous*: "O'Hara's imaginary solution to the problem of having a style," he writes, "was to imagine poems that had no style, and were therefore not actual poems" (Izenberg 2011, 112). Izenberg's larger argument places O'Hara in an irregular tradition of poets who aspire to make poems that are undone, as artifacts, by the social relations they bring into being.

§19: Nelson Goodman explores the problem of establishing likeness by common features in his article "Seven Strictures on Similarity" (Goodman 1972, 437–46).

§21: There are three comprehensive, modern biographies of Wyatt: Kenneth Muir's *Life and Letters of Sir Thomas Wyatt* (1963), which reproduces most of his prose; Patricia Thomson's excellent *Sir Thomas Wyatt and His Background* (1964), the most literary account of the life and times; and, recently, Susan Brigden's *Thomas Wyatt: The Heart's Forest* (2012), the most detailed and archivally resourceful. Greg Walker's *Writing under Tyranny* (2005) gives Wyatt's life in briefer compass, with particular attention to his career under Henry. Jason Powell's first volume of the *Collected Works* (2016) is full of useful context, as are his many articles. (I regret that the forthcoming second volume, containing the poems, is not yet available as I write.) Nicola Shulman has also written an excellent popular biography, *Graven with Diamonds* (2013). I have accepted Brigden's date for Wyatt's birth. She, like the other biographers, handles the story of the lion with appropriate reserve; it was told by John Bruce in *Gentleman's Magazine* in 1850, taken from family papers, collected in the British Library Wyatt MSS, that contain a number of other otherwise unsubstantiated anecdotes. **"Courage and heat"** (Bruce 1850, 237). Most biographies report Wyatt's first appearance at court as 1516, serving as sewer (or petitioner) extraordinary, but Brigden has determined that that list has been misdated, and belongs to ca. 1533 (Brigden 2012, 586 n. 110).

§22: **"Use the word"** (Strunk and White 1959, 14). Mark Garvey's *Stylized* (2009) offers a history of the book's publication and influence.

§23: **"Would that you"** (letter to Kenneth and Janice Koch, January 29, 1957). **"A system of"** (Perloff 1997, 131). Lists like Perloff's are familiar in writing about O'Hara: see for example Mark Silverberg's catalog of "misplaced modifiers . . . fragmented clauses . . . shifts in pronoun . . . and shifts in tone," to which he attributes "the work's high level of stylisation" (Silverberg 2006, 42–43). O'Hara is himself a great poetical list maker.

§24: **"I believe that"** (Wittgenstein 2009, 93e). Wittgenstein's German is "u.s.w.," the abbreviation for *und so weiter*.

§25: **"The only way,"** from "Poetry" (O'Hara 1995, 49).

§26: "**Into this scene,**" from "Larry Rivers: A Memoir" (O'Hara 1983, 170).

§27: "**I find no**" (Wyatt 1978, 80).

§28: "**The mystery of**" (quoted in Mason 1959, 179). "**Greatly polished our**" (Puttenham 2007, 148). Puttenham says: "And ye shall find verses, made all of monosyllables, and do very well, but lightly: they be iambics, because for the more part the accent falls sharp upon every second word rather than contrariwise, as this of Sir Thomas Wyatt's: I find no peace" (ibid., 208). Puttenham does, elsewhere, observe that Wyatt's translations of Petrarch do not keep a strict syllable count, "strained perchance out of their original"; but "we must think he did it of purpose, by the odd syllable to give greater grace to his meter" (ibid., 214). "**I fly aloft**" (Tottel 2011, 59). The most detailed discussion of Wyatt's meter is in George Wright's chapter on "expressive pentameters" in his *Shakespeare's Metrical Art*; he treats Wyatt's line as a combination of Lydgate's pentameter and Italian hendecasyllabics, and concludes that "Wyatt appears to be absorbed much more deeply in the problems of assembling phrases into lines than in the problems of arranging those lines into groups that flow melodiously" (Wright 1988, 34). Maura Nolan also discusses Wyatt's Lydgatian "jointed line" (Nolan 2010, 411), and emphasizes small matters of metrical difference, intersections between individual idiosyncrasy and the horizon of the historically possible; she speculates, with James Simpson, that tyranny may drive experiment to "ever smaller units of interpretation (the word, the syllable, the letter)" (ibid., 418).

§29: "**One must say**" (Auden 1962, 46–47). Auden is commenting particularly on Wyatt's meter: "Of course I know that all the historical evidence suggests that Wyatt was trying to write regular iambics," but this made him good for us. "Our problem in the twentieth century is not how to write iambics but how not to write in them from automatic habit when they are not to our genuine purpose" (ibid., 47).

§31: "**Quick! a last,**" "On Rachmaninoff's Birthday" (O'Hara 1995, 159).

§32: Style is often treated as a compromised variant of normal or pure language; see discussions below of the idea of style as deviation. Puttenham warns that the figures of speech are ornaments, but also "in a sort abuses, or rather trespasses, in speech, because they pass the ordinary limits of common utterance" (Puttenham 2007, 238). William Poole provides a general account of stylistic excess and error in the Renaissance, and takes rhetoricians in the period to be more interested in such problems than their classical sources are; see "The Vices of Style" (Poole 2011, 237–51). Taking a wider view, Gilles Deleuze says that "style is managing to stammer in your own language. . . . Not being a stammerer in one's speech, but being a stammerer of language itself. Being like a foreigner in one's own language" (Deleuze and Parnet 1987, 4). Style only emerges, on this account, when fluency is disrupted.

§33: Wyatt has traditionally been placed at Saint John's College, Cambridge, but Susan Brigden makes the case for Christ's (Brigden 2012, 88–92).

§34: **"Whoso list to"** (Wyatt 1978, 77).

§35: **"Deem as ye"** (Wyatt 1978, 247). **"Grudge on who"** (ibid., 275). **"Stand whoso list"** (ibid., 94). **"Grudge who likes"** (Herman 2002, 217). R. G. Siemens notes that the king's ballad, "Pastime with Good Company," had been current in court since 1510; possibly it was the inspiration for a motto Anne Boleyn took on in 1530, *"Ainsi sera, groigne qui groigne"* (what will be, will be, grudge who may) (Siemens 1997, 26). Wyatt's gesture of ambivalent resignation becomes still more pointed in that context. It should be said, the king's original is not very serious, or at least, not until you cross him; it is a defense of his love of court recreations, whatever anyone else may have to say about it. John Stevens discusses the song and its setting in his *Music and Poetry in the Early Tudor Court* (Stevens 1961, 112).

§36: **"Have you forgotten"** (O'Hara 1995, 30). Charles Molesworth writes, "Like all great improvisational artists, O'Hara thrives in the realm of nostalgia, in a looking back that can never for a moment become true regret" (Molesworth 1990, 209).

§38: **"Society is alienated"** (Goodman 1951, 361). **"The physical reestablishment"** (ibid., 375). **"Clearly an act"** (ibid., 376–77). **"The only pleasant"** (letter to Jane Freilicher, August 1, 1951). Goodman regards the intimacy as a mixed blessing: "given the estrangement of the aliens from one another, it will also seem (and be) hostile, an intolerable invasion of privacy and a forcing of unwanted attention" (Goodman 1951, 377). This avant-garde impulse to mingle art and life is strong among the New York School poets, with their improvisations and collaborations. Peter Bürger's *Theory of the Avant-Garde* is now the classic theoretical treatment of such movements (Bürger 1984, 35–54), but as Lytle Shaw points out, O'Hara's teacher at Harvard, Renato Poggioli, was interested in the same questions (Shaw 2006, 243 n. 14). Poggioli published his *Teoria dell'Arte d'Avanguardia* in four installments between 1949 and 1951, when O'Hara was taking his course on the symbolist movement (O'Hara 1977, 151). Harold Rosenberg saw the same idea in action painting in 1952: "The act-painting is of the same metaphysical substance as the artist's existence. The new painting has broken down every distinction between art and life" (Rosenberg 1994, 28).

§39: **"Memorize the rules"** (Erasmus 1974–, 24: 670). **"As much wit"** (Muir 1963, 6). As Kathy Eden observes, a preoccupation with style was virtually constitutive of humanism as a movement; she quotes Ronald Witt: "a litmus test for identifying a humanist was his intention to imitate ancient Latin style" (Eden 2012, 2 n. 5; Witt 2000, 22).

§40: **"Sensitive literary matters"** (Gruen 1972, 26). In the decades after its foundation, the *Partisan Review* had moved from its early radicalism toward what its editors would come to call the "vital center"; "More and more writers have ceased to think of themselves as rebels and exiles," they proclaimed in 1952. "They now believe that their values, if they are to be realized at all, must be realized in America and in relation to the actuality of American life" (Bloom 1986, 178). The magazine became an easy synecdoche for institutional intellectual culture, with one foot in the universities, and a byword for what O'Hara and company did not want to become. Still, O'Hara published "On Looking at *La Grande Jatte*, The Czar Wept Anew" there in 1952, and "Ode to Joy" in 1958 (O'Hara 1995, 523, 540). "**I have always**" (Hamilton 1982, 377).

§41: "**Without eyen I**" (Wyatt 1978, 80). "**Even or equal**" (Sherry 1550, D5r). Richard Foster Jones tells the story of the adaptation of classical rhetoric to the vernacular in *The Triumph of the English Language*; Sean Keilen offers a more recent and nuanced account of the "vulgar eloquence" that English poets cultivated over the course of the sixteenth century, compound of classical fluency and native rudeness (Keilen 2006). Recent studies of the subject tend to pick up the story at midcentury, for example Catherine Nicholson's *Uncommon Tongues* (2014) and Jenny Mann's *Outlaw Rhetoric* (2012).

§42: "**Et ò in**" (Petrarch 1976, 272–73).

§43: "**Their intimacy sweetly**," from "Two Epitaphs" (O'Hara 1995, 153).

§44: Elaine Scarry gives an influential account of pain as a limit to language in *The Body in Pain* (1986).

§45: "**Scheme is a**" (Sherry 1550, B5r). "**A certain comely**" (Wilson 1553, Gg2r). Wilson emphasizes decorum as the law of gesture, another basic commonalty with style: "The gesture of man, is the speech of his body, and therefore reason it is, that like as the speech must agree to the matter, so must also the gesture agree to the mind. . . . When we see a man look red in the eyes, his brows bent, his teeth biting his upper lip, we judge that he is out of patience" (ibid., Gg2v). Giorgio Agamben, in his essay "Notes on Gesture," gives an account of gesture as neither acting nor making, but a third category that "opens the sphere of ethos as the more proper sphere of that which is human" (Agamben 2000, 56). See also Lytle Shaw's account of Frank O'Hara's resistance to the heroic, existential gestures of action painting, in favor of the local gestures of coterie (Shaw 2010, 47).

§46: "**And after salutations**" (Wyatt 1968, 27). "**Desirous to see**" (Brigden 2012, 103). Brigden tells the story at length, pp. 103–27.

§47: "**Favour an indefinite**" (Stamatakis 2012, 203); he argues that "thematic interest in latent performance," that is, in baffled, unconsummated action, "goes some way to explaining why the grammar of these poems often involves modal verbs and conditional phrases expressing some state of potentiality" (ibid.). For a concise definition of the distinctions among the three parts of the trivium, grammar, logic, and rhetoric, see Mack 2011, 6–8. I am using the word *grammar* as a modern would, to refer to the systematic principles of construction that govern agreed-upon usage. This is not so different, for present purposes, from the "grammar rules and teachings" (Lily 2013, 158) that William Lily sought to impart in his *Introduction of the Eyght Partes of Speech* (1542), the book that came to be known as *Lily's Grammar*. Ian Michael gives the subject a more thorough treatment in *English Grammatical Categories and the Tradition to 1800* (Michael 1970, 149–200); Brian Cummings explores its literary potential in *The Literary Culture of the Reformation: Grammar and Grace* (Cummings 2002, 20–26).

§48: **"There was never"** (Wyatt 1978, 87). **"Anglica lingua fuit"** (Leland 1542, A5v). **"The English tongue"** (Muir 1963, 266).

§49: **"An action is"** (Rosenberg 1994, 38).

§51: **"The colloquial have"** (Strunk and White 1959, 39). **"Style is a"** (Barthes 1971, 6). Tzvetan Todorov discusses the style-as-deviation theory in detail in "The Place of Style in the Structure of the Text" (Todorov 1971, 29–39); a proper structuralist, he is dissatisfied with a definition of style as "infraction, transgression of a norm" (30) on the grounds that it depends on the construction of an ideal which may not be proper to the text or to the text's field of discourse, cannot be found there, and hence cannot be adequately formalized. See also Charles Altieri's essay "Style" (Altieri 1989, 423). Graham Hough discusses Charles Bally's stylistic theory as a "method" for considering the "living characters of language as deviations from a norm," where the norm is defined as the Saussurian *langue* (Hough 1969, 27). See also Mario Aquilina's chapter on "Traditional Theories of Style," where he treats deviation in the course of an excellent survey of the history of the concept (Aquilina 2014, 13).

§52: **"Johnny and Alvin,"** from "Poem" (O'Hara 1995, 225).

§53: For Morelli's drawings, see the ears in *Die Werke Italienischer Meister* (Lermolieff 1880, 94); they are reproduced in the English translation (Morelli 1897, 90). **"My adversaries like"** (quoted in Ginzburg 1989, 101).

§54: Kathy Eden discusses Aristotle's conception of style as a matter of distance between interlocutors (Eden 2012, 12–14); see also Carlo Ginzburg's *Wooden Eyes: Nine Reflections on Distance* (Ginzburg 2001, 139–56).

§55: **"It seems to"** (Freud 1997, 134). **"In each case"** (Ginzburg 1989, 101). See also Richard Wollheim's "Giovanni Morelli and the Origins of Scientific Connoisseurship," which résumés Morelli's remarkable career (he accompanied Louis Agassiz on his glacier expeditions, was a combatant in the turbulence of the Risorgimento, and later a senator). Wollheim's discussion of the limitations of Morelli's method is useful, especially the concentration on individual elements at the expense of syntax (Wollheim 1973, 201). Morelli wrote his *Die Werke Italienischer Meister* in German, under a pseudonym, Ivan

Lermolieff, an irascible, anagrammatic Russian. Sigmund Freud's "The Moses of Michelangelo" was published anonymously. A footnote observes that "the author . . . moves in psycho-analytic circles, and . . . his mode of thought has in point of fact a certain resemblance to the methodology of psycho-analysis" (Freud 1997, 122).

§57: "**Avising the bright**" (Wyatt 1978, 81). "**Incoherency and elusiveness**" (Padelford 1907, xxii). "**It is impossible**" (Heale 1998, 97).

§59: Kenny's *The Computation of Style* finds word length a more workable proxy (Kenny 1982, 61–71); his book is a disciplined approach to standards of statistical evidence in a field that has burgeoned since he wrote it. "**Relatively little meaning**" (Joula 2006, 255). On the promise of computational approaches to syntax see Daniel Shore, "Shakespeare's Constructicon" (2015). Michael Witmore, whose blog *Wine Dark Sea* is an ongoing diary of findings in the quantitative analysis of literary texts, argues that, "When taken as objects of quantitative description, texts possess qualities that—at some point in the future—could be said to have existed in the present, *regardless* of our knowledge of them" (Witmore 2011). Or indeed, could always have existed without our ever knowing it.

§60: "**When your left**," "Poem" (O'Hara 1995, 133).

§63: "**Excitement-prone Kenneth**" (O'Hara 1995, 328). "**A true description**" (ibid., 496). "**Candidly. The past**" (ibid., 146). "**Continuing to write**" (ibid., 496). "**I don't know**" (ibid., 497). Andrew Epstein discusses the "ongoing, head-to-head competition" (Epstein 2006, 104) of the two writing their poems, and has an illuminating discussion of O'Hara's temporary turning away from such "rococo" surrealism as it is described in the 1954 poem "To a Poet" (ibid., 104–6). Oren Izenberg detects a particular anxiety about style in the poem's dissociations, the fear "that having a style at all makes one subject to endless opportunities for determination" (Izenberg 2006, 119).

§64: "**Nature hides**": in Robin Waterfield's translation, "The true nature of a thing tends to hide itself" (Waterfield 2009, 40).

§65: "**So chanceth it**," from "Caesar, when that the traitor of Egypt" (Wyatt 1978, 76).

§66: "**First observing details**" (Spitzer 1948, 19). "**The 'axiom' of**" (ibid., 24).

§67: Ina Blom's study of what she calls "the style site" considers the holistic drift of style in relation to works of contemporary art that show a shaping interest in the social ambience, the living style, in which the works participate and which they create; a "stylistics of the life-environment" (Blom 2007, 12). "The artwork or art event," she argues, "could equally be understood as a social space rather than an object" (ibid., 15), and "style itself as a site that marks *the changing historical conditions for the very formation of social identities*" (ibid., 19).

§68: "**Oh! kangaroos, sequins**," from "Today" (O'Hara 1995, 15).

§69: **"Every age had"** (Loos 2000, 289). Angus Fletcher discusses ornament as the "cosmic image" in his study *Allegory: The Theory of a Symbolic Mode* (Fletcher 1964, 69–146; see esp. 108–9 on the complex of words *kosmos, ornatus, decoratio*). Alina Payne's *From Ornament to Object* (2012) surveys the history of the idea into the twentieth century; Spyros Papapetros's review of her book follows the story through Gottfried Semper, Aloïs Riegl, and Aby Warburg (Papapetros 2012, 5–9). **"Methodological postulate"** (Genette 1993, 113).

§70: **"Why do I"** (Spitzer 1948, 26). He goes on: "This first step is the awareness of having been struck by a detail, followed by a conviction that this detail is connected basically with the work of art; it means that one has made an 'observation,'—which is the starting point of a theory, that one has been prompted to raise a question—which must find an answer" (ibid., 26–27).

§71: **"In any random"** (Auerbach 2013, 547). **"Vital unity of"** (ibid., 443). On the idea of period style, see below. Schleiermacher first develops his idea of a hermeneutic circle in his 1799 *On Religion*, "the harmony of the universe, the wondrous and great unity in its eternal work of art" (Schleiermacher 1996, 41). On the inward-guiding spiral in Heidegger's work, and his debt to ideas of the hermeneutic circle, see George Steiner's *Martin Heidegger* (Steiner 1989, 20–21). Gadamer treats the subject of style in an appendix to *Truth and Method* (Gadamer 2004, 494–97).

§75: On Katherine's changing fortunes at court, and the corresponding changes in ceremony around her, see Giles Tremlett's biography (Tremlett 2010, 257–65, 361–67). Brigden discusses possible connections between Katherine and Wyatt, and observes the risk of his gift, "at the moment when she had greatest need of friends, even young, untested ones" (Brigden 2012, 143).

§76: Nancy Christiansen offers an account of the dualist tradition in style studies in her *Figuring Style*; she takes it to be the fundamental structure of Aristotle's thought about style in the *Rhetoric* (Christiansen 2013, 29–33).

§77: **"By superfluous often"** (Wyatt 2016, 17).

§79: **"But ideas are,"** from "Poem Read at Joan Mitchell's" (O'Hara 1995, 266–67). The poem departs from Apollinaire's "Poème lu au Mariage d'André Salmon" (Gooch 1993, 293). **"Like Kenneth Koch"** (letter to Ned Rorem, October 16, 1959).

§80: **"We accuse wicked"** (Wyatt 2016, 30).

§81: **"I am sober,"** from "To a Poet" (O'Hara 1995, 185).

§82: Wyatt had been a beneficiary of the queen's patronage, and was one of her defenders during the elaborate chivalric pageantry of the Castle of Loyalty, over the Christmas holidays in 1524 (Brigden 2012, 42–51). **"Its sentence structure"** (Thomson 1962, 147). **"Each sentence [is] primitive"** (Brilliant 1971, 4).

§83: G. L. Hendrickson, in his article "The Origin and Meaning of the Ancient Characters of Style," argues that the three levels develop from an earlier, binary distinction, which is, in Aristotle's *Rhetoric*, effectively between style and no style. Stylelessness is a philosophical ideal, style a rhetorical necessity (Hendrickson 1905, 254–55; see also Christiansen 2013, 29, and Eden 2012, 11–48). Aristotle's virtue of styleless philosophical clarity becomes, when it is folded into later rhetorics, the plain style; the ideal of stylelessness in turn becomes one pole of the larger debate between philosophy and rhetoric. They are two enterprises that Cicero, in his *De Oratore*, took to have been disjoined by Socrates, and that he sought himself to reunite; for a history of the debate though the Renaissance, see Jerrold Seigel's *Rhetoric and Philosophy in Renaissance Humanism*. Humanism as a movement is partly constituted by a refusal of the distinction. "Eloquence is one," writes Cicero, "*Una est . . . eloquentia*," in the *De Oratore* (Cicero 1942a, 18–19).

§84: I am adapting the idea of aspect here from Wittgenstein's *Philosophical Investigations* (in particular its second part, known in recent editions as *Philosophy of Psychology—a Fragment*); see §111–261 (Wittgenstein 2009, 203–25).

§85: "**Throughout the world**" (Wyatt 1978, 101).

§86: "**The finding out**" (Wilson 1553, A3v). "**An apt bestowing**" (ibid.). "**An applying of**" (ibid., A4r). "**Framing of the**" (ibid.). "**It might be**" (Erasmus 1974–, 24: 301).

§87: "**I speak as**," from "For James Dean" (O'Hara 1995, 228).

§89: "**My Poyntz, I,**" from "Mine own John Poyntz" (Wyatt 1978, 186–87).

§90: Muir and Thomson print Alamanni's poem and discuss Wyatt's debts to it, including the anaphoric "I cannot" (Wyatt 1969, 347–50); Jason Powell observes that Wyatt's "'honesty' is often less a moral success than a failure of effective dissimulation" (Powell 2009c, 194). "**Felix qui poterit**" (Brigden 2012, 245–46). Brigden's biography reproduces Hans Holbein's portrait of Poyntz, which shows a sober, plain-featured man with his eyes tilted upward in an attitude almost devotional.

§92: "**The Tarzans**," from "To the Film Industry in Crisis" (O'Hara 1995, 232).

§94: "**Always, as long**" (Erasmus 1974–, 24: 354–64).

§95: "**The more we**" (Hough 1969, 4). "**Spilled milk**" (Hirsch 1975, 566). "**Ontological queerness of**" (Ohmann 1964, 427). Charles Altieri critiques Ohmann's approach in his article "Style" (Altieri 2009, 424–25).

§96: "**Each time my**," from "Meditations in an Emergency" (O'Hara 1995, 197).

§97: "**Distinctness of style**" (Goodman 1975, 800). "**To save style**" (Compagnon 2004, 141).

§101: "**The long love**" (Wyatt 1978, 76). John Kerrigan captures the challenge of reading such poems: "A Wyatt poem is typically plain (advertising the sincerity of its self in a world that is otherwise) and extraordinarily opaque (reserving the self to itself)" (Kerrigan 1981, 7); he adds, "it could be argued that Wyatt's reticence makes all his poems, to some degree, riddles" (ibid., 9).

§102: Alfred Gell writes wonderfully about "traditional" art, "'traditional' in the sense that innovation was constrained within strict parameters of stylistic coherence. This is not to say that in these art-producing traditions innovation did not occur; it did so, continuously. But it was not associated with artistic identity, only with virtuosity" (Gell 1998, 158). His immediate examples are Maori tattoo artists. I have written elsewhere about how Sir Philip Sidney stages encounters between the skill-culture of his shepherds and the style-culture of his aristocrats in the pastoral of *Arcadia* (Dolven 2013, 87–94).

§103: "**Love that doth**" (Surrey 1964, 3).

§104: "**Amor, che nel**" (Petrarch 1976, 285). "**Friendly competition . . . as**" (Wyatt 1816, 2.cliv).

§105: "**I am standing,**" from "Life on Earth" (O'Hara 1995, 158).

§106: "**A subtle tool**" (Hughley 1960, 1.332). "**What should I**" (Sessions 1994, 176).

§107: "**We'll open with**" (O'Hara 1975, 149). "**About Dada—style**" (ibid., 154). In his brief history of the Club, Irving Sandler quotes the art historian Robert Goldwater, who used to attend meetings: "The proceedings always had a curious air of unreality. One had a terrible time following what was going on. The assumption was that everyone knew what everyone else meant, but it was never put to the test; no one ever pointed to an object and said, see, that's what I'm talking about (and like or don't like)" (Sandler 1990, 55). One could read this as a description of a community of style, by someone not quite naturalized to it, someone looking for fixed points of reference in what others were prepared to accept as ways of constituting and continuing the community. I borrow my ad hoc definition of seriousness here from Richard Lanham, who begins *The Motives of Eloquence* with a distinction between *Homo seriosus* and *Homo rhetoricus*. The premises of *Homo seriosus* include: "Every man possesses a central self, an irreducible identity. These selves combine into a single, homogeneously real society which constitutes a referent reality for the men living in it. This referent society is in turn contained in a physical nature itself referential, standing 'out there,' independent of man. Man has invented language to communicate with his fellow man. He communicates facts and concepts about both nature and society" (Lanham 1976, 1). The basic structure of serious style is referential.

§109: "**Joan says Norman**" (O'Hara 1975, 152). "**George says Mayakovsky**" (ibid.). "**Milton says somebody**" (ibid.). "**Ernestine Lassaw told**" (ibid., 151). "**Elaine says sharpening**" (ibid.). "**The cult of**" (ibid., 153). "**The race to**" (ibid.). "**Frank says: Style**" (ibid., 149).

§110: "**Few of his**" (Tottel 1965, 2: 76–77). "**There is no**" (Spearing 1985,

280). **"An idiom that"** (Greene 1982, 246–47). **"The drabness of"** (ibid., 256). Mario Domenichelli places Wyatt's refusal of the higher diction of his sources in the context of contemporary Italian debates about the proper idiom for courtly writing, whether it should be based in speech, as Castiglione argued, or on Petrarch's sophistications, of which Pietro Bembo was champion; "a language *d'eccezione*," on the one hand, "or as the shaping of an aristocratic common language *d'uso*," on the other, the latter "emphasizing the everyday spoken language of the court" (Domenichelli 2002, 73). Wyatt's plainness leads Domenichelli to regard him as an anti-Petrarchan, a position shared by some other scholars who emphasize diction over other continuities with Petrarch's work (e.g., Blevins 1999).

§111: **"The divine Oscar"** (Gooch 1993, 140). **"In all unimportant"** (Wilde 2008, 572). Mario Aquilina considers Wilde as a radical thinker about style, whose interest is "counteractive to traditional criticism"; he quotes Wilde's essay "The Decay of Lying": "Truth is entirely and absolutely a matter of style" (Aquilina 2014, 21).

§113: **"Rumor hath it"** (Rivers 1992, 221).

§114: The first drawing is to be found in the *Philosophical Investigations* (Wittgenstein 2009, 204); the second in the October 23, 1892, edition of *Fliegende Blätter*. For Lanham's views on looking through and looking at, and the question of aspect, see his *Analyzing Prose* (Lanham 2003, 191–95).

§115: **"This letter, in"** (Rivers 1992, 221).

§116: **"And for the,"** from "The knot which first my heart did strain" (Wyatt 1978, 127).

§117: On style as symptom in an art historical context, see Antoine Compagnon's survey of style's definitions. He says: "According to this modern conception, inherited from Romanticism, style is associated with *genius* much more than *genre*" (Compagnon 2004, 127).

§118: One could also point to Aloïs Riegl's *Stilfragen*, of 1893, usually translated as *The Problem of Style*, or the subtitle of Heinrich Wölfflin's 1915 *Principles of Art History: The Problem [das Problem] of the Development of Style in Later Art*; or to 323,000 Google search hits for the phrase, as of this writing.

§119: **"In all unimportant"** (Wilde 2008, 572). **"A really well"** (ibid.). **"The first duty"** (ibid.).

§120: **"Such a peak"** (Erasmus 1974–, 24: 313). **"Splendid power of"** (Cicero 1939, 318–19). **"Explaining everything and"** (ibid.). **"Neglegentia . . . diligens"** (ibid., 362–63). **"Medius et quasi"** (ibid., 318). **"Neither the intellectual"** (ibid., 319). The *Rhetorica ad Herennium* offers an account of the levels that is at least as influential on English versions: the grand style (*gravis*) uses "the most ornate words . . . impressive thoughts . . . figures of thought and figures of diction which have grandeur" (Cicero 1954, 254–55); in the middle (*mediocris*), "we have somewhat relaxed our style, and yet have not descended to the most ordinary prose" (ibid., 258–59); the simple (*adtenuatus*) is "brought down to the most ordinary speech of every day" (ibid., 260–61). It is the *Rhetorica* that links the levels to the orator's motives, the *officia oratoris*: *movere, conciliare* (*delectare*), *docere*. G. L. Hendrickson's articles from the beginning of the last century are still the best account of the development of the threefold distinction in ancient rhetoric, "The Peripatetic Mean of Style and the Three Stylistic Characters" (1904) and "The Origin and Meaning of the Ancient Characters of Style" (1905). See also George Kennedy's "The Evolution of a Theory of Artistic Prose" (1989).

§121: "**Perhaps it is**," from "Sleeping on the Wing" (O'Hara 1995, 235). "**Unquenchable inspiration**": Schuyler described the composition to Don Allen in a letter of August 12, 1969 (ibid., 536). In such matters of emotional self-regulation as a poetic project, I owe a debt to Jeff Nunokawa's *Tame Passions of Wilde* (2003).

§122: On the levels as postures, I am influenced by Mark Johnson's *The Meaning of the Body*, which argues that concepts have "their roots in movement and other bodily experiences at a pre-reflective level" (Johnson 2007, 26), basic physical experiences like tension, linearity, amplitude, projection, force, and resistance. Johnson in turn is indebted to John Dewey.

§123: "**There are iii**" (Wilson 1553, Z2r). Debora Shuger goes so far as to say that Wilson "advocates a single 'classless' style as the linguistic corollary of English national self-consciousness" (Shuger 1999, 184).

§124: "**Wyatt, I tell**" (Muir 1963, 18).

§125: Richard Lanham identifies four variables, speaker, subject, audience, and situation; I have separated out situation into occasion and motive (Lanham 2003, 166).

§127: "**Disbelieving your own**," from "Ode to Mike Goldberg ('s Birth and Other Births)" (O'Hara 1995, 293–94).

§128: "**And if it**" (Muir 1963, 18). "**Conversation with the**" (Greenblatt 1980, 136–37).

§129: Philosophers typically call such accounts of truth as the match between a proposition and its referent "correspondence theories." A correspondence theory of style finds truth in decorum, as though the style could be matched or mismatched with the content, and hence true or false. Derrida offers a very different account of the relation between style and truth in his short book *Spurs* (1981), a meditation on Nietzsche's claim that truth is a woman; the English title, suggesting both trace and goad, allows him to explore the ambiguous gendering of style and of the stylus that is its chief metaphor.

§130: "**But really there**" (Quintilian 2002, 5: 316–19). Demetrius wrote sometime between the second century BCE and the first CE; Doreen Innes surveys the question of date and authorship in her edition (Aristotle, Longinus, and Demetrius 1995, 312–15). In support of an earlier date she observes that "there is no mention of a three-style theory in the defense of four styles against those who allow only two" (ibid., 313). See also George Kennedy, "The Evolution of a Theory of Artistic Prose" (Kennedy 1989, 196–98). My description of Hermogenes scants much of the complexity of the system: force (*deinotēs*), for example, is not so much a distinct type as the gift of using the others purposefully. His translator Cecil Wooten summarizes these interactions in his edition of *On Types of Style* (Hermogenes 1987, xi–xvii); see also Annabel Patterson's *Hermogenes and the Renaissance: Seven Ideas of Style* (Patterson 1970, 44–68). "**Since it is**" (Hermogenes 1987, 7).

§131: "**PS We must**" (O'Hara, letter to Grace Hartigan, July 2, 1957).

§132: "**Indeed, imitation and**" (Hermogenes 1987, 1). "Structural man," writes Roland Barthes, "takes the real, decomposes it, then recomposes it" (Rowe 1995, 35). On the practice of *imitatio*, the classic article is by G. W. Pigman, "Versions of Imitation in the Renaissance" (1980); Anthony Grafton and Lisa Jardine discuss its common practice as "an overwhelming preoccupation with a profusion of tiny details" (Grafton and Jardine 1986, 20), an atomization of style. I consider the pedagogical protocols of Renaissance imitation in *Scenes of Instruction* (2007), 15–64.

§133: "**For it is**" (Aristotle 1941, 1403a15). "**The inevitable rise**" (Hendrickson 1905, 268). On the ancient history of a mean of style see Hendrickson's "The Peripatetic Mean of Style and the Three Stylistic Characters." Richard Lanham discusses the middle style as a mean between two significant alternatives, "a little idea": "the three-level distinction has stuck around with the remarkable pertinacity reserved, probably, for categories based on tacit bargaining principles rather than on any clear, universally accepted content" (Lanham 2003, 164). David Wilson-Okamura provides the most detailed and adventurous account of the middle style in early modern literature in *Spenser's International Style*: he explores its associations, in rhetorical theory and in practice, with sweetness and with lyric poetry itself (Wilson-Okamura 2013, 79–136).

§134: "**Each man me**" (Wyatt 1978, 86).

§135: The sense of structure as "the arrangement and organization of mutually connected and dependent elements in a system or construct" is a late-sixteenth-century usage, according to the OED (3.a), but it is the twentieth-century project in anthropology and literary studies to which I refer here: as Barthes puts it, "a *simulacrum* of the object, but a directed, *interested* simulacrum, since the imitated object makes something appear which remained invisible, or if one prefers, unintelligible in the natural object" (Rowe 1995, 35). The three levels can be understood as such a model of linguistic interaction.

§136: "**The purpose of**" (Erasmus 1974–, 24: 301).

§137: **"Our motive's not,"** from "Ode on Saint Cecilia's Day" (O'Hara 1995, 28).

§138: I draw here on the classic critique of structuralism in Fredric Jameson's *The Prison-House of Language*: he takes Saussure's founding distinction between synchronic and diachronic perspectives to be a "static antithesis" (Jameson 1972, 36), one that results in a temporal model that consists of "a series of complete systems succeeding each other in time; . . . language is for him a perpetual present, with all the possibilities of meaning implicit in its every moment" (ibid., 6). John Carlos Rowe takes up this concern in his survey of structuralism's fortunes: it aspires to historical specificity, he argues, but struggles with change; "Although this characterization of 'structure' as historically specific is *theoretically* true for most structuralists, in practice many fail to live up to their own theoretical ideals" (Rowe 1995, 25). See also Bourdieu's *The Logic of Practice*, on the tendency of models "to exist in the mode of temporal existence which is that of theoretical objects, that is, *tota simul*, as a totality in simultaneity" (Bourdieu 1990, 35).

§139: **"But you that,"** from "Each man me telleth" (Wyatt 1978, 86).

§140: **"Whatever its sophistication"** (Barthes 1977, 10–11).

§141: **"They flee from"** (Wyatt 1978, 116–117).

§142: "They flee from me" was Stephen Spender's "favorite of all poems" (Leeming 1999, 216), a mark of its currency in Auden's circle.

§143: **"O'Hara's work is"** (Clune 2005, 182). **"Valuing as such"** (Izenberg 2011, 128). **"A poet who"** (ibid., 119). **"O'Hara opens a"** (Clune 2005, 182). **"This is free"** (ibid., 185). **"Abstract is not"** (Nelson 2007, 5). Clune and Izenberg both make complex arguments about the meaning of this choice: for Izenberg, it is the almost Kantian commonalty that is disclosed by the shared faculty of judgment, only visible in the act of choosing; Clune makes an economic analysis of this disposition, as a rejection of rational choice per Friedman, but not necessarily of the climate of rationality implicit in the price system, per Hayek. On either account, it is possible to see how style might constrain that abstract choice intolerably. A style is not a reason, but it narrows (and focuses) the market. Nelson's abstraction resists being a single style because of its many variations, the mostly male action painters but also Gertrude Stein (ibid., 10–11).

§144: On Anne in the Low Countries and in France, see Eric Ives's biography, *The Life and Death of Anne Boleyn*, 18–36. Ives describes Anne's taste in fashion, 252–55. It is Nicholas Sander who declared her **"the model and the mirror"** (Sander 1877, 25) at court, though the recusant historian, writing in Latin fifty years later, means it as an accusation. **"For the last"** (Tremlett 2010, 369).

§145: **"They flee from"** (Rivers 1992, 282). Ashbery is telling Rivers how the sculptor Ibram Lassaw "made some reference to words just being abstractions for things not present, which called forth some non-abstract words from me; after all in poems the words are all there, and they refer to each other and back, not to absent chairs tables and sentiments—'They flee from me who one time did me seek': isn't that emotion itself, not the memory of it."

§147: "**Frank says: Style**" (O'Hara 1975, 149).

§148: "**I'm not going**," from "My Heart" (O'Hara 1995, 231).

§149: "**A way of**" (Robinson 1985, 227). "**We are interested**" (Wollheim 1987, 186–87). "**Someone with a**" (ibid., 188). "**Style—individual style**" (ibid., 189).

§151: "**Thus stylistic qualities**" (Robinson 1985, 232). Arthur Danto offers a similar definition of style in *The Transfiguration of the Commonplace*: given "the intuition that style is the man, that while there may be various external and transient properties of a person, style at least comprises those of his qualities which are necessarily his" (Danto 1981, 204). He draws an analogy to ethics, and Aristotle's distinction between a man doing a temperate action and a temperate man (ibid., 202). The phrase "practical identity" I borrow from the ethicist Christine Korsgaard, particularly as it is taken up by Jonathan Lear in *A Case for Irony* (Lear 2011, 4–5).

§152: "**Discipline et personnalité**" (letter to Kenneth and Janice Koch, January 29 1957). "**I just read**" (James Schuyler papers, undated; box 3, folder 30). The brief letter from O'Hara to Schuyler bears no date; the archive proposes 1960, but it is tempting to date it to 1957, between the letter to the Kochs and Schuyler's use of the phrase in the Resnick review. "**His credo might**" (Schuyler 1998, 181).

§153: "**A hand that**" (Surrey 1964, 27). "**It seemed to**" (O'Hara 1983, 17). "**Physiognomic style**" (Gombrich 1968, 15: 358). In his article "Cathedrals and Shoes," Frederic Schwartz discusses Heinrich Wölfflin's sense of the body as the site of style: "We *feel* forms by analogy to our bodies, and forms are created as the unconscious expression of the corporeal feeling of an age: 'the psychic is *directly* transformed into bodily form'" (Schwartz 1999, 10).

§154: The most complete survey of the development of the word from its Latin root is Willibald Sauerländer's "From Stilus to Style: Reflections on the Fate of a Notion." See also Kathy Eden's *The Renaissance Rediscovery of Intimacy* (2012), especially chapters 2 and 3.

§155: "**So all things**" (Wyatt 2016, 31).

§157: "**We go eat**," from "Personal Poem," the poem described in the essay "Personism" (O'Hara 1995, 336). "**O'Hara has proved**" (Izenberg 2011, 115).

§160: "**Nay, I warrant**" (Muir 1963, 29–30).

§161: "**A common tendency**" (Schapiro 1961, 109–10). "**More often than**" (Gombrich 1968, 358). "**The less collateral**" (ibid.). "**Kroeber offers as**"

(Schapiro 1959, 305). Schapiro's essay was first published in 1953; Gombrich cites it in his 1960 essay, "On Physiognomic Perception." Otto Spengler seems to have been responsible for introducing the phrase "physiognomic style" to English in *The Decline of the West*, as translated by Charles Francis Atkinson (Spengler 1926, 1: 145). Spengler trades freely in the sort of civilizational essentialism that Gombrich and Schapiro deplore. Physiognomic style as a set of assumptions about race and nation is deep in the history of stylistic criticism; see for example the introduction to Wölfflin's *Principles of Art History* (1915), which promises that "art history has grateful tasks before it as soon as it takes up systematically this question of the national psychology of form. Everything hangs together. . . . Epoch and race interact" (Wölfflin 1950, 9).

§162: "**Then if an**," from "Was I never yet of your love grieved" (Wyatt 1978, 77–78).

§163: "**I was open**" (Baraka 1984, 157). "**Kind of openness**" (quoted in Epstein 2006, 197). Epstein treats the two men's friendship at length in his chapter, "'Against the Speech of Friends': Baraka's White Friend Blues" (ibid., 194–232).

§165: I borrow the immanent and transcendent distinction from Theodor Adorno's essay "Lyric Poetry and Society"; as he argues there, "Social ideas should not be brought to works from without but should, instead, be created out of the complete organized view of things present in the works themselves" (Adorno 2000, 214).

§166: "**Yet I do**," from "Pistachio Tree at Château Noir" (O'Hara 1995, 403).

§168: "**I grant I**" (Wyatt 2016, 317). "**Queen's abomination**" (Brigden 2012, 279). "**If they take**" (Wyatt 2016, 311–12).

§171: "**Grace to be**," from "In Memory of My Feelings" (O'Hara 1995, 256).

§173: "**French Zen**" (O'Hara 1995, ix). Ashbery writes, in his introduction to the *Collected Poems*, "What was needed was a vernacular corresponding to the creatively messy New York environment to ventilate the concentrated Surrealist imagery" (ibid., x). "**I call to**" (ibid., 305). "**I consider myself**" (ibid., 468). The last line is from the 1963 poem "Answer to Voznesensky and Evtushenko," in which he rebukes the Soviet poets for their blanket condemnation of American racism (Roberts 2015, 200). "**Lives in the**" (ibid., 305). O'Hara's attitudes to race over his career are complicated, "less didactic than libidinal, less a matter of sociology than sex," as Benjamin Friedlander puts it (Friedlander 2001, 129), but he felt a deep sympathy between the oppressive situations of race and of homosexuality in American society. In a carefully balanced essay Peter Stoneley writes that "O'Hara's rebellious gesture was not to approximate and usurp black languages and modes"—he was not, that is, a conspicuous imitator of available styles of blackness—"but to focus on the fantastical element of primitivism—to

recognize the primitive as a white fantasy, and to explore its libidinal compo-
nents" (Stoneley 2012, 497). "For him the primitive is not a finite and knowable
other, but an opportunity for a polymorphous experimentation" (ibid., 504).

§174: "**Rain, wind, or**," from "Sighs are my food, drink are my tears" (Wyatt
1978, 99).

§175: "**Yet Solomon said**" (Surrey 1964, 32). On Bryan's career see Susan
Brigden's entry in the *Oxford Dictionary of National Biography* and Jason
Powell's "Thomas Wyatt and Francis Bryan: Plainness and Dissimulation"
(Powell 2009c, 194–98). Bryan was the dedicatee of another of Wyatt's satires
("A spending hand"); he had served as Henry's broker in Rome during the di-
vorce negotiations, and later helped to bring about Anne Boleyn's execution;
the nickname "vicar of hell" was given to him by Thomas Cromwell, whom he
outlived. Sessions takes Surrey to have written his poem to Thomas Radcliffe
from the battlefield in France in 1544, where he had a command in Boulogne
(Sessions 1999, 300). Bryan's one known poem was his sententious "Proverbs
of Salmon," or Solomon; perhaps, in using Wyatt's line as a corrective, Surrey
was making a distinction between his model Wyatt and the king's vicar. Perez
Zagorin discusses Bryan's poem and his translation of Antonio de Guevara's
court satire, *Menosprecio de Corte* (Zagorin 1993, 113–16).

§176: "**There was also**" (Gruen 1972, 152).

§178: "**Watch what is**" (Gooch 1993, 261). "**I don't care**" (ibid.). On O'Hara's
entanglements with French poetry, see Andrew Epstein's account of his French
poem "Choses Passagères" (Epstein 2000, 144–61). Peter Stoneley describes
his movement away from surrealism as he traveled more in Europe, and found
love in the United States: over time he "no longer needs to be 'French' in order
to be homosexual" (Stoneley 2010, 139).

§179: "**Discipline et personnalité**" (letter to Kenneth and Janice Koch,
January 29, 1957). "**Style at its**" (O'Hara 1975, 149). "**Every man . . . must**"
(Wyatt 2016, 31). "**If only the**" (letter to Kenneth and Janice Koch, January 29,
1957).

§181: "**Down the dark**," from "At the Old Place" (O'Hara 1995, 223–24).

§182: "**Mixture of frivolousness**" (Vendler 1972, 8). "Interestingly, it took a
woman, the redoubtable Helen Vendler, to recognize the poem's special quality
and straightforward narrative" (LeSueur 2003, 55). D. A. Miller, writing about
Jane Austen, understands saving us from shame to be among the most basic
functions of style: "In the instant of being shamed, style learns that (as we say
of a fashion mistake) it isn't working. . . . So intrinsically does shame control
belong to the experience of style (on the part of the practitioner, victim, and
spectator alike)" (Miller 2003, 49).

§183: "**By style is**" (Schapiro 1961, 81). "**A system of**" (ibid.). "**Formed
style**" (Wollheim 1987, 188). "**Formally or formalistically**" (ibid., 192). Arthur

Danto, who draws on Wollheim, puts the collaboration in its strongest form: "It is as if the style were the Platonic essence of the artist which, as such forms 'participate' in individual things, participate in individual works" (Danto 1991, 208).

§184: **"Jane's picture pointed"** (Hartigan 2009, 118). Hartigan's biographer Cathy Curtis notes that Hartigan sometimes cited George Sand and George Eliot as her inspiration, and sometimes credited John Myers with giving her George as a camp name; above all she seems to have been reluctant to be known as a "woman painter," though her identity was never secret (Curtis 2015, 74).

§186: **"My heart is"** (Herman 2002, 218). On the history and social life of Wyatt's forms, see Patricia Thomson's literary biography, *Sir Thomas Wyatt and His Background*, which has chapters that canvass his classical and vernacular influences—for example, the strambotto, of which he wrote about thirty after Serafino (Thomson 1964, 211).

§187: **"You were there,"** from "Biotherm" (O'Hara 1995, 442).

§188: **"Matter out of"** (Douglas 1984, 36), with a nod to William James.

§189: **"How beautiful it"** (O'Hara 1995, 268). **"And here I"** (ibid., 11). In her article "Frank O'Hara and the Aesthetics of Attention," Marjorie Perloff explores the link between the concepts; she cites Shklovsky on the power of art to defamiliarize "so as to make the act of perception more difficult and to prolong its duration" (Perloff 1990, 160). She writes powerfully too about what was for O'Hara "the duty to be attentive" (ibid., 172). Helen Vendler has an acute sense of the demands of such a posture: "We can attend to life in this hyperattentive way for only a short time, and then our energy flags," and yet "O'Hara was stubborn enough to wish . . . that life could always be lived on the very edge of loss, so that every instant would seem wistfully precious" (Vendler 1972, 6).

§190: **"And she me"** (Wyatt 1978, 117).

§192: **"How I wish"** (letter to Larry Rivers, September 28, 1956). **"When tired mortally"** (O'Hara 1995, 234). Bill Berkson quotes O'Hara on the sculptor David Smith, "the slightest loss of attention leads to death" (Berkson 1990, 226), turning the remark back on its author.

§194: **"When a thing"** (Ginzburg 2002, 136). Ginzburg quotes Weil on this question of the singularity of beauty, and also Adorno: "Beauty, as single, true and liberated from appearance and individuation, manifests itself not in the synthesis of all works . . . but only as a physical reality" (ibid., 137). Frederic Schwartz cites the art historian O. K. Werckmeister: "all great art, even before modernism, stands in a negative relation to style" (Schwartz 1999, 43). See also Ina Blom's commentary on the opposition between style and art for Susan Sontag and Dick Hebdige (Blom 2007, 20).

§195: **"When I want,"** from "Les Luths" (O'Hara 1995, 343).

§196: **"Nor I am,"** from "Mine own John Poyntz" (Wyatt 1978, 188–89). **"I never saw" (Muir 1963, 55). Greg Walker states with confidence that at least the first two satires "were written at Allington in the second half of 1536" (Walker 2005, 296), and William Rossiter agrees, following a tradition that includes editors Rebholz, Daalder, and Powell (Rossiter 2014, 127 n. 24). Susan Brigden is more circumspect: "At some time and in some place unknown Thomas Wyatt addressed two verse epistles to his 'owne Jhon poyntz'" (Brigden 2012, 245). Walker argues that he turned to longer poems after being "deprived of regular access to the courtly circles that had provided both the subject matter and the audience for his amatory lyrics" (Walker 2005, 296). For Stephen Greenblatt, the satires were a "struggle to clear himself from the entanglements that had nearly brought him to the scaffold and to discover a new mode of 'address'" (Greenblatt 1980, 127). Kenneth Muir puts it simply: "The fashionable courtier and writer of ballets was superseded by the hard-working diplomat, by the writer of satires and penitential psalms" (Muir 1963, 35). Colin Burrow gives a helpful account of the Horatian strain in Wyatt's satires, mark of the humanist Wyatt, and of the appeal of Horace to a restless, homeless ambassadorial class, for whom there might be an "identification of home and something like a political value" (Burrow 1993, 33).

§197: "**After all it's**" (O'Hara 1975, 107–8). Joe LeSueur tells the story of the painting in his *Digressions*: Porter gave it to O'Hara, but took it back some years later to sell it, needing the cash; when LeSueur had to listen to another friend describe its new home in a wealthy collector's house in Beverley Hills, it was too much: "I never spoke to that person again: that was how much the painting meant to me—not as a possession, but as an integral part of my life with Frank" (LeSueur 2003, 80).

§198: "**My Poyntz, I**" (Wyatt 1969, 88); the reading "from me" is attested in the Devonshire MS; Egerton, and Rebholz's edition, have "frame my" (Wyatt 1978, 188). "**Thou hast no**" (ibid., 73). "**Though I my**" (ibid., 80). "**She from myself**" (ibid., 85). As Nigel Blake observes, "In fact it is characteristic of prepositions at an earlier period of the language that they all had a much wider range of meanings than we are accustomed to today" (Blake 1983, 111). Still Wyatt is a flagrant case.

§199: "**Form is what**" (Barthes 1982, 234). Angela Leighton discusses this remark in her book *On Form* (Leighton 2007, 20). "**Purposiveness without a**" (Kant 2002, 112), translated in Guyer's edition as "purposiveness without an end." Kant develops his account of form in the "Analytic of the Beautiful" in his *Critique of the Power of Judgment*; see especially §11–17 (ibid., 106–20). Leighton puts his conception in the context of the development of the word in the West (Leighton 2007, 4–6). Jacques Rancière regards aesthetics as a regime for the reception of works of art that enacts Kant's failure of a concept; aesthesis begins when we can no longer distinguish between fine art and the sound of the water pump (Rancière 2009, 14).

§201: **"I can't even,"** from "Meditations in an Emergency" (O'Hara 1995, 197).

§202: **"Called such because"** (O'Hara 1983, 41).

§203: **"But since that,"** from "They flee from me" (Wyatt 1978, 117).

§205: **"From styles whose"** (O'Hara 1983, 43). **"I must think"** (O'Hara 1977, 103). **"Stylistic preoccupation often"** (O'Hara 1983, 46). **"The other enemy"** (O'Hara 1977, 103).

§207: **"It makes me"** (letter to Fairfield Porter, August 5, 1954).

§208: **"Here I am"** (O'Hara 1995, 11). **"But as for"** (Wyatt 1978, 77). **"Tired mortally tired"** (O'Hara 1995, 234). For a counterargument to this idea of beauty as outside of time, see Alexander Nehamas's *Only a Promise of Happiness*: there, the experience of beauty entails a strong desire to spend time with the beautiful object or person, and one of the things one might do to fill that time is interpret, or understand (Nehamas 2007, 126–30). The point of the present study is not to refute such a position; it is enough to establish that the sense of beauty outside of time is commonplace and might animate a poet and affect his or her audience. That said, I believe that to see something or someone as beautiful is always to take, as O'Hara might say, a step away. We might wish to draw nearer, or stay longer, but the experience of beauty itself is vulnerable to proximity and duration, and that is no bad thing. I take beauty to be a necessarily intermittent condition rather than a constant attitude. Consider the moment of saying *you are beautiful* to a lover: it may be delightful to say it, and to hear it said, but it is a momentary interruption of the texture of being together; it is outside ordinary conversation; there is no easy thing to say back. The constant experience of beauty would make intimacy impossible.

§209: **"But if my,"** from "In Spain" (Wyatt 1978, 112).

§214: **"I am sober,"** from "To a Poet" (O'Hara 1995, 185).

§215: **"Isocrates had grace"** (Cicero 1942b, 22–25). *De Oratore* is a dialogue, set thirty-six years before the book's composition in 55 BCE; these lines are spoken by Lucius Licinius Crassus, the great orator of his age and Cicero's teacher. **"New cognitive model"** (Ginzburg 2002, 113). Ginzburg argues that "diversity of historical style, although conceived in ahistorical terms, contributed to the development of an idea of historical awareness that remains substantially current today" (ibid., 112): Cicero's questions would bear fruit in the analysis of style specific not only to individuals, but to places and times. Kathy Eden follows this passage through classical and into Renaissance rhetoric (Eden 2012, 28–48).

§217: **"Behold in painting"** (Castiglione 1561, G3r). Ludovico goes on to paraphrase Cicero directly, "As it is written among the Grecians, of Isocrates, Lysias, Eschines and many other, all excellent, but yet like unto none saving themselves" (ibid.). "**Every one is**" (ibid.). Edmund Bonner asked to borrow a copy of Castiglione from Cromwell in 1530; it was said that Charles V loved to read only three books, Machiavelli's *Discorsi*, Polybius, and the *Cortegiano* (Brigden 2012, 121, 336). "**Quis cuiusdam nisi**" (Cicero 1942b, 22–23).

§218: "**Ah, Robin, jolly**" (Wyatt 1978, 175). John Stevens discusses the song, which also appears in the Devonshire MS: "It is not impossible that he wrote the trifle which Cornish set (Cornish lived until 1523). But another explanation which fits the facts is that Wyatt's poem is a later handling and amplification of a popular song already known at court" (Stevens 1961, 111).

§219: "**Physical reestablishment of**" (Goodman 1951, 375). Arthur Marotti's *Manuscript, Print, and the English Renaissance Lyric* offers a valuable survey of the "manuscript system" as it developed in several scenes of Tudor life, court, university, and the law schools known as the Inns of Court; lyrics were "part of social life, associated with a variety of social practices in polite and educated circles" (Marotti 1995, 2); "poems were an extension of artful, polite behavior and, at the same time, ways of formulating actual or wished-for social transactions" (ibid., 9). Chris Stamatakis summarizes the manuscript circulation of Wyatt's poems in the prologue to his study *Sir Thomas Wyatt and the Rhetoric of Rewriting* (Stamatakis 2012, 1–34). He argues generally that Wyatt's poems both participate in and thematize a culture in which literary value depends upon rewriting, on the availability of text to transcription, imitation, and appropriation: "Reading and rewriting become closely entwined practices" (ibid., 30).

§222: "**It's 5:03 a.m.**" (Berrigan 2005, 117). The postcard is reported in Alice Notley's chronology of Berrigan's life (ibid., 20); Brad Gooch gives an account of their first meeting (Gooch 1993, 399). Oren Izenberg reads Ron Padgett's elegy "Strawberries in Mexico" in similar terms, for its conflation of thinking about and thinking like O'Hara: "'liking' O'Hara (in the sense of finding him to your *taste*) is hard to differentiate from being *like* O'Hara" (Izenberg 2006, 117).

§223: "**He could do**" (Ashbery 2005, 289). "**Seems to be**" (Berkson 1988, 10). "**It is a**" (Winnicott 1965, 186).

§224: Rollins describes the many changes between the first and second printing (Tottel 1965, 2: 10); the volume's popularity led to at least seven editions. Powell describes the "decade of carping" (Ellen Caldwell's phrase) in a thoughtful survey, "Editing Wyatts" (Powell 2009a, 94). The decade bracketed by Muir and Thomson's *Collected Poems* (1969) and R. A. Rebholz's *Complete Poems* (1978) also included Richard Harrier's transcription of the Egerton manuscript, *The Canon of Sir Thomas Wyatt's Poetry* (1975), and Joost Daalder's

Collected Poems (1975). Important shortcomings in Muir and Thompson set the debate going. **"Does not consider"** (Mason 1976, 681). **"The only criterion"** (Daalder 1973, 402). **"While they do"** (Caldwell 1989, 242).

§226: **"So much of"** (Schuyler 2004, 9). E. H. Gombrich observes that the Romans "would speak of an 'accomplished style' much as later generations spoke of a 'fluent pen'" (Gombrich 1960, 9). *Disertus* is typically the Latin word: see for example Cicero in the *De Oratore*, 1.21 and 1.49 (Cicero 1942a, 68–69, 152–53). **"Achieved style"** (Schuyler 1998, 193). **"Has developed this"** (ibid., 201). **"Has evolved a"** (ibid., 218). **"By how formed"** (ibid., 163). Schuyler was not insensitive to the risks of mannerism: his notice for Frankenthaler praises "a show that, without violating her achieved style, made a remarkable shift in the character of her work" (ibid., 193); of a show of paintings by Paul Klee, he writes, "chosen as the works are here, one has a chance to view freshly an artist whose styles may have become too familiar" (ibid., 293).

§227: The Comte de Buffon delivered his *"Discours"* to the Académie Française in 1753. His address is a defense of the individuality of style, contrasted with the universality of content, especially scientific knowledge: "Only those works that are well written will pass down to posterity. The quantity of knowledge, the singularity of the facts, even the novelty of discoveries, will not be sure guarantees of immortality . . . for the knowledge, the facts, the discoveries are easily removed and carried off, and even gain by being placed in more able hands. Those things are outside the man, but the style is the man himself [*le style c'est l'homme même*]; the style cannot be stolen, transported, or altered" (Durant 1965, 574; Buffon 1923, 13). Wittgenstein comments on the *"même,"* taking it for a disruption of the idea of simple identity, one that might allow us to understand "a man's style" as a "picture [*Bild*] of him" (Wittgenstein 1984, 78), in his rich sense of picture as a form of life. Charles Altieri comments sympathetically in his article "Style as the Man" (Altieri 1989, 69–72). See also Alexander Nagel, who offers an ingenious reading of the stylus as seismometer, and comments on Lacan's skepticism about Buffon's phrase (Nagel 2010, 259).

§228: **"In frozen thought"** (Wyatt 1978, 81). **"I find no"** (ibid., 80). The OED illustrates this necessity: the first definition of *like* reads, "Having the same or comparable characteristics or qualities as some other person or thing." Perhaps it is in the nature of language to work this way, insofar as it brings the sameness of names to the infinity of actual difference.

§229: **"And of myself"** (Wyatt 2016, 64). **"Brought me into"** (ibid.). **"He shall be sure"** (ibid.). **"Have your friends"** (ibid.). **"To gather a"** (ibid., 67–68). **"Think that I"** (ibid., 65). Brigden describes the letter's circumstances (Brigden 2012, 299–302).

§231: **"And we drift,"** from "How to Get There" (O'Hara 1995, 370).

"Fragrant after-a-French-movie-rain," from "F.M.I. 6/25/61" (ibid., 410). Both appear in *Locus Solus* III–IV, the short-lived journal published in Geneva in 1961 by Harry Matthews, this number edited by John Ashbery.

§232: "**Never to be**," from "How to Get There" (O'Hara 1995, 370). "**Unlike Larry Rivers**" (Gooch 1993, 330). "**You never come**," from "St. Paul and All That" (O'Hara 1995, 407).

§233: "**Twenty-five questions**" (Bourdieu 1984, 506). "**Continuously generates practical**" (ibid., 173).

§234: "**Natural to man**" (Aristotle 1941, 1448b5). "**It is also**" (ibid.). Bourdieu offers a particularly powerful account of ethical mimesis in his *Logic of Practice*: "the practice of acquisition—a practical *mimesis* (or mimeticism) which implies an overall relation of identification and has nothing in common with an *imitation* that would presuppose a conscious effort to reproduce a gesture, an utterance or an object explicitly constituted as a model—and the process of reproduction—a practical reactivation which is opposed to both memory and knowledge—tend to take place below the level of consciousness, expression and the reflexive distance which these presuppose. The body believes in what it plays at . . . the body is thus constantly mingled with all the knowledge it reproduces" (Bourdieu 1990, 73).

§235: "**Wyatt is in**" (Brewer 1893, 13.2.237). "**Fish out the**" (Walker 2005, 335). "**The king looked**" (Bergenroth 1888, 5.2.530). "**Witty he is**" (Wyatt 2016, 330). Walker provides a valuably concise summary of Wyatt's diplomatic brief at the beginning of his chapter on "Wyatt's Embassy" (Walker 2005, 335-40).

§236: "**Nothing but a**," from Benjamin's 1933 essay, "On the Mimetic Faculty" (Benjamin 2003, 1: 720). "**Magical correspondences and**" (ibid., 1: 721).

§237: "**He was thin**" (Rivers 1992, 228).

§239: "**Temptation by space**" (Caillois 1984, 28). "**Life seems to**" (ibid., 32). Caillois's description of the moth is worth quoting in full: "The case of the Phyllia is even sadder: they browse among themselves, taking each other for real leaves, in such a way that one might accept the idea of a sort of collective masochism leading to mutual homophagy, the simulation of the leaf being a provocation to cannibalism in this kind of totem feast" (ibid., 25). His ecology is arguable, but his essay is a powerful meditation on the desire of the figure to return to ground. On Caillois and Freud see Michael Taussig's *Mimesis and Alterity*; he also compares Caillois to the notion of "active yielding" in Adorno and Horkheimer's *Dialectic of Enlightenment* (Taussig 1992, 46).

§241: "**What rage is**" (Wyatt 1978, 150-51).

§242: The classic, modern account is Gilbert Ryle's "Knowing How and Knowing That" (1971); Alva Noë offers a strongly argued defense of the difference (annexing many *thats* to *how* along the way) in his essay "Against Intellectualism" (2005).

§243: **"But that's not,"** from the essay "Personism" (O'Hara 1995, 498).

§244: On the inks in Egerton and their relation to Wyatt's travels, see Jason Powell's resourceful study, "Thomas Wyatt's Poetry in Embassy" (Powell 2004). He identifies the faded inks with Wyatt's time abroad, mixed from a travel-ready, make-do recipe; his diplomatic correspondence shows the same fading, in contrast with the sturdy black of the letters he received from England. Helen Baron has made a study of the additions and corrections to "What rage" in an effort to establish a rough chronology of the poem's composition (Baron 1976). **"Running day and"** (Wyatt 1978, 192). **"But out of"** (Wyatt 2016, 138). **"I never saw"** (Muir 1963, 55).

§245: **"If you live,":** from "Larry Rivers: A Memoir" (O'Hara 1995, 513). Amiri Baraka offers an expert portrait of the seductions of Kline's style in his *Autobiography*: "Franz Kline's style, not only his painting but his personal idiosyncrasies, we set out to emulate. Kline always seemed a little smashed, drink in hand, cigarette dangling, talking in drunken parody as abstractly as he painted. Basil King, Dan Rice, Joel Oppenheimer, and Fee Dawson used to do takes on this style, personalized but legitimately drunk. To talk in a fragmented, drunken but hopefully profound ellipsis was the goal" (Baraka 1984, 155).

§246: **"Memorize the rules"** (Erasmus 1974–, 24: 670).

§247: **"To 'give style'"** (Nietzsche 2001, 163). Nietzsche continues: "It is practiced by those who survey all the strengths and weaknesses that their nature [*Natur*] has to offer and then fit them into an artistic plan [*künstlerischen Plane*] until each appears as art and reason and even weaknesses delight the eye" (ibid.). There is no voice stronger and clearer for the virtue of an individual style. By force of will, however, Nietzsche strips the concept of its basic irony, the tension between self-imitation and the imitation of others. The strong and domineering natures (*Naturen*) he loves best will be "perfected under their own law" (ibid., 164). The language is Kantian, the moral autonomy that converges, in Kant's third *Critique*, with the free play of aesthetic judgment. Nietzsche could be understood to make an attempt to rescue the concept of style from its interdependences, and there is a question whether what is left is style at all, or whether he celebrates instead a great personal beauty.

§248: **"Later on, imitate"** (O'Hara 1975, 98). **"Quis cuiusquam nisi"** (Cicero 1942b, 22–23). Perhaps the playful title, "How to Proceed in the Arts," recalls Paul Goodman's serious formulation, from his "Advance-Guard Writing, 1900–1950": "this was the 'existential' problem for the artist: not what to think nor what kind of person to be, but how to persist at all, being an artist. (As usual, the advance-guard problem has slightly anticipated the current general problem: how to persist, being alive)" (Goodman 1951, 370). Larry Rivers looked back on the composition in his autobiography with a keen sense of the double agenda of self-loss and self-preservation: "we collaborated on a piece of writing, 'How to Proceed in the Arts,' driven to it by articles on art, half of them incomprehensible, by name-dropping exhibitions, and of course by other artists and their statements about art receiving more attention than we could bear. Almost thirty-five years later I can still recognize which lines are mine and which are Frank's. I could point them out, but I am inhibited by the collaborator's code, which frowns upon naming lines and goes back to the *Iliad*" (Rivers 1992, 241–42).

§252: "**Act as if**" (O'Hara 1975, 97).

§253: "**The ideal types**" (Cicero 1942b, 28–29). These lines again are spoken by Crassus. "**Looking now at**" (Quintilian 2002, 5: 286–87).

§254: "**An orange sky**" (O'Hara 1997, 110). Lytle Shaw discusses the line as a variation on Oscar Wilde's "life imitates art" (Shaw 2006, 30), and cites another line, "the clouds are imitating Diana Adams," from "Variations on Pasternak's 'Mein Leibchen, Was Willst Du Noch Mehr?'" (O'Hara 1995, 339).

§255: "**Wherever I go**" (Baraka 2015, 114). "**As an African**" (Baraka 1984, 156).

§257: "**I remember feeling**" (Londry 1997, 119–20). Koch's reminiscences are from a 1997 interview with Michael Londry. Koch was the most deliberately promiscuous imitator in the group, and often taught poetry at Columbia by assigning exercises in *imitatio* to students. The practice came back to trouble his ghost, when Kent Johnson undertook a serio-ludic investigation into whether Koch might have been the true author of O'Hara's poem, "A True Account of Talking to the Sun on Fire Island." (After O'Hara died, Koch had discovered the poem among O'Hara's manuscripts.) The controversy eventually resulted in a book on the subject, called *A Question Mark above the Sun*, where Johnson claims that Marjorie Perloff wrote him to say she had come to the same conclusion by "the sound of it, 'by internal evidence'" (Johnson 2012, 180).

§258: Neuroscientists dispute the role of mirror neurons in social life, particularly their relation to empathy, but there is agreement that some neurons fire both when an animal acts and when the animal observes the same action in another animal. Mark Johnson offers a sensible account of the humanistic possibilities of such an account in his discussion, in *The Meaning of the Body*, of the idea that "understanding requires simulation" (Johnson 2007, 164). Among the anthropologists, Alfred Gell draws on James Frazer and Michael Taussig when he writes, "To see (or to know) is to be sensuously filled with what is perceived, yielding to it, mirroring it—and hence imitating it bodily" (Gell 1998, 100).

§260: Georg Simmel articulates a version of this arbitration: "Finally, style is the aesthetic attempt to solve the great problem of life: an individual work or behaviour, which is closed, a whole, can simultaneously belong to something higher, a unifying encompassing context" (Simmel 1991, 70).

§262: "**I am alive**" (O'Hara 1995, 406). "**You never come**" (ibid., 407).

§264: The concept of irony here is not the forensic irony of Socrates or Kierkegaard, a tactic for the radical questioning of ordinary life (as in Jonathan Lear's *A Case for Irony*); rather, it is the double consciousness of our practical accommodations to social and political contradictions. It makes a contrast with dialectic, insofar as dialectic is progressive, a recurring sublation of contradiction; irony is a set of strategies for maneuver within contradiction. See below for a discussion of style and history.

§265: "**The pillar perished**" (Wyatt 1978, 86).

§267: "**I am ashamed**" (Scarisbrick 1968, 370). "**Oh, gentle Wyatt**" (Hume 1889, 104). "**Oh, Wyatt, do**" (ibid.). Brigden's account of the scene at the scaffold is taken primarily from the commonplace book of Bishop Cox of Ely; she allows that "the Spanish chronicler—usually unwaveringly unreliable—may veer toward truth as he relates Cromwell's farewell to his grief-stricken friend" (Brigden 2012, 525–26, 682 n. 154). The sonnet "The pillar perished," an imitation of Petrarch's lament for his patron Cardinal Giovanni Colonna, is often taken to be an elegy for Cromwell. Brigden reserves judgment (ibid., 527–28), but Walker is more confident (Walker 2005, 279–82), as is Mason (Mason 1986, 244–55); Rossiter observes that Vellutello's commentary on Petrarch would have informed Wyatt of the identity of Petrarch's pillar (Rossiter 2014, 120).

§268: "**I definitely don't**" (O'Hara 1995, 510). The passage is taken from what Allen calls a "Statement for Paterson Society," likely Paterson, New Jersey, the town chronicled by William Carlos Williams in his book-length poem. Allen avers that it was never sent. "**And now it**," from *Leaves of Grass* (Whitman 1992, 31). "**I hope the**" (O'Hara 1995, 497). "**Rarely spoke about**" (Rivers 1992, 215–16).

§270: "**Cooptation must always**" (McGann 1983, 2). McGann's *Romantic Ideology* was an influential reproach to a previous generation of Romanticists, whom he accused of the "uncritical absorption . . . in Romanticism's own self-representations" (ibid., 1).

§271: "**God knoweth what**" (Wyatt 2016, 294). "**Although he is**" (Muir 1963, 176). "**That same Wyatt**" (Wyatt 2016, 300).

§273: "**For in this**" (Wyatt 2016, 308). "**Again 'fall out'**" (ibid.). Jason Powell surveys the textual history and the historical situation of both the "Declaration" and the "Defense" in his edition of the prose (Wyatt 2016, 269–92).

§274: "**A long history**," from "Biotherm" (O'Hara 1995, 446). William Arrowsmith's review of Ashbery's *Some Trees* captures this particular frustration, finding "an impossibly fractured brittle private world, depersonalized and discontinuous, whose characteristic emotional gesture is an effete and cerebral whimsy" (Arrowsmith 1956, 294). "Privileging juxtaposition over metaphor—a typical New York School move," as Maggie Nelson puts it (Nelson 2007, 26).

§275: "**Kenneth did it**": recorded by John Gruen (Gruen 1972, 149).

§276: Happy Hooligan is borrowed from John Ashbery's poem, "Soonest Mended" (Ashbery 1997, 231).

§277: "**Sighs are my**" (Wyatt 1978, 99).

§278: O'Hara picks up "An ugly NEW WORLD WRITING" in "The Day Lady Died" (O'Hara 1995, 325).

§281: "**For though he**" (Wyatt 2016, 305). Revisited without a difference—scratching it, bewailing it, like Philoctetes's wound—a scar is only repetition. Repetition is a continuing, but not the continuing of style. There can be no style of trauma if trauma is without a difference, the return of an event neither forgotten nor remembered. Style's answer to the scar is not the same, it should be said, as learning how to narrate the story of how you got it, another idea of what it means to move on, and one more usually associated with the theory of trauma. But perhaps it is not less effective, and perhaps more available when the writing of an adequate narrative is not entirely in your hands.

§283: "**At a streetcorner**," from "F. (Missive and Walk) I. #53" (O'Hara 1995, 420).

§285: "**Yet Solomon said**" (Surrey 1964, 32). I follow Sessions in taking the poem to have been written in France, where Surrey was at the siege of Montreuil (Sessions 1999, 300). Over the course of his own short life, Surrey was suspected of sympathy with the peasant-pilgrims' cause in the Pilgrimage of Grace, and consigned to house arrest in Windsor castle afterward (ibid., 123–29); he may have challenged a courtier named John à Leigh to a duel in 1542, and was at all events imprisoned in the Fleet (ibid., 230). In the strangest episode of his career of miscreance, he spent a rowdy night in the company of Wyatt's son, breaking windows with a stone bolt. He later wrote a poem excusing the spree as a fit of "fervent zeal" (Surrey 1964, 31) meant to waken the citizens of London from religious error (Dolven 2014, 100–103; Sessions 1999, 234–38).

§286: "**Style is the**" (Genette 1993, 105). He adopts Nelson Goodman's distinction between exemplification and denotation as basic functions of language (Goodman 1975, 804–6). Antoine Compagnon comments sympathetically, but regards exemplification as a broader category than style: "The effort, however, remains commendable. What is unquestionably new, and not at all negligible, is that the substitution of the exemplificatory function for the poetic function necessarily revives the importance of semantic and pragmatic considerations generally kept at a distance by poetics and semiology" (Compagnon 2004, 144).

§287: Kendall Walton remarks, "it is not clear to me that there could be just one work in a given style" (Walton 2008, 233); he is right, but he does not take account of the possibility that the other works lie in the future.

§288: **"Oh dear I"** (letter to John Ashbery, October 13, 1959). **"Mother was walking"** (Koch 2006, 133).

§289: Nietzsche's famous dictum is rendered in the recent Cambridge translation, by Kate Sturge, as, "facts are just what there aren't, there are only interpretations" (Nietzsche 2003, 139). Sontag distinguishes her account from Nietzsche's: "Of course, I don't mean interpretation in the broadest sense, the sense in which Nietzsche (rightly) says, 'There are no facts, only interpretations.' By interpretation, I mean here a conscious act of the mind which illustrates a certain code, certain 'rules' of interpretation" (Sontag 1966, 5). **"The world, our"** (ibid., 7). My attempt to distinguish between stylistic recognition and interpretation could be said to be an argument with Stanley Fish, whose two essays with the title "What Is Stylistics and Why Are They Saying Such Terrible Things about It?" make the claim that style is a product of interpretation. "Here my thesis is that formal patterns are themselves the products of interpretation and that therefore there is no such thing as a formal pattern, at least in the sense necessary for the practice of stylistics" (Fish 1980, 267). I want to argue for a recognition that can usefully be understood to precede interpretation, a recognition that is fundamentally imitative, rather than propositional, representational, semiotic, etc.

§291: **"He forbeareth not"** (Wyatt 2016, 329). **"But by cause"** (ibid., 310). **"But let them"** (ibid., 312–13).

§292: **"Precise personal light"** (O'Hara 1975, 67). Forgeries of Motherwell's work have attracted recent scandal: see for example "Motherwell Painting Declared a Forgery," in the *New York Times*, October 11, 2011.

§294: **"Frank's poetry undergoes"** (LeSueur 2003, 237–38). **"That Muir volume"** (Bill Berkson in discussion with the author, June 16, 2011). Wyatt was fuel for their collaborations: "While he would be typing, I would be raiding his bookshelves looking for fuel to keep up with him—and that was one I would dip into and dip into" (ibid.). Berkson mentions Wyatt in a catalog of the "general education" that friendship with O'Hara gave him: "the Stravinsky-Balanchine *Agon* (and Edwin Denby's essay on it), Satie (we created four-hand annoyances at various apartments, once played for Henze in Rome). Feldman, *Turandot*, a certain Prokofiev toccata. Virgil Thomson (I had heard a recording of *Four Saints* at Harry Smith's, Providence, 1957), movies . . . we read Wyatt together, recited Racine, skipped through galleries" (Gooch 1993, 365–66).

§295: **"He confessed upon"** (Muir 1963, 210). **"O Lord, since"** (Wyatt 1978, 197). **"Pour estre personnage"** (Muir 1963, 210).

§297: **"How do you"** (Allen 1999, 424). **"Openness"** (Epstein 2006, 197). Andrew Epstein discusses the friendship between O'Hara and Baraka at length in his *Beautiful Enemies*: "O'Hara is an important marker in Baraka's verbal and mental landscape, a magnetic force he is drawn towards and repulsed by—an attractive symbol of the avant-garde, whiteness, and homosexuality he will later feel compelled to renounce" (197).

§298: "**The images have**" (O'Hara 1975, 45). This account of Kline introduces the reprinting of an interview he had published six years before in the *Evergreen Review*. On the influence of Hofmann, who taught so many of the abstract expressionists, see Dore Ashton's *The New York School* (1973), 79–84.

§299: Franz Kline's sudden, calligraphic strokes were carefully planned, but what matters for style is the impression they give. Kendall Walton, considering the "styles of action" legible in a painting, is careful on this point: "The idea I wish to pursue is that it is how a work *appears* to have been made, what sort of action or actions it looks or sounds or seems as though the artist performed in creating it, which is crucial to the work's style" (Walton 2008, 228). Lytle Shaw discusses action, gesture, and the dangers of style, in painting and writing, in a reading of O'Hara's "Far from the Porte des Lilas and the Rue Pergolèse." He quotes O'Hara: "and the danger of being Proustian / and the danger of being Pasternakesque" (O'Hara 1995, 311; Shaw 2006, 162–63).

§300: "**I find very**" (Puttenham 2007, 150). "**Sweet, and worthy**" (Muir 1963, 262); in Leland's original Latin, "*dulce decus linguae vel iuste*" (Leland 1542, A2r).

§301: Compared to the purposeful movement of narrative, description can seem ungoverned, idle, "a risky 'drift,'" as Philippe Hamon puts it, "from detail to detail" (Hamon 1981, 11). Because it takes time, it can function as a brake; its details, however arbitrarily ordered, still must wait in the line of sentences. But just as that slowing down can be a way of controlling style, so it can be a way of enjoying it, spending time with it.

§302: "**It's so original**": O'Hara is writing about marriage, in his "Poem Read at Joan Mitchell's" (O'Hara 1995, 265). "**I'm getting rather**" (ibid., 274).

§303: O'Hara was famously free with proper names; Lytle Shaw gives an influential account of their indeterminate position between the irrecoverably particular, and the appropriable, even universal; the sense of coterie they make "should be understood not as a symbolic stand against time but as a fluid and experimental way of conceptualizing literary and social linkage" (Shaw 2006, 37). To treat the names as adjectives is a slightly different game, liberating personality into virtuosity. So his virtuoso description of Larry Rivers's influences: "Larry was chiefly involved with Bonnard and Renoir at first, later Manet and Soutine; Joan Mitchell—Duchamp; Mike Goldberg—Cézanne-Villon-de Kooning; Helen Frankenthaler—Pollock-Miró; Al Leslie—Motherwell; De Niro—Matisse; Nell Blaine—Helion; Hartigan—Pollock-Guston; Harry Jackson—a lot of Matisse with a little German Expressionism; Jane Freilicher—a more subtle combination of Soutine with some Monticelli and Moreau appearing through the paint" (O'Hara 1995, 513).

§304: "**Medicine of cherries**" (Sidney 2009, 227). On the history of the word *taste*, see Denise Gigante's *Taste*, especially pp. 1–21. Jeffrey Masten explores the intimacy and homoerotic potential of the word *sweet* in "Toward a Queer Address" (2004). Matthew Harrison's dissertation "Tear Him for His Bad Verses" discusses *sweet* as a value term.

§305: "**Like a struggle**" (O'Hara 1975, 45). "**Emotive Fruition is**" (O'Hara 1995, 232).

§306: "**We don't even**" (Lanham 2003, xv). In his preface, Lanham is particularly concerned about the confusion between evaluative and descriptive language, between "'sincere,' 'fast-moving,' 'lean,'" and "hypotactic nominal style" (ibid.).

§308: "**By a little**" (Mason 1959, 171). "**Stony heart**" (Wyatt 1978, 71, 116, 145, 173). "**'Twixt hope and dread**" (ibid., 84, 124, 153, 226, 249, 354, 305). "**Whoso list**" (ibid., 77, 94, 182, 268). "**It has little**" (Lewis 1954, 230).

§309: "**I have been**" (letter to James Schuyler, February 11, 1956). "**Let's face it**" (Berkson 1988, 20). Three years later O'Hara confessed to Allen Ginsberg, in a letter, "I do have a thing when drunk about superlatives which consists in showing how much I like something by saying I like it or am moved by it even MORE than by something else I assume everyone knows I'm crazy about" (letter to Allen Ginsberg, February 20, 1959). Lytle Shaw discusses the Harvard episode in the context of the friends' avowed preference for minor art and auxiliary traditions, and O'Hara's use of proper-name-dropping to create emergent communities (Shaw 2006, 17–20).

§311: "**Jimmy and I**" (letter to Kenneth Koch, April 1956).

§312: "**The diminution of**" (Goodman 1958, 291). LeSueur recounts the debate in his *Digressions* (LeSueur 2003, 117–18). Irving Howe judged the Goodman of the later 1950s "an example of asphyxiating righteousness" (Bloom 1986, 315); though see Susan Sontag's affecting memorial, and her effort to separate the man from his works (Sontag 1972, 3–12). For Goodman's relationship with O'Hara see also the entry in Diggory's *Encyclopedia* (Diggory 2009, 200–202) and his essay on community in the New York School (Diggory 2001, 18–21); also Gooch's *City Poet* (Gooch 1993, 187, 201, 268). The concert, on the night of February 15, 1957, featured a new work by Ned Rorem, "The Poet's Requiem," which set texts by Goodman and others. According to Howard Taubman's review in the next day's *New York Times*, Haydn and Brahms were on the program, but not Prokofiev. Perhaps O'Hara brought him up. "**I liked him**" (LeSueur 2003, 117). "**As we got**" (ibid., 118).

§313: On Surrey's appropriation of the royal arms, see Sessions's biography (Sessions 1999, 404–6). The accusation stood in for many accumulated crimes of ambition. In Wyatt's paraphrase, the plural "complaints" seems to be the subject of the singular verb "distills"; Aretino's image of the heart as a still is awkwardly handled: his plaints condense on every side of the organ? Greg Walker offers a concise and illuminating account of the tradition and sources of Wyatt's psalms; he sees Wyatt as creating "a David who is both a mouthpiece for the poet's own spiritual quest and a vehicle for satirical criticism, counsel, and imagined redemption of the King" (Walker 2005, 360). For Aretino's original texts, see Muir and Thomson's notes (Wyatt 1969, 356–90).

§314: "**I am always**" (Ashbery 1983, 48). Ashbery revolves the problem in his prose poem, "The System," which continues and continues by dint of its wonderfully ruminative, self-qualifying sentences, but still worries that it will stop: "They were correct in assuming that the whole question of behavior in life has to be rethought each second; that not a breath can be drawn nor a footstep taken without our being forced in some way to reassess the age-old problem of what we are to do here and how did we get here, taking into account our relations with those about us and with ourselves, and the ever-present issue of our eternal salvation, which looms larger at every moment—even when forgotten it seems to grow like the outline of a mountain as one approaches it" (Ashbery 1997, 346).

§315: "**His harp he**" (Wyatt 1978, 196–97).

§317: "**John Ashbery, Barbara**" (O'Hara 1983, 169). "**Abstract Expressionism is**" (O'Hara 1975, 6). Maggie Nelson analyzes the "gender at play" in the ways that O'Hara et al. defined themselves against the self-consciously major and emphatically masculine first-generation painters; in a tour de force synopsis of what made the New York School a school, she cites, inter alia, "a mixture of high/low sensibilities, including the impertinent habit of venerating 'minor' artistic figures over 'major' ones . . . a distaste for grandiosity of all kinds, from institutional pretense to linguistic tropes that grope at metaphysical symbolism; a love of chatter, via such ephemeral modes of communication as lunch dates, telephone calls, and postcards; an interest in collaborative practices which complicate or erase the possibility of the original genius author . . . and so on" (Nelson 2007, 55).

§318: "**The whole is**" (Eliot 1946, 11). "**It is not**" (ibid., 10). Philip Sidney treats the poet's work as a "second nature, which in nothing [the poet] showeth so much as in poetry, when with the force of a divine breath he bringeth things forth surpassing [nature's] doings" (Sidney 2009, 217). O'Hara comments with familiar half-pretended weariness on the demands of important art in his "Ode (to Joseph LeSueur)" in 1958: "(you're right to go to Aaron's PIANO FANTASY, but I'm not up to it this / time, too important a piece not to punish me / and it's raining" (O'Hara 1995, 300).

§320: "**Gathering his sprites**" (Wyatt 1978, 201). "**On sonour chords**" (ibid., 206).

§321: Philip Fisher's *The Vehement Passions* treats rage and grief as thorough passions, "monarchical" (Fisher 2002, 43) and admitting no mixture.

§322: "**Someone else's Leica**" (O'Hara 1995, 393–94). O'Hara admired Berkson's way with a typewriter; he wrote to him in August 1962, "As Winthrop Sargeant said of you at lunch this weekend, 'Bill Berkson makes the typewriter sing like Sutherland!'" (O'Hara to Berkson, August 10, 1962). Lettrism is a French avant-garde movement, indebted to Dada, established by Isidore Isou in the mid-1940s.

§323: "**Cramped space**" (Deleuze and Guattari 1986, 17). "**There is nothing**" (ibid., 26). Subsequent scholarship has undermined their claims about Kafka's language, which bears fewer marks of Prager Deutsch than their argument calls for; see Stanley Corngold's essay, "Kafka and the Dialect of Minor Literature" (Corngold 1994, 89–90). Aloïs Riegl's *Stilfragen* treats "the minor arts as the site where 'the birthplace of a new style must be sought'" (Schwartz 1999, 11).

§324: Georg Simmel titles an essay "The Problem of Style," but nonetheless speaks of "the calm happiness of a style" (Simmel 1991, 69).

§326: "**His sentence is**" (O'Hara 1995, 33). In his *Rhetoric* Aristotle explains that "the period must . . . not be completed until the sense is complete" (Aristotle 1984, 1409b5). Ian Robinson discusses the history of Aristotle's idea (Robinson 1998, 6–8), and argues that the notion of grammatical completeness ("the syntactic domain of a finite verb" [ibid., 2]) is an Enlightenment development.

§327: "**In order to**" (Rivers 1992, 45).

§328: "**In times of**," from "To the Film Industry in Crisis" (O'Hara 1995, 232).

§329: Vasari does not name his periods, but they structure his *Lives* and are explained in the preface to part two (Vasari 2008, 48–49). For Winckelmann, see his *History of the Art of Antiquity* (2006). Hegel discusses the three phases in a set of introductory lectures from the 1820s translated as *Introductory Lectures on Aesthetics* (Hegel 2004, 78–88). Focillon outlines his stages in *The Life of Forms in Art* (Focillon 1992, 53–61). Schapiro is surveying available resources, not making his own taxonomy (Schapiro 1961, 93). Considering the development of O'Hara's short career, Helen Vendler sees "everywhere a breakdown of logical categories" at the beginning, "sometimes only in a false imitation of Dada, but later in the [*Collected Poems*] in a true attempt to synthesize all of American experience, taking even a wider field than Whitman" (Vendler 1972, 15); Wayne Koestenbaum says, "In the late 1950s, O'Hara deliberately forewent the semantically pyrotechnical elevations of 'Second Avenue' and other earlier poems and chose, instead, a relatively plain style (the *Lunch Poems* voice), thus enacting, in the development of his poetics, a movement from a congested and spiked excitement to a toned-down ebullience" (Koestenbaum 2011). See also Charles Molesworth's taxonomy, the "personal madcap," the "directly surrealist," the personal, and the sentimental (Molesworth 1990, 214–17).

§330: "**Whatever Constantine's donation**" (Bergenroth 1862–, 5.2.421). Brigden describes the episode (Brigden 2012, 362–64). "**With dishonorable words**" (Sowerby 2010, 200).

§331: "**Whose character is**" (Auerbach 2013, 443). Frederic Schwartz explores this problem in his essay "Cathedrals and Shoes: Concepts of Style in Wölfflin and Adorno." He argues that Wölfflin is a shrewd diagnostician of the transformation of style into fashion, but he "can articulate no proper *theory* of stylistic change. This crucial section of the book," his *Principles of Art History*, "shows in the end that he can not *explain* formal development; he can only postulate laws about it, which is something quite different" (Schwartz 1999, 34).

§333: "**It's eight in**," from "Early on Sunday" (O'Hara 1995, 404–5).

§334: "**Resisted change deliberately**" (Huxley 1961).

§335: "**He, then inflamed**" (Wyatt 1978, 204). The heart leans to the left, as Wyatt knew.

§336: "**The sun is**" (Baraka 2016, 132). "**You part of**" (Baraka 1984, 189). "**Seeking revolution**" (ibid., 201). Baraka's distrust of style as a category is audible elsewhere in his autobiography: of *The System of Dante's Hell*, which he started writing in 1960, he says, "It was as if I wanted to shake off the stylistic shackles of the gang I'd hung with and styled myself after. I consciously wrote as deeply into my psyche as I could go" (ibid., 166); though he respects how his friend Tim Poston "developed a distinctive style" (ibid., 132).

§338: "**An action is**" (Rosenberg 1994, 38).

§339: "**Let me again**" (Wyatt 1978, 209).

§341: "**Transferring the concept**" (Gadamer 2004, 497). My understanding of explanation as a matter of establishing causal chains is shaped, here and elsewhere, by David Lewis's "Causal Explanation." Michael Strevens's *Depth* develops the idea of a "causal story" (Stevens 2009, iv). His final, speculative chapter on the aesthetics of explanation as a matter of recognizing pattern raises some deep questions about the opposition between style and explanation (ibid., 473–76).

§343: Alina Payne, in "Vasari, Architecture, and the Origins of Historicizing Art," describes the importance for Vasari of "the narrative format—the story that has a beginning, a middle, and an end" (Payne 2001, 51); see also Philip Sohm, who carries the story forward in "Ordering History with Style" (Sohm 2000, 44–45). E. H. Gombrich was a staunch opponent of Hegelianism in art history, both its expressivism (taking artifacts as crystallizations of their historical moment) and its historicism (the large-scale developmental scheme to which those expressivist details were entailed). He gives a useful history of these assumptions in *Art and Illusion* (Gombrich 1960, 12–22) and "The Psychology of Styles" (Gombrich 1979, 196–201). David Summers offers perspective and background in "E. H. Gombrich and the Tradition of Hegel" (Summers 2002, 139–50). For a defense of the idea that styles have a natural life, that a narrative of origin, development, and limit is intrinsic to them, see Arthur Danto's "Narrative and Style": "What I want . . . is a sense of beginning and ending in which we can see, afterward, the later works of an artist already visible in his or her earlier work though they would not have been visible to us were we contemporary with these works" (Danto 1991, 206). He counts himself a narrative realist, and style is one of the real sites where he takes narrative to be inscribed. See also Jonathan Gilmore's *The Life of a Style* (2000), which builds on Danto.

§344: **"Now the past"** (O'Hara 1995, 445–46).

§345: **"What may I,"** from "The long love that in my thought doth harbour" (Wyatt 1978, 77).

§346: **"Bohemian artworld of"** (Gooch 1993, 13). **"I didn't want"** (ibid.). **"I am an"** (O'Hara 1995, 11).

§347: Helen Vendler finds this true of O'Hara's career, which changes but does not have a familiar narrative trajectory: "we are offered glimpses of relation, happy and sad, but no continuous curve of a life-spiral" (Vendler 1972, 10). Charles Altieri, in another early response, finds him "in no way a traditional narrative poet" (Altieri 1973, 93). Such an account of style touches significant recent work on queer temporalities, the way time and narrative work differently when you do not easily find yourself or fit within traditional, heteronormative frameworks. As Judith Halberstam (now Jack) put it in 2007, "Queer time for me is the dark nightclub, the perverse turn away from the narrative coherence of adolescence–early adulthood–marriage–reproduction–child rearing–retirement–death, the embrace of late childhood in place of early adulthood or immaturity in place of responsibility" (Dinshaw et al. 2007, 182). The nightclub and late childhood are only two possible alternatives, but they would likely have been recognizable to the O'Hara of "The Old Place": "Down the dark stairs drifts the steaming cha- / cha-cha" (O'Hara 1995, 223).

§350: The single sheet is in the Frank O'Hara Papers in the Museum of Modern Art Archives, file 4. The painters are Nell Blaine, Amando de Ossorio, Esteban Vicente, Philip Pearlstein, Ad Reinhardt, John Grillo, Mark Rothko, Philip Guston, Grace Hartigan, and Rafael Ferrer. O'Hara's abbreviations designate styles and movements, abstract ("ab"), figurative ("fig"), surrealist ("sur"), allover à la Jackson Pollock ("allover"), lyrical ("lyr"), geometrical ("geo"), and symbolist ("symb"). I remain uncertain about "neo p."

§351: Georg Simmel puts it bluntly: in his essay "Fashion," published in English in 1957, he writes that fashion "signalizes the lack of personal freedom;

hence it characterizes the female and the middle class, whose increased social freedom is matched by intense individual subjugation" (Simmel 1957, 541).

§352: "**For we have**," from "In Memory of My Feelings" (O'Hara 1995, 254–55).

§353: "**Historical sensation does**," in F. R. Ankersmit's translation (Ankersmit 2005, 121). "**The concept of**" (Gadamer 2004, 494). Wölfflin articulates the kind of explanation style offers: "To *explain* a style can mean nothing other than to place it in its general historical context and to verify that is speaks in harmony with the other organs of its age" (Schwartz 1999, 7). But is this explanation? Ankersmit's *Sublime Historical Experience* offers a radical, alternative account of history-as-experience, "ontological rather than epistemological" (Ankersmit 2005, 225); he understands the study of the past to be motivated by the possibility of a kind of fusion with it. Such experience is not given us by storytelling, nor any other mode of representation: "Where we have narrative, experience is impossible; and experience excludes narrative" (ibid., 172). He follows a line of thinkers—Nietzsche and Agamben among them—who take experience to be possible only by an annulment not only of narrative but of epistemology. Huizinga is one of his masters, too.

§354: Here Bourdieu's concern about structuralism and time returns: "to exist in the mode of temporal existence which is that of theoretical objects, that is, *tota simul*, as a totality in simultaneity" (Bourdieu 1990, 35). Structuralist anthropology has flourished in describing cultures that anthropologists want not to change; one might say that they are concerned to preserve an experience, for the native and for the participant-observer.

§355: "**If there is**" (O'Hara 1959, 12).

§358: Fredric Jameson maintains that "history is what hurts" in *The Political Unconscious* (Jameson 1981, 102). "**Articulating the past**" (Benjamin 2003, 4: 391). For an account of style's potential to activate such a disruption, an account sympathetic to Walter Benjamin's sense of the disruptive potential of fashion, see Andrew Benjamin's *Style and Time* (2006), especially chapter 1. As Ina Blom paraphrases: "Fashion may suppress the untimely or interruptive event, but even so it cannot help pointing to the critical question of the temporality of appearance, the possibility of unforeseen appearances and unaccounted-for events. It has, as Walter Benjamin puts it, 'a sense of time'" (Blom 2007, 16).

§360: "**Wyatt had cast**" (Muir 1963, 209). Brigden speculates that "the Brooke family were seeking Elizabeth's rehabilitation, demanding that Wyatt acknowledge her" (Brigden 2012, 548).

§361: "**At the height**" (Hoffman 1961). "**The French Revolution**" (Benjamin 2003, 4: 395). In steering style away from the category of event, I am mindful of the arguments made by Mario Aquilina in *The Event of Style in Literature*. He develops from Derrida an account of "the eventhood of literature, the undecidability between the absolutely singular and its iterability or translatability that generates the force of the poetic or the literary" (Aquilina 2014, 134); literature, that is, is the kind of writing that most solicits and most resists imitation. Style can be thought of as arising, always anew, in the eventhood of the work, within the "undecidability between auto- and hetero-reference" (ibid., 135). I prefer to separate style and aesthesis, and to reserve to aesthesis the power of event, of interruption; style, on such an account, is the web of likeness in which the event is already entangled. But my position is neither more nor less than an analytic preference for greater separation between the terms; to understand how style works it is also necessary to consider attempts, theoretical and vernacular, to remap, reverse, and collapse them, of which Aquilina's is one. See also Andrew Benjamin's *Style and Time*, which makes a similar investment in style as historical interruption, following his namesake: "Only by allowing for the interarticulation of style and time can a distinction be drawn between simple novelty and the possible realization of an actual interruption" (Benjamin 2006, xvi). Dick Hebdige's *Subculture: The Meaning of Style* (1979) offers another way of thinking about style's dissidence, invested more than my account in the language of semiotics: "the challenge to hegemony which subcultures represent is not issued directly by them. Rather it is expressed obliquely, in style. The objections are lodged, the contradictions displayed . . . at the profoundly superficial level of appearances: that is, at the level of signs" (Hebdige 1979, 17).

§363: "**With hot dogs**," from "Early on Sunday" (O'Hara 1995, 404–5).

§366: "**By nightly plaints**" (Wyatt 1978, 199). "**Et duro campo**," literally, "and the bed is a harsh battlefield" (Petrarch 1976, 382–83). Powell writes: "Wyatt began paraphrasing the Penitential Psalms in Spain or before, since Brereton begins copying one of them on folio 65v. . . . He continued them in a blank portion of Egerton, from folio 86r (which gave more room for the composition of this longer work) in Spain or after" (Powell 2004, 279).

§368: "**But we will**" (O'Hara 1995, 438). "**They hadn't read**" (ibid., 513). "The freedom to" (Arendt 1961, 151). Susan Stewart has adapted this argument to poetry in *The Poet's Freedom*, the "affirmative freedom involving making without prior rules" (Stewart 2011, 25). "**Continuez, même stupide**" (O'Hara 1995, 438). Gertrude Stein could be said to fight the distinction I am making, between freedom-as-beginning and the continuing of style, in her great essay "Composition as Explanation": composition is "a continuous present using everything and beginning again" (Stein 1993, 499). The essay treats the postwar period as a moment when a style can be recognized as a new start even at the moment of its arrival, when her way of writing can be an aesthetic event, and still be a way of continuing. She acknowledges, however, that history has afforded her a rare opportunity.

§369: **"We think by,"** from "Cento: A Note on Philosophy" (Berrigan 2005, 443).

§370: **"Tender fracas"** (O'Hara 1995, 79). Roethke's question is "What is there to know?" (Roethke 1975, 104). **"Melodic sighs"** (Berrigan 2005, 39). Alice Notley gives the biographical background in her edition of Berrigan's *Collected* (ibid., 19–24). **"A particular poem"** (Berkson and LeSueur 1988, 210).

§371: **"I've been painting"** (letter to Jane Freilicher, August 8, 1952). O'Hara joined Grace Hartigan and others for a "sketch group" that fall in her studio: "It was a good group—Larry, Miles, Jane, Fairfield, Nell B, Allen K, Wolfe K & his girl, Al Kresch and Frank and Kenneth K" (Hartigan 2009, 47).

§373: **"In ship, freight"** (Surrey 1964, 21). Sessions dates the poem to 1544 (Sessions 1999, 417).

§374: Kendall Walton offers a strong argument for style as a maker's knowledge: "I would suggest that styles of works of art are to be understood in terms of the notion of styles of action. Specifically, attributing a style to a work involves, somehow, the idea of the manner in which it was made, the act of creating it," or at least "how a work *appears* to have been made" (Walton 2008, 222, 228). **"In imitation the"** (Cave 1979, 35). Recall Chris Stamatakis's assertion that for Wyatt, "reading and rewriting become closely entwined practices" (Stamatakis 2012, 30). **"I read simply"** (O'Hara 1995, 406).

§376: **"My galley charged"** (Wyatt 1978, 81).

§377: **"More regard for"** (Muir 1963, 216).

§379: **"I wanted to"** (O'Hara 1995, 217).

§380: Brad Gooch begins his biography with an account of the funeral (Gooch 1993, 3–11). **"Always coming back"** (Ashbery 1997, 233).

§382: **"In storms and"** (O'Hara 1995, 217).

§383: **"I think that"** (Gooch 1993, 464).

§385: **"And every oar"** (Wyatt 1978, 81).

§387: **"My wallpaper and"** (Ellman 1988, 581).

§389: Larry Rivers tested his audience's limits at O'Hara's funeral, describing O'Hara's injuries in terrible detail (Gooch 1993, 9).

§390: **"To you I"** (O'Hara 1995, 217).

§392: **"I finally cried"** (Diggory 2001, 14). Tabak was a chronicler of the period she wept for: her novel *But Not for Love* (1960) was a satiric account of a group of painters and writers between New York City and the Hamptons in the 1950s.

§395: **"A rain of"** (Wyatt 1978, 81).

BIBLIOGRAPHY

Frank O'Hara's letters are quoted from the Donald Allen Collection of Frank O'Hara Letters at the Thomas J. Dodd Research Center at the University of Connecticut, Storrs, unless otherwise specified.

Other O'Hara letters, and some letters by James Schuyler, are quoted from the James Schuyler Papers, 1947–91, MSS 0078, Special Collections and Archives, University of California, San Diego.

Ackerman, James. 1963. "A Theory of Style." *Journal of Aesthetics and Art Criticism* 20(3): 227–37.

Adorno, Theodor. 2000. "Lyric Poetry and Society." In *The Adorno Reader*, edited by Brian O'Connor, 211–29. Malden, MA: Blackwell.

Agamben, Giorgio. 2000. "Notes on Gesture." In *Means without End: Notes on Politics*, 49–62. Translated by Vincenzo Binetti and Cesare Casarino. Minneapolis: University of Minnesota Press.

Allen, Donald. 1999. *The New American Poetry*. Berkeley: University of California Press.

Altieri, Charles. 1973. "The Significance of Frank O'Hara." *Iowa Review* 4 (1): 90–104.

———. 1989. "Style as the Man: From Aesthetics to Speculative Philosophy." In *Analytic Aesthetics*, edited by Richard Shusterman, 59–84. Oxford: B. Blackwell.

———. 2009. "Style." In *The Oxford Handbook of Philosophy and Literature*, edited by Richard Eldridge, 420–41. Oxford: Oxford University Press.

Ankersmit, F. R. 2005. *Sublime Historical Experience*. Stanford, CA: Stanford University Press.

Aquilina, Mario. 2014. *The Event of Style in Literature*. New York: Palgrave Macmillan.

Arendt, Hannah. 1961. "What Is Freedom?" In *Between Past and Future*, 143–71. New York: Viking Press.

Aristotle. 1984. *The Complete Works of Aristotle*. Edited by Jonathan Barnes. 2 vols. New York: Random House.

Aristotle, Longinus, and Demetrius. 1995. "On Style." In *Aristotle: Poetics, Longinus: On the Sublime, Demetrius: On Style*. Edited by Stephen Halliwell et al. Cambridge, MA: Harvard University Press.

Arrowsmith, William. 1956. "Review: Nine New Poets." *Hudson Review* 9 (2): 289–97.

Ashbery, John. 1983. "The Art of Poetry XXXIII: John Ashbery." Interview by Peter Stitt. *Paris Review* 90: 30–59.

———. 1997. *The Mooring of Starting Out: The First Five Books of Poetry*. New York: Ecco.

———. 2005. *Selected Prose*. Ann Arbor: University of Michigan Press.

Ashton, Dore. 1973. *The New York School: A Cultural Reckoning*. New York: Viking.

Auden, W. H. 1962. *The Dyer's Hand*. New York: Random House.

Auerbach, Erich. 2013. *Mimesis: The Representation of Reality in Western Literature*. Translated by Willard Trask. Princeton, NJ: Princeton University Press.

Baraka, Amiri. 1984. *The Autobiography of LeRoi Jones*. New York: Freundlich Books.

———. 2016. *SOS: Poems 1961–2013*. New York: Grove Press.

Baron, Helen. 1976. "Wyatt's 'What Rage.'" *The Library*, 5th ser., 31: 188–204.

Barthes, Roland. 1971. "Style and Its Image." In *Literary Style: A Symposium*, edited by Seymour Chatman. New York: Oxford University Press.

———. 1977. *Writing Degree Zero*. Translated by Annette Lavers and Colin Smith. New York: Hill and Wang.

———. 1982. *The Responsibility of Forms: Critical Essays on Music, Art, and Representation*. Translated by Richard Howard. Oxford: Blackwell.

Benjamin, Andrew. 2006. *Style and Time*. Evanston, IL: Northwestern University Press.

Benjamin, Walter. 1996–2003. *Selected Writings*. 4 vols. Edited by Howard Eiland and Michael Jennings. Cambridge, MA: Harvard University Press.

Bergenroth, G. A., et al. 1862–. *Calendar of Letters, Despatches and State Papers*

Relating to the Negotiations between England and Spain, Preserved in the Archives at Simancas and Elsewhere. London: Longman, Green, Longman and Roberts.

Berkson, Bill. 1990. "Frank O'Hara and His Poems." In *Frank O'Hara: To Be True to a City*, edited by Jim Elledge, 226–233. Ann Arbor: University of Michigan Press, 1990.

Berkson, Bill, and Joe LeSueur, eds. 1988. *Homage to Frank O'Hara*. Bolinas, CA: Big Sky Books.

Berrigan, Ted. 2005. *The Collected Poems of Ted Berrigan*. Edited by Alice Notley. Berkeley: University of California Press.

Berryman, John. 1989. *Collected Poems, 1937–1971*. Edited by Charles Thornbury. New York: Farrar, Straus, and Giroux.

Blake, Nigel F. 1983. *The Language of Shakespeare*. New York: Macmillan.

Blevins, Jacob. 1999. "The Catullan Lyric and Anti-Petrarchism in Sir Thomas Wyatt." *Classical and Modern Literature: A Quarterly* 19 (3): 279–85.

Blom, Ina. 2007. *On the Style Site: Art, Sociality, and Media Culture*. New York: Sternberg.

Bloom, Alexander. 1986. *Prodigal Sons: The New York Intellectuals and Their World*. New York: Oxford University Press.

Bourdieu, Pierre. 1984. *Distinction: A Social Critique of the Judgement of Taste*. Translated by Richard Nice. Cambridge, MA: Harvard University Press.

———. 1990. *The Logic of Practice*. Translated by Richard Nice. Stanford, CA: Stanford University Press.

Brewer, J. S., and J. Gairdner. 1862–1910. *Letters and Papers, Foreign and Domestic, of the Reign of Henry VIII*. 21 vols. London: Longman, Green, Longman and Roberts.

Brigden, Susan. 2008. "Bryan, Sir Francis." *Oxford Dictionary of National Biography*. Oxford University Press, online edition. http://www.oxforddnb.com/view/article/3788, accessed November 11, 2015.

———. 2012. *Thomas Wyatt: The Heart's Forest*. London: Faber and Faber.

Brilliant, A. N. 1971. "The Style of Wyatt's *Quyete of Mynde*." *Essays and Studies* 24: 1–21.

Bruce, John. 1850. "Unpublished anecdotes of Sir Thomas Wyatt the Poet, and of Other Members of that Family." *Gentleman's Magazine* 34: 235–41.

Buffon, Georges-Louis Leclerc, comte de. 1923. *Discours sur le Style*. Paris: Hatier.

Bürger, Peter. 1984. *Theory of the Avant-Garde*. Translated by Michael Shaw. Minneapolis: University of Minnesota Press.

Burrow, Colin. 1993. "Horace at Home and Abroad: Wyatt and Sixteenth-Century Horatianism." In *Horace Made New: Horatian Influences on British Writing from the Renaissance to the Twentieth Century*, edited by Charles

Martindale and David Hopkins, 27–49. Cambridge: Cambridge University Press.

Caillois, Roger. 1984. "Mimicry and Legendary Psychasthenia." *October* 31: 16–32.

Caldwell, Ellen. 1989. "Recent Studies in Sir Thomas Wyatt." *English Literary Renaissance* 19 (2): 226–46.

Castiglione, Baldassare. 1561. *The Courtyer of Count Baldessar Castilio*. Translated by Sir Thomas Hoby. London.

Cave, Terence. 1979. *The Cornucopian Text: Problems of Writing in the French Renaissance*. Oxford: Oxford University Press.

Chatman, Seymour. 1987. "The Styles of Narrative Codes." In *The Concept of Style*, edited by Berel Lang, 230–44. Ithaca, NY: Cornell University Press.

Christiansen, Nancy L. 2013. *Figuring Style: The Legacy of Renaissance Rhetoric*. Columbia: University of South Carolina Press.

Cicero. 1939. *Brutus, Orator*. Translated by G. L. Hendrickson and H. M. Hubbell. Cambridge, MA: Harvard University Press.

———. 1942a. *On the Orator, Books 1–2*. Translated by E. W. Sutton and H. Rackham. Cambridge, MA: Harvard University Press.

———. 1942b. *On the Orator: Book 3. On Fate. Stoic Paradoxes. Divisions of Oratory*. Translated by H. Rackham. Cambridge, MA: Harvard University Press.

———. 1954. *Rhetorica ad Herrennium*. Translated by Harry Caplan. Cambridge, MA: Harvard University Press.

Clune, Michael. 2005. "'Everything We Want': Frank O'Hara and the Aesthetics of Free Choice." *PMLA* 120 (1): 181–96.

Compagnon, Antoine. 2004. *Literature, Theory, and Common Sense*. Translated by Carol Cosman. Princeton, NJ: Princeton University Press.

Corngold, Stanley. 1994. "Kafka and the Dialect of Minor Literature." *College English* 21 (1): 89–101.

Cummings, Brian. 2002. *The Literary Culture of the Reformation: Grammar and Grace*. Oxford: Oxford University Press.

Curtis, Cathy. 2015. *Reckless Ambition: Grace Hartigan, Painter*. Oxford: Oxford University Press.

Daalder, Joost. 1973. "Editing Wyatt." *Essays in Criticism* 23 (4): 399–413.

Danto, Arthur Coleman. 1981. *The Transfiguration of the Commonplace: A Philosophy of Art*. Cambridge, MA: Harvard University Press.

———. 1991. "Narrative and Style." *Journal of Aesthetics and Art Criticism* 49 (3): 201–9.

Deleuze, Gilles, and Félix Guattari. 1986. *Kafka: Toward a Minor Literature*. Translated by Dana Polan. Minneapolis: University of Minnesota Press.

Deleuze, Gilles, and Claire Parnet. 1987. *Dialogues II*. Rev. ed. Translated by

Hugh Tomlinson and Barbara Habberjam. New York: Columbia University Press.

Derrida, Jacques. 1981. *Spurs: Nietzsche's Styles*. Translated by Barbara Harlow. Chicago: University of Chicago Press.

Diggory, Terence. 2001. "Community 'Intimate' or 'Inoperative': New York School Poets and Politics from Paul Goodman to Jean-Luc Nancy." In *The Scene of My Selves: New Work on New York School Poets*, edited by Terence Diggory and Stephen Paul Miller, 13–34. Orono, ME: National Poetry Society.

———. 2009. *Encyclopedia of the New York School Poets*. New York: Facts on File.

Dinshaw, Carolyn, et al. 2007. "Theorizing Queer Temporalities: A Roundtable Discussion." *GLQ: A Journal of Lesbian and Gay Studies* 13 (2–3): 177–95.

Dolven, Jeff. 2007. *Scenes of Instruction in Renaissance Romance*. Chicago: University of Chicago Press.

———. 2013. "Hardly They Heard." In *Shakespeare Up Close: Reading Early Modern Texts*, edited by Russ McDonald, Nicholas Nace, and Travis Williams, 87–94. New York: Bloomsbury.

———. 2014. "Surrey's Black Eye." *Cabinet* 53: 100–103.

Domenichelli, Mario. 2002. "Sir Thomas Wyatt's Translations from Petrarch and the 'Lingua Cortigiana.'" *Textus: English Studies in Italy* 15 (1): 65–86.

Douglas, Mary. 1984. *Purity and Danger: An Analysis of the Concepts of Pollution and Taboo*. London: Routledge and Kegan Paul.

Durant, Will and Ariel. 1965. *The Age of Voltaire*. New York: Simon and Schuster.

Eden, Kathy. 2012. *The Renaissance Rediscovery of Intimacy*. Chicago: University of Chicago Press.

Eliot, T. S. 1946. "What Is Minor Poetry?" *Sewanee Review* 54: 1–18.

Ellman, Richard. 1988. *Oscar Wilde*. New York: Vintage.

Epstein, Andrew. 2000. "Frank O'Hara's Translation Game." *Raritan* 19 (3): 144–61.

———. 2006. *Beautiful Enemies: Friendship and Postwar American Poetry*. Oxford: Oxford University Press.

Erasmus, Desiderius. 1974–. *Collected Works of Erasmus*. 89 vols. Toronto: University of Toronto Press.

Fish, Stanley. 1980. "What Is Stylistics and Why Are They Saying Such Terrible Things about It? Part II." In *Is There a Text in This Class*, 246–67. Cambridge, MA: Harvard University Press.

Fisher, Philip. 2002. *The Vehement Passions*. Princeton, NJ: Princeton University Press, 2002.

Fletcher, Angus. 1964. *Allegory: The Theory of a Symbolic Mode*. Ithaca, NY: Cornell University Press.

Focillon, Henry. 1992. *The Life of Forms in Art*. Translated by George Kubler. New York: Zone.

Freud, Sigmund. 1997. "The Moses of Michelangelo." In *Writings on Art and Literature*, 122–50. Stanford, CA: Stanford University Press.

Friedlander, Benjamin. 2001. "Strange Fruit: O'Hara, Race, and the Color of Time." In *The Scene of My Selves: New Work on New York School Poets*, edited by Terence Diggory and Stephen Paul Miller, 123–41. Orono, ME: National Poetry Society.

Gadamer, Hans-Georg. 1977. "Aesthetics and Hermeneutics." In *Philosophical Hermeneutics*, translated and edited by David E. Linge, 95–104. Berkeley: University of California Press.

———. 2004. *Truth and Method*. Translated by W. Glen-Doepel, Joel Weinsheimer, and Donald G. Marshall. London: Continuum.

Garvey, Mark. 2009. *Stylized: A Slightly Obsessive History of Strunk and White's The Elements of Style*. New York: Touchstone.

Gell, Alfred. 1998. *Art and Agency: An Anthropological Theory*. Oxford: Oxford University Press.

Genette, Gérard. 1993. "Style and Signification." In *Fiction and Diction*, translated by Catherine Porter, 85–141. Ithaca, NY: Cornell University Press.

Gigante, Denise. 2005. *Taste: A Literary History*. New Haven, CT: Yale University Press.

Gilmore, Jonathan. 2000. *The Life of a Style*. Ithaca, NY: Cornell University Press.

Ginzburg, Carlo. 1989. "Clues: Roots of an Evidential Paradigm." In *Clues, Myths, and the Historical Method*. Baltimore: Johns Hopkins University Press.

———. 2001. *Wooden Eyes: Nine Reflections on Distance*. New York: Columbia University Press.

Gombrich, E. H. 1960. *Art and Illusion*. New York: Pantheon.

———. 1968. "Style." In *International Encyclopedia of the Social Sciences*, 17 vols., 15: 352–61. New York: Macmillan.

———. 1979. "The Psychology of Styles." In *The Sense of Order*, 193–216. Ithaca, NY: Cornell University Press.

Gooch, Brad. 1993. *City Poet: The Life and Times of Frank O'Hara*. New York: Alfred A. Knopf.

Goodman, Nelson. 1972. "Seven Strictures on Similarity." In *Problems and Projects*, 437–46. Indianapolis: Bobbs-Merrill.

———. 1975. "The Status of Style." *Critical Inquiry* 1 (4): 799–811.

Goodman, Paul. 1951. "Advance-Guard Writing, 1900–1950." *Kenyon Review* 13 (3): 357–80.

———. 1958. "Reflections on Literature as a Minor Art." *Dissent* (Summer): 291–93.

Grafton, Anthony, and Lisa Jardine. 1986. *From Humanism to the Humanities.* Cambridge, MA: Harvard University Press.

Gray, Douglas, ed. 2003. *The Oxford Companion to Chaucer.* Oxford, UK: Oxford University Press.

Greenberg, Clement. 1940. "Towards a Newer Laocoon." *Partisan Review* 7 (4): 296–310.

———. 1989. *Art and Culture.* Boston: Beacon Press.

Greenblatt, Stephen. 1980. *Renaissance Self-Fashioning: From More to Shakespeare.* Chicago: University of Chicago Press.

Greene, Thomas M. 1982. *The Light in Troy.* New Haven, CT: Yale University Press.

Gruen, John. 1972. *The Party's over Now.* New York: Viking Press.

Hamilton, Ian. 1982. *Robert Lowell: A Biography.* New York: Random House.

Hamon, Philippe. 1981. "Rhetorical Status of the Descriptive." Translated by Patricia Baudoin. *Yale French Studies* 61: 1–26.

Harrier, Richard. 1975. *The Canon of Sir Thomas Wyatt's Poetry.* Cambridge, MA: Harvard University Press.

Harrison, Matthew. 2015. "Tear Him for His Bad Verses." PhD thesis, Princeton University.

Hartigan, Grace. 2009. *The Journals of Grace Hartigan, 1951–1955.* Edited by William T. La Moy and Joseph P. McCaffrey. Syracuse, NY: Syracuse University Press.

Heale, Elizabeth. 1998. *Wyatt, Surrey, and Early Tudor Poetry.* London: Longman.

Hebdige, Dick. 1979. *Subculture: The Meaning of Style.* London: Routledge.

Hegel, Georg Wilhelm Friedrich. 2004. *Introductory Lectures on Aesthetics.* Translated by Bernard Bosanquet. London: Penguin.

Hendrickson, G. L. 1904. "The Peripatetic Mean of Style and the Three Stylistic Characters." *American Journal of Philology* 25 (2): 125–46.

———. 1905. "The Origin and Meaning of the Ancient Characters of Style." *American Journal of Philology* 26 (3): 249–90.

Herman, Peter S., ed. 2002. *Reading Monarchs Writing: The Poetry of Henry VIII, Mary Stuart, Elizabeth I, and James VI/I.* Tempe: Arizona Center for Medieval and Renaissance Studies.

Hermogenes. 1987. *Hermogenes' on Types of Style.* Translated by Cecil Wooten. Chapel Hill: University of North Carolina Press.

Hickman, Ben. 2013. "'Our Program Is the Absence of Any Program': The New York School Reading the Past." In *New York School Collaborations: The*

Color of Vowels, edited by Mark Silverberg, 17–34. New York: Palgrave Macmillan.

Hirsch, E. D., Jr. 1975. "Stylistics and Synonymity." *Critical Inquiry* 1 (3): 559–79.

Hoffman, Paul. 1961. "Folk Singers Riot in Washington Square." *New York Times*, April 10.

Hough, Graham. 1969. *Style and Stylistics*. London: Routledge and Kegan Paul.

Hughley, Ruth, ed. 1960. *The Arundel-Harrington Manuscript of Tudor Poetry*. 2 vols. Columbus: University of Ohio Press.

Hume, Martin A. Sharp, trans. 1889. *Chronicle of King Henry VIII of England*. London: G. Bell and Sons.

Huxley, Elspeth. 1961. "Two Tribes Tell Africa's Story." *New York Times*, April 30.

Izenberg, Oren. 2011. *Being Numerous: Poetry and the Ground of Social Life*. Princeton, NJ: Princeton University Press.

Jakobson, Roman. 1990. *Language in Literature*. Edited by Krystyna Pomorska and Stephen Rudy. Cambridge, MA: Harvard University Press.

Jameson, Fredric. 1972. *The Prison-House of Language*. Princeton, NJ: Princeton University Press.

———. 1981. *The Political Unconscious: Narrative as a Socially Symbolic Act*. Ithaca, NY: Cornell University Press.

Janson, H. W. 1962. *History of Art*. New York: Abrams.

Johnson, Kent. 2012. *A Question Mark above the Sun*. Buffalo, NY: Starcherone Books.

Johnson, Mark. 2007. *The Meaning of the Body: Aesthetics of Human Understanding*. Chicago: University of Chicago Press.

Joula, Patrick. 2006. "Authorship Attribution." *Foundations and Trends in Information Retrieval* 1 (3): 233–334.

Kant, Immanuel. 2002. *Critique of the Power of Judgment*. Edited by Paul Guyer. Cambridge: Cambridge University Press.

Keilen, Sean. 2006. *Vulgar Eloquence*. New Haven, CT: Yale University Press.

Kennedy, George. 1989. "The Evolution of a Theory of Artistic Prose." In *The Cambridge History of Literary Criticism*. Vol. 1, *Classical Criticism*, 184–99. Cambridge: Cambridge University Press.

Kenny, Anthony. 1982. *The Computation of Style: An Introduction to Statistics for Students of Literature and Humanities*. Oxford: Pergamon Press.

Kerrigan, John. 1981. "Wyatt's Selfish Style." *Essays and Studies* 34: 1–18.

Koch, Kenneth. 1991. "Frank O'Hara and His Poetry: An Interview with Kenneth Koch." Interviewed by Richard Kostelanetz. In *American Writing Today*, edited by Richard Kostelanetz, 201–11. Troy, NY: Whiston.

———. 2006. *The Collected Poems of Kenneth Koch*. New York: Alfred A. Knopf.

Koestenbaum, Wayne. 2011. "'Oh! Kangaroos, Sequins, Chocolate Sodas!':
Frank O'Hara's Excitement." *Academy of American Poets.* https://www.
poets.org/poetsorg/text/oh-kangaroos-sequins-chocolate-sodas-frank-
oharas-excitement, accessed May 24, 2016.

Kubler, George. 1967. "Style and the Representation of Historical Time." *Annals
of the New York Academy of Sciences* 138: 849–55.

———. 1987. "Toward a Reductive Theory of Visual Style." In *The Concept of
Style,* edited by Berel Lang, 163–73. Ithaca, NY: Cornell University Press.

———. 2008. *The Shape of Time: Remarks on the History of Things.* New Haven,
CT: Yale University Press.

Lanham, Richard. 1976. *The Motives of Eloquence: Literary Rhetoric in the Renaissance.* New Haven, CT: Yale University Press.

———. 2003. *Analyzing Prose.* 2nd ed. New York: Continuum.

Lear, Jonathan. 2011. *A Case for Irony.* Cambridge, MA: Harvard University
Press.

Leeming, David. 1999. *Stephen Spender: A Life in Modernism.* New York: Henry
Holt.

Leland, John. 1542. *Naeniae in Mortem Thomae Viati Equitis Incomparabilis.*
London.

Lermolieff, Ivan [Giovanni Morelli]. 1890. *Die Werke Italienischer Meister in
den Galerien von München, Dresden und Berlin.* Leipzig: E. A. Seeman.

Lessing, Gotthold Ephraim. 1984. *Laocoön: An Essay on the Limits of Painting and Poetry.* Translated by Edward Allen McCormick. Baltimore: Johns
Hopkins University Press.

LeSueur, Joe. 2003. *Digressions on Some Poems by Frank O'Hara.* New York:
Farrar, Straus, and Giroux.

Lewis, C. S. 1954. *English Literature in the Sixteenth Century Excluding Drama.*
Oxford: Oxford University Press.

Lewis, David. 1986. "Causal Explanation." In *Philosophical Papers,* 2: 214–40.
Oxford: Oxford University Press.

Lily, William. 2013. *Lily's Grammar of Latin in English.* Edited by Hedwig
Gwosdek. Oxford: Oxford University Press.

Londry, Michael. 1997. "The New York School Poets at Harvard." PhD diss., University of Alberta.

Loos, Adolf. 2000. "Ornament and Crime." In *The Theory of Decorative Art: An
Anthology of European and American Writings, 1750–1940,* edited by Isa-
belle Frank, 288–94. New Haven, CT: Yale University Press.

Mack, Peter. 2011. *A History of Renaissance Rhetoric, 1380–1620.* Oxford: Oxford University Press.

Mann, Jenny. 2012. *Outlaw Rhetoric: Figuring Vernacular Eloquence in Shakespeare's England.* Ithaca, NY: Cornell University Press.

Marotti, Arthur. 1995. *Manuscript, Print, and the English Renaissance Lyric.* Ithaca, NY: Cornell University Press.

Mason, H. A. 1959. *Humanism and Poetry in the Early Tudor Period.* London: Routledge and Kegan Paul.

———. 1976. "Editing Wyatt." *Sewanee Review* 84 (4): 675–83.

———. 1986. *Sir Thomas Wyatt: A Literary Portrait.* Bristol: Bristol Classical Press.

Masten, Jeffrey. 2004. "Toward a Queer Address: The Taste of Letters and Early Modern Friendship." *GLQ: A Journal of Lesbian and Gay Studies* 10 (3): 367–84.

McGann, Jerome. 1983. *The Romantic Ideology: A Critical Investigation.* Chicago: University of Chicago Press.

Michael, Ian. 1970. *English Grammatical Categories and the Tradition to 1800.* Cambridge: Cambridge University Press.

Miller, D. A. 2003. *Jane Austen, or the Secret of Style.* Princeton, NJ: Princeton University Press.

Molesworth, Charles. 1990. "'The Clear Architecture of the Nerves': The Poetry of Frank O'Hara." In *Frank O'Hara: To Be True to a City,* edited by Jim Elledge, 209–25. Ann Arbor: University of Michigan Press.

Morelli, Giovanni. 1880. *Die Werke Italienischer Meister.* Leipzig: E. A. Seemann.

———. 1897. *Italian Painters: Critical Studies of Their Works.* Translated by Constance Jocelyn Ffoulkes. London: Spottiswoode.

Muir, Kenneth. 1963. *Life and Letters of Sir Thomas Wyatt.* Liverpool: Liverpool University Press.

Nagel, Alexander. 2010. "Questions of Style." *Artforum* 49 (1): 258–59.

Neer, Richard. 2005. "Connoisseurship and the Stakes of Style." *Critical Inquiry* 32 (1): 1–26.

Nehamas, Alexander. 2007. *Only a Promise of Happiness: The Place of Beauty in a World of Art.* Princeton, NJ: Princeton University Press.

Nelson, Maggie. 2007. *Women, the New York School, and Other True Abstractions.* Iowa City: University of Iowa Press.

Nicholson, Catherine. 2014. *Uncommon Tongues: Eloquence and Eccentricity in the English Renaissance.* Philadelphia: University of Pennsylvania Press.

Nietzsche, Friedrich. 2001. *The Gay Science.* Translated by Josefine Nauckhoff. Cambridge: Cambridge University Press.

———. 2003. *Writings from the Late Notebooks.* Edited by Rüdiger Bittner. Cambridge: Cambridge University Press.

Noë, Alva. 2005. "Against Intellectualism." *Analysis* 65 (4): 278–90.

Nolan, Maura. 2010. "Style." In *Cultural Reformations: Medieval and*

Renaissance in Literary History, edited by Brian Cummings and James Simpson, 396–419. Oxford: Oxford University Press.

Nunokawa, Jeff. *Tame Passions of Wilde: The Styles of Manageable Desire.* Princeton, NJ: Princeton University Press, 2003.

O'Hara, Frank. 1959. *Jackson Pollock.* New York: George Braziller.

———. 1975. *Art Chronicles 1954–1966.* New York: George Braziller.

———. 1977. *Early Writing.* Edited by Donald Allen. Bolinas, CA: Grey Fox Press.

———. 1983. *Standing Still and Walking in New York.* Edited by Donald Allen. San Francisco: Grey Fox Press.

———. 1995. *The Collected Poems of Frank O'Hara.* Edited by Donald Allen. Berkeley: University of California Press.

———. 1997. *Amorous Nightmares of Delay: Selected Plays.* Baltimore: Johns Hopkins University Press.

Ohmann, Richard. 1964. "Generative Grammar and the Concept of Literary Style." *Word* 20: 423–39.

Padelford, F. M. 1907. *Early Sixteenth Century Lyrics.* Boston: D. C. Heath.

Papapetros, Spyros. 2012. "Ornament and Object—Ornament as Object." *Journal of Art Historiography* 7: 1–12.

Patterson, Annabel. 1970. *Hermogenes and the Renaissance: Seven Ideas of Style.* Princeton, NJ: Princeton University Press.

Payne, Alina. 2001. "Vasari, Architecture, and the Origins of Historicizing Art." *RES: Anthropology and Aesthetics* 40: 51–76.

———. 2012. *From Ornament to Object: Genealogies of Architectural Modernism.* New Haven, CT: Yale University Press.

Peirce, Charles Sanders. 2011. *Philosophical Writings of Peirce.* Edited by Justus Buchler. New York: Dover.

Perloff, Marjorie. 1990. "Frank O'Hara and the Aesthetics of Attention." In *Frank O'Hara: To Be True to a City*, edited by Jim Elledge, 156–88. Ann Arbor: University of Michigan Press, 1990.

———. 1997. *Frank O'Hara: Poet among Painters.* Rev. ed. Chicago: University of Chicago Press.

Petrarch. 1976. *Petrarch's Lyric Poems.* Translated by Robert Durling. Cambridge, MA: Harvard University Press.

Pigman, G. W. 1980. "Versions of Imitation in the Renaissance." *Renaissance Quarterly* 33 (1): 1–32.

Poole, William. 2011. "The Vices of Style." In *Renaissance Figures of Speech*, edited by Sylvia Adamson, Gavin Alexander, and Katrin Ettenhuber, 237–51. Cambridge: Cambridge University Press.

Powell, Jason. 2004. "Thomas Wyatt's Poetry in Embassy: Egerton 2711 and the

Production of Literary Manuscripts Abroad." *Huntington Library Quarterly* 67 (2): 261–82.

———. 2005. "'For Caesar's I Am': Henrician Diplomacy and Representations of King and Country in Thomas Wyatt's Poetry." *Sixteenth Century Journal* 36 (2): 415–31.

———. 2009a. "Editing Wyatts: Reassessing the Textual State of Sir Thomas Wyatt's Poetry." *Poetica* 71: 93–104.

———. 2009b. "Marginalia, Authorship, and Editing in the Manuscripts of Thomas Wyatt's Verse." *English Manuscript Studies 1100–1700* 15: 1–40.

———. 2009c. "Thomas Wyatt and Francis Bryan: Plainness and Dissimulation." In *The Oxford Handbook of Tudor Literature: 1485–1603*, edited by Mike Pincombe and Cathy Shrank, 187–202. Oxford: Oxford University Press.

Puttenham, George. 2007. *The Art of English Poetry by George Puttenham: A Critical Edition*. Edited by Frank Whigham and Wayne A. Rebhorn. Ithaca, NY: Cornell University Press.

Quintillian. 2002. *The Orator's Education*. 5 vols. Edited and translated by Donald A. Russell. Cambridge, MA: Harvard University Press.

Rancière, Jacques. 2009. *Aesthetics and Its Discontents*. Malden, MA: Polity.

Rivers, Larry. 1992. *What Did I Do: The Unauthorized Autobiography*. New York: Thunder's Mouth Press.

Roberts, Luke. 2015. "Strikers with Poems." In *Modernist Legacies: Trends and Faultlines in British Poetry Today*, edited by Abigail Lang and David Nowell Smith, 193–204. New York: Palgrave Macmillan.

Robinson, Ian. 1998. *The Establishment of Modern English Prose in the Reformation and the Enlightenment*. Cambridge: Cambridge University Press.

Robinson, Jenefer M. 1985. "Style and Personality in the Literary Work." *Philosophical Review* 94 (2): 227–47.

Roethke, Theodore. 1975. *The Collected Poems of Theodore Roethke*. New York: Anchor.

Rosenberg, Harold. 1994. *The Tradition of the New*. Cambridge, MA: Da Capo Press.

Rosset, Barney, ed. 2011. *The Evergreen Review Reader: 1957–1966*. New York: Arcade Publishing.

Rossiter, William T. 2014. *Wyatt Abroad: Tudor Diplomacy and the Translation of Power*. Cambridge: D. S. Brewer.

Rowe, John Carlos. 1995. "Structure." In *Critical Terms for Literary Study*, 2nd ed., edited by Frank Lentricchia and Thomas McLaughlin, 23–38. Chicago: University of Chicago Press.

Ryle, Gilbert. 1971. "Knowing How and Knowing That." In *Collected Papers*, 2: 212–25. New York: Barnes and Noble.

Sander, Nicholas. 1877. *Rise and Growth of the Anglican Schism*. London: Burns and Oates.

Sandler, Irving. 1990. "The Club." In *Abstract Expressionism: A Critical Record*, edited by David Schapiro and Cecile Schapiro, 48–58. Cambridge: Cambridge University Press.

Sauerländer, Willibald. 1983. "From Stilus to Style: Reflections on the Fate of a Notion." *Art History* 6 (3): 253–70.

Scarisbrick, J. J. 1968. *Henry VIII*. Berkeley: University of California Press.

Scarry, Elaine. 1985. *The Body in Pain*. New York: Oxford University Press.

Schapiro, Meyer. 1959. Review of A. L. Kroeber, *Style and Civilizations*. *American Anthropologist*, n.s., 61 (2): 303–5.

———. 1961. "Style." In *Aesthetics Today*, edited by Morris Philipson, 81–113. Cleveland: World Publishing.

Schleiermacher, Friedrich. 1996. *On Religion: Speeches to Its Cultured Despisers*. Edited by Richard Crouter. Cambridge: Cambridge University Press.

Schuyler, James. 1983. Interview by Mark Hillinghouse. Interviewed on April 3, 8, 22. From James Schuyler Papers, University of California, San Diego, MSS 78, box 1, folder 2.

———. 1998. *Selected Art Writings*. Edited by Simon Pettet. Santa Rosa, CA: Black Sparrow Press.

———. 2004. *Just the Thing: Selected Letters of James Schuyler, 1951–1991*. Edited by William Corbett. New York: Turtle Point Press.

Schwartz, Frederic J. 1999. "Cathedrals and Shoes: Concepts of Style in Wölfflin and Adorno." *New German Critique* 76: 3–48.

Seigel, Jerrold. 1968. *Rhetoric and Philosophy in Renaissance Humanism: The Union of Eloquence and Wisdom, Petrarch to Valla*. Princeton, NJ: Princeton University Press.

Sessions, W. A. 1994. "Surrey's Wyatt: Autumn 1542 and the New Poet." In *Rethinking the Henrician Era*, edited by Peter C. Herman, 168–92. Urbana: University of Illinois Press.

———. 1999. *Henry Howard, The Poet Earl of Surrey: A Life*. Oxford: Oxford University Press.

Shaw, Lytle. 2006. *Frank O'Hara: The Poetics of Coterie*. Iowa City: University of Iowa Press.

———. 2010. "Gesture in 1960: Toward Literal Solutions." In *Frank O'Hara Now: New Essays on the New York Poet*, edited by Robert Hampson and Will Montgomery, 29–48. Liverpool: Liverpool University Press.

Sherry, Richard. 1550. *A Treatise of Schemes and Tropes*. London.

Shore, Daniel. 2015. "Shakespeare's Constructicon" [*sic*]. *Shakespeare Quarterly* 66: 113-136.

Shuger, Debora K. 1988. *Sacred Rhetoric: The Christian Grand Style in the English Renaissance*. Princeton, NJ: Princeton University Press.

———. 1999. "Conceptions of Style." In *The Cambridge History of Literary Criticism*. Vol. 3, *The Renaissance*, edited by Glyn P. Norton, 176–86. Cambridge: Cambridge University Press.

Shulman, Nicola. 2013. *Graven with Diamonds: The Many Lives of Thomas Wyatt; Poet, Lover, Statesman, and Spy in the Court of Henry VIII*. Hanover, NH: Steerforth.

Sidney, Sir Philip. 2009. *Sir Philip Sidney: The Major Works*. Edited by Katherine Duncan-Jones. Oxford: Oxford University Press.

Siemens, R. G. 1997. "Thomas Wyatt, Anne Boleyn, and Henry VIII's Lyric 'Pastime with Good Company.'" *Notes and Queries* 44 (1): 26–27.

Silverberg, Mark. 2006. "Working in the Gap between Art and Life: Frank O'Hara's Process Poems." In *Neo-Avant-Garde*, edited by David Hopkins, 37–47. Leiden: Brill.

Simmel, Georg. 1957. "Fashion." *American Journal of Sociology* 62 (6): 541–58.

———. 1991. "The Problem of Style." *Theory, Culture, and Society* 8: 63–71.

Sohm, Philip. 2000. "Ordering History with Style." In *Antiquity and Its Interpreters*, edited by Alina Payne et al., 40–54. New York: Cambridge University Press.

Sontag, Susan. 1966. *Against Interpretation and Other Essays*. New York: Farrar, Straus, and Giroux.

———. 1972. *Under the Sign of Saturn*. New York: Farrar, Straus, and Giroux.

Sowerby, Tracey A. 2010. *Renaissance and Reform in Tudor England: The Careers of Sir Richard Morrison*. Oxford: Oxford University Press.

Spearing, A. C. 1985. *Medieval to Renaissance in English Poetry*. Cambridge: Cambridge University Press.

Spengler, Oswald. 1926. *The Decline of the West*. 2 vols. Translated by Charles Francis Atkinson. New York: Knopf.

Spitzer, Leo. 1948. *Linguistics and Literary History: Essays in Stylistics*. Princeton, NJ: Princeton University Press.

Stamatakis, Chris. 2012. *Sir Thomas Wyatt and the Rhetoric of Rewriting*. Oxford: Oxford University Press.

Stein, Gertrude. 1993. *A Gertrude Stein Reader*. Edited by Ulla E. Dydo. Evanston, IL: Northwestern University Press.

Steiner, George. 1989. *Martin Heidegger*. Chicago: University of Chicago Press.

Stevens, John. 1961. *Music and Poetry in the Early Tudor Court*. London: Methuen.

Stewart, Susan. 2011. *The Poet's Freedom: A Notebook on Making*. Chicago: University of Chicago Press.

Stoneley, Peter. 2010. "Frank O'Hara and 'French in the Pejorative Sense.'" *Journal of Modern Literature* 34 (1): 125–42.

———. 2012. "O'Hara, Blackness, and the Primitive." *Twentieth Century Literature* 58 (3): 495–514.

Strevens, Michael. 2009. *Depth*. Cambridge, MA: Harvard University Press.

Strunk, William Jr., and E. B. White. 1959. *The Elements of Style*. New York: Macmillan.

Summers, David. 1989. "'Form,' Nineteenth-Century Metaphysics, and the Problem of Art Historical Description." *Critical Inquiry* 15 (2): 372–406.

———. 2002. "E. H. Gombrich and the Tradition of Hegel." In *A Companion to Art Theory*, edited by Paul Smith and Carolyn Wilde, 139–49. Oxford: Blackwell Publishing.

Surrey, Henry Howard, Earl of. 1964. *Surrey: Poems*. Edited by Emrys Jones. Oxford: Oxford University Press.

Taussig, Michael. 1992. *Mimesis and Alterity: A Particular History of the Senses*. New York: Routledge.

Thomson, Patricia. 1962. "A Note on Wyatt's Prose Style in *Quyete of Mynde*." *Huntington Library Quarterly* 25 (2): 147–56.

———. 1964. *Sir Thomas Wyatt and His Background*. Stanford, CA: Stanford University Press.

Todorov, Tzvetan. 1971. "The Place of Style in the Structure of the Text." In *Literary Style: A Symposium*, edited by Seymour Chatman, 29–39. New York: Oxford University Press.

Tottel, Richard. 1965. *Tottel's Miscellany*. Edited by Hyder Rollins. 2 vols. Cambridge, MA: Harvard University Press.

———. 2011. *Tottel's Miscellany: Songs and Sonnets of Henry Howard, Earl of Surrey, Sir Thomas Wyatt and Others*. Edited by Amanda Holton and Tom MacFaul. London: Penguin.

Tremlett, Giles. 2010. *Catherine of Aragon*. London: Faber and Faber.

Vasari, Giorgio. 2008. *The Lives of the Artists*. Translated by Julia Conaway Bondanella and Peter Bondanella. Oxford: Oxford University Press.

Vendler, Helen. 1972. "The Virtues of the Alterable." *Parnassus: Poetry in Review* 1 (1): 5–20.

Walker, Greg. 2005. *Writing under Tyranny: English Literature and the Henrician Reformation*. Oxford: Oxford University Press.

Walton, Kendall. 2008. "Style and the Products and Processes of Art." In *Marvelous Images: On Value and the Arts*, 220–48. Oxford: Oxford University Press.

Waterfield, Robin, ed. 2009. *The First Philosophers: The Presocratics and Sophists*. Oxford: Oxford University Press.

Whitman, Walt. 1992. *Leaves of Grass*. New York: Vintage Books/Library of America.

Wilde, Oscar. 2008. *Oscar Wilde: The Major Works*. Edited by Isobel Murray. Oxford: Oxford University Press.

Wilson, Thomas. 1553. *The Arte of Rhetorique*. London.

Wilson-Okamura, David Scott. 2013. *Spenser's International Style*. Cambridge: Cambridge University Press.

Winckelmann, Johann Joachim. 2006. *History of the Art of Antiquity*. Translated by Harry Mallgrave. Los Angeles: Getty Research Institute.

Winnicott, D. W. 1965. "Communicating and Not Communicating Leading to a Study of Certain Opposites." In *The Maturational Processes and the Facilitating Environment*. New York: International Universities Press.

Witmore, Michael. 2011. "The Ancestral Text." *Wine Dark Sea*. http://wine-darksea.org/?p=979.

Witt, Ronald. 2000. *"In the Footsteps of the Ancients": The Origins of Humanism from Lovato to Bruni*. Leiden: Brill.

Wittgenstein, Ludwig. 1984. *Culture and Value*. Translated by Peter Winch. Chicago: University of Chicago Press.

———. 2009. *Philosophical Investigations*. Translated by G. E. M. Anscombe et al. 4th ed. Oxford: Wiley-Blackwell.

Wölfflin, Heinrich. 1950. *Principles of Art History: The Problem of the Development of Style in Later Art*. Translated by M. D. Hottinger. Mineola, NY: Dover Books.

Wollheim, Richard. 1973. "Giovanni Morelli and the Origins of Scientific Connoisseurship." In *On Art and the Mind: Essays and Lectures*, 177–201. London: Allen Lane.

———. 1987. "Pictorial Style: Two Views." In *The Concept of Style*, edited by Berel Lang, 183–204. Ithaca, NY: Cornell University Press.

Wright, George T. 1988. *Shakespeare's Metrical Art*. Berkeley: University of California Press.

Wyatt, George. 1968. *The Papers of George Wyatt, Esq.* Edited by D. M. Loades. London: Royal Historical Society.

Wyatt, Sir Thomas. 1969. *Collected Poems of Sir Thomas Wyatt*. Edited by Kenneth Muir and Patricia Thomson. Liverpool: University of Liverpool Press.

———. 1975. *Collected Poems*. Edited by Joost Daalder. Oxford: Oxford University Press.

———. 1978. *The Complete Poems*. Edited by R. A. Rebholz. Harmondsworth: Penguin.

———. 2016. *The Complete Works of Sir Thomas Wyatt the Elder*. Vol. 1. Edited by Jason Powell. Oxford: Oxford University Press.

Wyatt, Sir Thomas, and Henry Howard. 1816. *The Works of Henry Howard, Earl of Surrey, and of Thomas Wyatt the Elder*. Edited by George Nott. 2 vols. London: Longman, Hurst, Orme, and Brown.

Zagorin, Perez. 1993. "Sir Thomas Wyatt and the Court of Henry VIII: The Courtier's Ambivalence." *Journal of Medieval and Renaissance Studies* 23 (1): 113–41.

INDEX

Proper names and concepts from the main text are indexed by page number. Substantial treatments of people or topics in the notes are treated the same way. Many section headings in the main text repeat; those that do are numbered (e.g. §114 **the aspect of style (2)**), and they are indexed here in bold by their section number (e.g. **aspect of style, the**, §84, §114) so that the reader who wishes to consider them as a sequence may easily do so.

Howard, Henry (Earl of Surrey). *See*
Surrey, Earl of (Henry Howard)
Huizinga, Johan, 165
humanism, 7, 20–21, 38, 45, 52–53,
99, 142, 175

imitating yourself, §216, §248,
§249, §252
imitatio, 21, 65, 83, 114, 167, 175
imitation, §132, §234; assimilation,
§239; harmony, §236; knowing,
§242, §246; Alfred Leslie, §254;
liking, §256, §259
imitation, 21, 26, 31, 65, 75, 83, 93,
99, 109, 110–20, 123, 125, 126,
133–34, 139, 140, 167, 174, 175–76,
182, 183
individual style, §215, §217
individual style, 5, 30, 64, 70, 72–73,
76, 98–120
in memory of my feelings, §171,
§352
interpretation, 14, 27, 32, 71, 76–77,
121–36, 139, 151, 176, 217. *See also*
explanation; sign
ironies of style, §73, §179, §260,
§325
irony, 16, 37, 82–83, 93, 120, 122–23,
152–53, 182
Izenberg, Oren, 70, 75

James, Henry, 75, 95
Jameson, Fredric, 167
Jones, LeRoi. *See* Baraka, Amiri
jujubes, §68, §72, §211
jujubes, 35, 36–37, 96, 132

Kant, Immanuel, viii, 92, 93, 95, 98,
167
Katherine of Aragon (queen), 38, 39,
41–42, 45, 61, 75–76, 125

Kenny, Anthony, 30
Kline, Franz, 52, 114, 139–40, 142–43
knowing what you are doing, §28,
§204, §206
Koch, Janice, 13, 73
Koch, Kenneth, 13, 32–33, 40, 73, 82,
103, 107, 118–19, 127, 128, 132–33,
145, 148, 177, 178; "You Were
Wearing," 132–33
Kooning, Elaine de, 51, 52, 105, 177
Kooning, Willem de, 91, 177
Kroeber, A. L., 77
Kubler, George, 2

Lanham, Richard, 56, 143, 199
Leclerc, Georges-Louis (Comte de
Buffon), 105
Leland, John, 26, 39, 141, 159
Leslie, Alfred, 116–17
LeSueur, Joe, 19, 60, 84–85, 137, 146,
151, 170
levels of style, §120, §123, §130, §133
levels of style, 57, 59, 60–62, 64, 65,
66, 67
Lewis, C. S., 144
life is beautiful, §189, §197
life of style, the, §381, §384
likeness, 5, 7, 9, 10, 11, 12, 14, 29,
36–37, 56, 78, 79, 93, 95, 96, 99,
101, 104, 105–7, 107, 108–9, 110–
11, 112–13, 115, 117–18, 119, 125,
129, 132, 133–34, 135, 139, 140,
141, 142–43, 152, 176. *See also*
metonymy
limits of style: action, §310; death,
§378; God, §357; helplessness,
§90; incoherence, §56; nature, §202; nature again, §250;
passion, §321; plainness, §83;
sameness, §240
Loos, Adolf, 35

Surrey, Earl of (Henry Howard), 7, 15–16, 49–50, 74, 81, 131, 140, 146, 159, 164, 174–75

Surrey, Earl of (Henry Howard), poems of: "The fancy which that I have served long," 7; "Love that doth reign and live within my thought," 49–50; "My Ratcliff, when thy reckless youth offends," 81, 131; "O happy dames that may embrace," 174–75; Penitential Psalms, 146; "Wyatt resteth here," 74

symptom, 28, 56, 57, 78, 82, 160

synesthesia, 89, 142, 143

synonymy, §93, §95, §97, §98, §100

synonymy, 46–48

time, 5–6, 11, 36, 44, 67, 78, 93, 99, 129, 130, 132, 141, 156, 216–17. *See also* alreadyness; history

time of style, the: after, §88; already, §20, §70, §280; to come, §287; past, §332

to the film industry in crisis, §92, §328

to the harbormaster, §379, §382, §390

Tottel, Richard, 8, 16, 50, 103, 144

truth, 44–45, 64, 79, 80, 87–88, 121, 135, 163, 167. *See also* fiction

Turberville, George, 50

Valla, Lorenzo, 155–56

Vendler, Helen, 85

vices of style, 12, 14, 16

Waldman, Anne, 102–3

Warren, Vincent, 2, 12, 108, 121–22, 137, 155

Weil, Simone, 89

we will begin again, §6, §368

Whitman, Walt, 117, 124, 158

whoso list, §34, §308

Wilde, Oscar, 53, 57, 58, 72, 179–80

Williams, Oscar, 21–22

Williams, William Carlos, 117, 118, 141, 158

Wilson, Thomas, 22, 24, 43, 61

Winckelmann, Johann Joachim, 155, 161

Winnicott, D. W., 103

Witmore, Michael, 32

Wittgenstein, Ludwig, 13, 55–56

Wollheim, Richard, 72–73, 85–86, 113

Wyatt, George, 64

Wyatt, Sir Henry, 11, 79

Wyatt, Sir Thomas: authorship, 3, 15, 100–101, 103–4; and Anne Boleyn, 8, 18, 71, 79; and Elizabeth Brooke, 168; childhood, 11; and Elizabeth Darrell, 38, 125, 168; death of, 176, 180; diplomacy, 18, 24–25, 106, 109–10, 112–113, 123–24, 126, 134–35, 155–56, 171, 176; education of, 7, 12, 21; Egerton manuscript, 15, 18, 100, 113; friendships, 90–91, 113; and Henry VIII, 61–64, 135, 176; imprisonments, 6, 7, 76, 79, 81, 90, 106, 126, 130, 134, 137–38; and Katharine of Aragon, 38–39, 41–42; marriage, 17, 168; meter, 15–16, 50; religion of, 159–60; son Thomas, 18, 106; style of, 18, 25–26, 29–30, 41–42, 45, 49–50, 52–53, 70, 86–87, 91, 130–31, 134–35, 140–41, 144, 147–48, 159, 171

Wyatt, Sir Thomas, works of: "Ah, Robin, jolly Robin," 100; "Avising the bright beams of these fair eyes," 29; "Caesar, when that the traitor of Egypt," 34; "Declaration," 126; "Defense," 126, 130; "Each man me telleth I change most my device," 66, 68; "I find no peace and all my war is done," 14–15, 17, 22–23; "In Spain," 96; "The knot which first my heart did strain," 56–57; "The long love that in my thought doth harbour," 49, 162; "Mine own John Poyntz," 44–45, 90; "My galley charged with forgetfulness," 5, 7, 8, 175, 179, 183; *Of the Quyete of Minde*, 38, 39, 40–41, 74–75, 82; Penitential Psalms, 138, 147, 149, 157–58, 159–60, 170–71; "The pillar perished is whereto I leant," 123; "Sighs are my food, drink are my tears," 81, 130; "There never was file half so well filed," 25–26; "They flee from me that sometime did me seek," 69–70, 71, 88, 93, 160; "Throughout the world, if it were sought," 43; "To make an end of all this strife," 2–4; "Was I never yet of your love grieved," 77; "What rage is this," 112, 113; "Whoso list to hunt, I know where is an hind," 18–19, 82, 95, 144

Wyatt, Sir Thomas, the younger (son of Sir Thomas Wyatt), 18, 106

Wyatt's forms, §186, §198

you were wearing, §288, §291

14 : reconcile
18 : mild
19 : faster
32 : not being able
45 : juice
81 : personality
103 : joy
107 : disappointment

parenthesis
isolation